More Praise for *Kindred Souls*

"Edna Gurewitsch's sensitive and poignant *Kindred Souls*, with its perceptive portrait of Eleanor Roosevelt, is an indispensable contribution to the Roosevelt literature."
—Arthur Schlesinger, Jr.

"A wonderful love story that opens to public view a fascinating chapter in Eleanor Roosevelt's life. Edna Gurewitsch has re-created Eleanor's last years with such remarkable empathy and such deep intuition that it seems as if Eleanor is alive once more."
—Doris Kearns Goodwin

"A love story of rare quality: intelligent, wise, and, above all, generous in spirit and understanding."
—*Kirkus Reviews*

"A sensitive and astute portrait of a 'rare and precious friendship.'"
—*Booklist*

"Gurewitsch has significantly expanded our understanding of the last years of the twentieth century's great American woman."
—*Publishers Weekly*

A native New Yorker, **Edna P. Gurewitsch** received her bachelor of science degree from New York University and taught art at the High School of Music and Art in New York. For many years, she was the vice president at the E. and A. Silberman Galleries in Manhattan. She has a daughter, three grandchildren, and a stepdaughter, and lives in New York City.

Eleanor Roosevelt as a young woman.

Inscribed "To David, from a girl he never knew. Eleanor Roosevelt."

KINDRED SOULS

The Devoted Friendship of
Eleanor Roosevelt and
Dr. David Gurewitsch

EDNA P. GUREWITSCH

INTRODUCTION BY GEOFFREY C. WARD

A PLUME BOOK

PLUME
Published by the Penguin Group
Penguin Putnam Inc., 375 Hudson Street, New York, New York 10014, U.S.A.
Penguin Books Ltd, 80 Strand, London WC2R 0RL, England
Penguin Books Australia Ltd, 250 Camberwell Road, Camberwell, Victoria 3124, Australia
Penguin Books Canada Ltd, 10 Alcorn Avenue, Toronto, Ontario, Canada M4V 3B2
Penguin Books (N.Z.) Ltd, 182–190 Wairau Road, Auckland 10, New Zealand

Penguin Books Ltd, Registered Offices: Harmondsworth, Middlesex, England

Published by Plume, a member of Penguin Putnam Inc. This is an authorized reprint of a hard-cover edition published by St. Martin's Press. For information address St. Martin's Press, 175 Fifth Avenue, New York, New York 10010.

First Plume Printing, January 2003
1   3   5   7   9   10   8   6   4   2

The letters of Eleanor Roosevelt are used with permission of the Eleanor Roosevelt Estate.

Frontispiece: Photograph of Eleanor Roosevelt as a young woman, courtesy of the Franklin D. Roosevelt Library.

Photographs follow pages 108 and 172. Most of the photographs selected were taken by Dr. David Gurewitsch. The photographs in which he himself appears were taken either by Edna P. Gurewitsch or Maureen Corr after the camera was adjusted by him. The portraits of him are in the collection of Edna P. Gurewitsch.

Ⓟ REGISTERED TRADEMARK—MARCA REGISTRADA

The Library of Congress has catalogued the St. Martin's Press edition as follows:

Gurewitsch, Edna P. (Edna Perkel)
    Kindred souls : the friendship of Eleanor Roosevelt and David
Gurewitsch / Edna P. Gurewitsch.
        p.   cm.
    ISBN 0-312-28698-8 (hc.)
    ISBN 0-452-28378-7 (pbk.)
    1. Roosevelt, Eleanor, 1884–1962.   2. Gurewitsch, A. David (Arno
David), 1902–1974.   3. Roosevelt, Eleanor, 1884–1962—Friends and
associates.   4. Presidents' spouses—United States—Biography.   5. Physicians—United
States—Biography.   6. Friendship—United States—Case studies.   I. Title.

E807.1.R48 G87 2002
973.917'0922—dc21

                                                                    2001048653

Printed in the United States of America

FOR MY MOTHER, BESSIE PERKEL,

IN LOVING MEMORY

CONTENTS

ACKNOWLEDGMENTS

I began to write this book about fourteen years ago shortly after I received a telephone call from my good friend Dr. William R. Emerson, who was then the director of the Franklin D. Roosevelt Library. "It is time *you* wrote a book about Eleanor Roosevelt," he said. To a hesitant would-be author, Bill urged: "Put down on paper everything you remember and include her letters." I think of the late Dr. Emerson with deep gratitude for his persistent, gentle prodding and for never losing faith that I would someday finish this task.

To my beautiful daughter, Maria, who has many outstanding qualities reminiscent of her father and who is so familiar with our story, I owe a debt of gratitude for the title of the book and for her useful critical comments on the manuscript. Many thanks also to Jacques Brand, my son-in-law. His interest in my writing and the warmth of his enthusiasm were very dear to me. I am grateful as well to my step-daughter, Grania G. Brolin, for sharing with me her own memories of Mrs. Roosevelt, and to my brother, Bertram Perkel, for plowing through an early book draft.

I wish to acknowledge special appreciation to my friend Dina Recanati for her patience in listening to me as I probed the complex character of Mrs. Roosevelt and for the clarity our countless conversations produced. Dina's discerning understanding of human nature, her own compassion, and her insightful observations have been invaluable to me.

To my friend Peggy Brooks, the first editor to whom I gave a lengthy, unwieldy early manuscript, go my deep thanks for making it coherent. My discussions with her were always helpful and her encouragement was extremely sustaining. I would also like to thank the editor Sally Arteseros, whose clear and astute marginal notes in my near-final copy kept me firmly within the bounds of my story.

Maureen Corr, Mrs. Roosevelt's primary secretary after Malvina Thompson, is another whose unfailing support of my endeavor is greatly appreciated. Maureen, David, and I enjoyed a special relationship that lasted after Mrs. Roosevelt died, and it continues with me until this day.

Among the Roosevelt family members whose friendship I valued through the years, I wish to particularly thank Eleanor Roosevelt Seagraves and her brother, Curtis Dall Roosevelt, Mrs. Roosevelt's eldest grandchildren. As they were old enough to appreciate direct closeness with their grandmother, their opinions were important to me. I cannot overestimate my gratitude for Ellie's encouragement as my writing progressed. Curtis's memories and insights into family relationships were always interesting, and I benefited immeasurably from his serious appraisals, generously shared. My thanks also to Nancy Roosevelt Ireland for permission to publish her grandmother's letters to David and me.

Among my original source material was my husband's medical history of Eleanor Roosevelt from which I excerpted data pertinent to my story. David's devoted younger colleague in the Department of Rehabilitation Medicine, New York Presbyterian Hospital Columbia-Presbyterian Center, Dr. John A. Downey, was kind enough to take the time to read my manuscript and review the medical information it contains. I warmly thank him for his help and greatly value his continued friendship. I also appreciate the talks I had with Dr. Stanley J. Myers, the A. David Gurewitsch Professor of Rehabilitation Medicine, New York Presbyterian Hospital Columbia-Presbyterian Center, for analyzing with me the development of the speciality of rehabilitation medicine.

I wish to express appreciation to my agent, Georges Borchardt, for his capable representation and wise counsel, as well as to Linda McFall at St. Martin's Press for the pleasure of working with her to bring this book to fruition.

And finally, to my good friends—you know who you are—who indulgently listened to my endless stories about David and Mrs. Roosevelt through the years, I offer my deepest thanks.

AUTHOR'S NOTE

The writing of this book was not always a labor of love. To decipher the flow of Eleanor Roosevelt's unusual handwriting on the hundreds of letters she wrote to my husband, David, was difficult. Since she did not have a formal education, her punctuation of lengthy sentences, when it existed, was not always helpful. You knew that the letters were not meant for posterity when they carried, for example, only the date: "Sunday"; or "Oct. 4." And while I found David's typed journals engrossing, though irregularly kept, there were times when his notes, written in a doctor's illegible hand, proved somewhat of a challenge. To me the effort was worth it. I hope the reader agrees.

The property called Val-Kill is located about a mile and a half from the Roosevelt estate in Hyde Park, New York. Val-Kill Cottage, Mrs. Roosevelt's residence, had first been a furniture factory founded by Mrs. Roosevelt and her friends, Nancy Cook and Marion Dickerman, with whom Mrs. Roosevelt had originally shared nearby Stone Cottage, also on the Val-Kill property. Mrs. Roosevelt later converted the furniture factory into her home. In David's and my time, Stone Cottage was the summer residence of the John Roosevelts and their children. The entire Roosevelt estate, which includes the Franklin D. Roosevelt Library, the family house, Springwood, and Mrs. Roosevelt's Val-Kill property, as well as the recently acquired Top Cottage—President Roosevelt's Hyde Park retreat—are presently National Historic Sites.

INTRODUCTION

One spring afternoon twenty years ago, I got a telephone call from Arthur Schlesinger, Jr. I was then the editor of *American Heritage* magazine. He'd just been up at the Franklin D. Roosevelt Library in Hyde Park, he said, and had read a remarkable oral history he thought might interest our readers. I sent for a copy right away. As usual, he was right. The interviewee was Edna P. Gurewitsch, the widow of Dr. A. David Gurewitsch, the empathetic, gifted, much younger man who had been both Eleanor Roosevelt's physician and her most intimate friend during the last fifteen years of her life. The story of Mrs. Roosevelt's closeness to him was not unknown; Joseph P. Lash had outlined it in the second volume of his *Eleanor: The Years Alone,* and he had also included letters between the two in A *World of Love: Eleanor Roosevelt and Her Friends, 1943–1962.* But, thanks to Mrs. Gurewitsch's dignified candor and the skill and sensitivity of interviewer Emily Williams, the Hyde Park document offered fresh insights into Mrs. Roosevelt's final years.

I got in touch with Mrs. Gurewitsch right away to see if I could persuade her to allow us to publish parts of the interview, along with answers to a few additional questions that had occurred to me after reading it. She was reluctant at first, unsure whether she should go on the public record, worried that what she said might be misconstrued and sensationalized. But she did eventually agree to see me, and we spent several mornings together at 55 East Seventy-fourth Street, the comfortable town house she and her husband had shared with Mrs. Roosevelt from 1959 until the latter's death in 1962. As we talked about Mrs. Roosevelt, reminders of her presence were everywhere: Two portrait busts, one a bronze by Jo Davidson, gazed benignly from their pedestals; her books, including several she had written, lovingly inscribed to the Gurewitsches, still occupied the shelves; Dr. Gurewitsch's black-and-white photographs taken during his travels with her covered several walls.

"Remembering Mrs. Roosevelt," the published result of our conversations, appeared in *American Heritage* in December 1981, but a good many questions inevitably remained unanswered. When I suggested to Edna—we were now on a first-name basis—that she might write a book based on her memories, she initially demurred, so I was pleased to see that just before the article appeared, she added a postscript to a note to me: "Perhaps," she wrote, "one day I may get more ambitious."

Two decades later, she has done so, and this book is the happy result, an important contribution to the growing library of volumes about the most influential American woman of the twentieth century, an intimate account of Eleanor Roosevelt's last years written by an eyewitness who took note of everything and everyone around her. The Mrs. Roosevelt whom Edna came to know so well was every bit as brave and tireless as the one the public thought it knew, just as committed to myriad causes, just as unfailingly courteous. (What other official visitor to Red Square would have insisted on standing in line with ordinary Soviet citizens to view Lenin in his tomb? Who else but Eleanor Roosevelt, barely conscious after being carried home from the hospital and within days of death, would still have worried aloud that she had forgotten to thank the men who bore her stretcher?) But she was also far more complex, more intensely human, than her millions of admirers ever knew: There is new evidence here, for example, that she never stopped battling depression and loneliness and sometimes even spoke of suicide when the turbulent lives led by her children became too much for her, and that her celebrated idealism was always healthily alloyed with hard-won political realism. (One of her favorite sayings—"Never antagonize anyone from whom you may someday want something"—could have been coined by her supposedly more pragmatic husband.)

Above all, *Kindred Souls* is a love story for and about grown-ups. It is told in two parts. First, there is a knowing, nuanced account of the complicated relationship between Mrs. Roosevelt and the man, eighteen years her junior, whom she herself said she loved "as I . . . have never loved anyone else." Then the author wryly describes her own oblique courtship by Dr. Gurewitsch, describes the impact on Mrs. Roosevelt of his decision to marry her, and illuminates the loving accommodation Eleanor Roosevelt subsequently made to include her as part of her innnermost circle. "I honor the human race," Mrs. Roosevelt wrote in her last book. "When it faces life head-on, it can almost remake itself . . . this I believe with all my heart: in the long run, we shape our lives. . . . The process never ends until we die." With grace and rare understanding, *Kindred Souls* reveals how triumphantly Eleanor Roosevelt embodied that creed to the very end of her life.

—GEOFFREY C. WARD

The people I love mean more to me than all the public things even if you do think that public affairs should be my chief vocation. I only do the public things because I really love all people, and I only *love* all people because there are a few people whom I love dearly and who matter to me above everything else. These are not so many, and of them, you are now one. And I shall just have to try not to bother you too much....

—*Letter from Eleanor Roosevelt*
to A. David Gurewitsch, April 17, 1948

KINDRED
SOULS

PROLOGUE

ON A BRIGHT SEPTEMBER day in 1959, the premier of the Soviet Union, Nikita S. Khrushchev, and his wife came to place a memorial wreath on the grave of President Franklin D. Roosevelt in the Rose Garden of the estate in Hyde Park, and to lunch with Eleanor Roosevelt at her cottage a mile and a half away. This was a return call. The Soviet premier and his wife had been hosts to Mrs. Roosevelt when she interviewed him in the Khrushchevs' country house in Yalta, on the Black Sea. Now, Mrs. Roosevelt's son John and his wife, Anne, stood beside her to receive the official party. So did my husband, David Gurewitsch.* Fluent in Russian, he had accompanied Mrs. Roosevelt to her interview with Mr. Khrushchev in Yalta two years before.

In a preliminary security inspection of the Roosevelt estate in advance of the Khrushchevs' visit, the Secret Service had wanted to have some trees on the property cut down for a clearer view of the main road. Mrs. Roosevelt adamantly refused. "You guarded my husband among those trees," she said indignantly, "and you will just have to do the same for Mr. Khrushchev."

There were other annoyances to be dealt with. The Republican State Department had not told Mrs. Roosevelt how many people she might

---

*Dr. Gurewitsch's first name, Arno ("Arni"), was used by his family and friends during his early years in Europe. After he settled in the United States, he was known to intimates by his middle name, David, which is how he will be referred to in this book.

1

expect that day. She guessed that they were piqued that Mr. Khrushchev had insisted on the visit to the Roosevelt Home and Library. In fact, the State Department had allocated the shortest possible time for the Hyde Park excursion before the Soviet leader's scheduled address to the United Nations back in New York City later that same day. The experienced Mrs. Roosevelt was, however, quite prepared to receive and feed the party, which she correctly surmised would number about three hundred.

I remember vividly Mr. Khrushchev's deeply respectful air as he placed flowers on the president's grave before the crowd set off across the gravel path for Mrs. Roosevelt's guided tour of the Franklin Roosevelt Library. A group of us then went on to nearby Val-Kill, Mrs. Roosevelt's cottage, for a hasty lunch.* As is usual with Russian officials, there were many elaborate toasts to world peace and friendship, and I noticed how tactfully Mr. Khrushchev masked his wife's refusal, for health reasons, of the proffered glass of champagne. Mockingly shaking his head at Mrs. Roosevelt, the Soviet premier quipped, "Don't you know she doesn't come from a free country? I never let my wife drink!" The luncheon was gulped down, given that time was so limited, and then Mr. Khrushchev, a roll of bread in hand, took his leave and the large party sped off in a long column of shiny black limousines, flags fluttering, accompanied by thunderous police motorcycles.

After Mr. Khrushchev left, Henry Morgenthau, Jr. (who had been President Roosevelt's secretary of the treasury) and his wife, Marcelle; John and Anne Roosevelt, Mrs. Roosevelt's son and daughter-in-law; my husband, David, and I; and several others settled down with Mrs. Roosevelt for tea. Earlier, Mr. Morgenthau had had a problem entering the Library, and it was only when Mrs. Roosevelt missed him in the crowd and sent someone to find him that the young state troopers allowed him in. In the peaceful aftermath of this whirlwind visit, a rather offended Mr. Morgenthau, gripping the arms of his chair, rose and exclaimed, "Eleanor, nobody there today knew who I was."

---

*The police escort, Secret Service men, and other escorts of the official party were served lunch in the Playhouse, a building adjacent to Mrs. Roosevelt's cottage.

"Henry, sit down," Mrs. Roosevelt replied, passing the teacups. "Do you think that if I stopped working for six months anyone would remember *me*?"

Nobody would be more surprised than Eleanor Roosevelt to learn that now, four decades after her death, she and her achievements are still a fresh inspiration to new generations working for world peace, human rights, and all manner of social justice, and her reputation continues to grow. The more that is known about her, the more accurate can be the appraisal of the remarkable wife of the thirty-second president of the United States. To this end, I am giving my account of Eleanor Roosevelt, and her relationship with my late husband, David Gurewitsch, her physician and friend, who played such an important role in the last fifteen years of her life.

She had written to David in 1962: "Above all others you are the one to whom my heart is tied." Though their extraordinary friendship has been summarized and interpreted elsewhere, I feel I can offer a deeper view, based on what I have experienced and reflected upon in the years since Mrs. Roosevelt and David died. Their spirit is here in this New York City house where I still live, which Mrs. Roosevelt, David, and I bought together and shared during her last years. I am surrounded, too, by tangible memories — by letters, books and notes, mementos, itineraries of trips taken together, hundreds of photographs, Mrs. Roosevelt's many gifts, including the blanket she knit for our newborn daughter, Maria, bedroom slippers she worked in needlepoint for David, and the seat cushion she stitched for his desk chair. I regularly use one of her kitchen forks, somehow left behind when she had something sent upstairs "to taste." I treasure the jars, which once contained rhubarb cooked at Hyde Park, that were lovingly left at our door, and I regularly serve guests on incised "Texas Centennial 1836–1936" glass dessert plates I strongly doubt I would otherwise have had.

I have included in this book selections of Mrs. Roosevelt's and David's correspondence and some of mine. While excerpts from it have appeared in other books, here letters are presented in context—the poignant ones Mrs. Roosevelt wrote to David before he and I were married and, later, her letters to both of us and to each of us individually. Many letters are missing, for David did not save all of his, and few of his to Mrs. Roosevelt exist. After she died, her daughter, Anna, who stayed on for a time to sort out things in her mother's apartment, burned David's letters in the bedroom fireplace.* They had been stored in Mrs. Roosevelt's desk. The relatively few that survived were found in her Hyde Park cottage bedroom and were returned to us by Franklin D. Roosevelt, Jr. While David's letters are warm and confidential, concerned with events of the day, his problems, and soul-searchings—the kind of letter one writes to an intimate friend—Mrs. Roosevelt's to him are open expressions of her deep love and need for him, courageous outpourings from a reserved lady so vulnerable to rejection in private life. In fact, Mrs. Roosevelt's letters to David are unique. They have little to do with her public duties; descriptions of famous people and events are written at times almost as chatty afterthoughts. They reveal the roots of her compassion, her inner life and motivation, and without understanding this, her story is incomplete.

It seems odd to me now that it was only in 1974, just after David had died, that I was drawn to read these letters of Mrs. Roosevelt's. They had always been available, and on one or two earlier occasions, I had made an attempt to read them. But because life had been so fully satisfying in the *present*, and there was little time to decipher Mrs. Roosevelt's unusual handwriting—penned on hundreds of sheets of paper, and sometimes covering both sides of a page—I simply postponed the project. When I did read them, twelve years after her death, they were a revelation. I read them voraciously, moved beyond measure by the power of her emotions and the grandeur of her unself-consciousness. My own loss of David at the time deepened my appreciation of that delicate balance that a woman keeps between her yearnings and her dignity, a consistent thread in Mrs. Roosevelt's letters to David.

---

*Told to me by Maureen Corr, who was present in the apartment at the time.

At one time, David had shown the letters to Mrs. Roosevelt's friend Esther Everett Lape for her opinion before turning them over to Joseph Lash in connection with a book he was writing.* Her reply encapsulates the relationship:

January 27, 1971
. . . I knew that Eleanor loved you deeply, pervasively, continuously. But only these letters convey the depth and magnitude of that love . . . You were dearer to her, as she not infrequently said, than anyone else in the world. Yes, she not only loved you, she was "in love" with you. You loved her and were not in love with her. But this is the story of a truly great love that confers nothing but honor upon you and upon her. I am impressed by how frequently her belief in your work appears, forming a basic substructure in her love for you. The truth of this is, to me, very important. . . . What history will know of [Eleanor Roosevelt] is of vast importance. . . . I hope you will some day let this record speak for itself. . . .

It might seem curious that David had not confided to me Mrs. Roosevelt's true feelings for him. But first of all, a doctor's discretion was ingrained in him. That, and David's respect for Mrs. Roosevelt, would have deterred him from describing anything intimate about her. Knowing how she felt about him would surely have made me self-conscious in my dealings with her, certainly in the beginning. He had prepared the way sufficiently for Mrs. Roosevelt to think she could handle having me in the picture, and he decided the less I knew about the involved nature of her love for him, the more natural I could feel with her. He himself did not dwell on that aspect of their relationship, keeping his awareness of how much she loved him at arm's length, so to speak. Explaining it to me would have unnecessarily complicated matters between us.

---

*Joseph P. Lash, *Eleanor: The Years Alone* (New York: W. W. Norton, 1972).

Be that as it may, the exceptional correspondence between Mrs. Roosevelt and David began when they parted company after an unduly long flight they had taken to Switzerland from New York on November 27, 1947 (two years after David had become Mrs. Roosevelt's doctor), and essentially ended with her farewell letter to him, written from Hyde Park in August 1962, three months before she died. Nothing unusual had developed in their association until 1947, when Mrs. Roosevelt was informed that David, her physician, was ill with tuberculosis and would be leaving his medical practice for a year's cure in his native Switzerland. Overwork and worries during the war years, as well as a disintegrating marriage and the thought of leaving his young daughter, Grania, had taken their toll. He was going to a sanitorium in the mountains above Davos. David noted in one of his journals: "When Mrs. Roosevelt first heard about my illness, she offered me the Stone Cottage next to her home in Hyde Park for the prescribed rest cure. I, however, preferred to be treated in the high altitude of the Swiss Alps, where I had been a sanitorium patient for a short time a good many years before." Since his departure coincided with the time Mrs. Roosevelt was scheduled to leave New York for United Nations meetings in Geneva, she invited him to join her on her flight to Switzerland, thinking she could make the journey easier for him. Eleanor Roosevelt and David Gurewitsch had known each other as patient and physician when their plane took off that November, each of them with a different Swiss destination and purpose. By the time they landed, however, after days of engine trouble and delays in the Newfoundland and Shannon airports due to bad weather, their relationship had markedly changed.

David and Mrs. Roosevelt found they needed each other. Deeply intuitive as they were, it was not long before they understood each other's hearts, yearnings, and subtle ways. As they grew closer, he helped dispel the infrequent dark moods that gripped her when she had irrational feelings of uselessness. Above all, he was the one who eased her loneliness and gave her the tenderness, so much a part of his nature, for which she had always longed. On her part, Mrs. Roosevelt fortified David's confidence, advised him about practical matters and impractical love affairs.

She commiserated with him regarding his indecisiveness and his complaints of overwork, toothaches, and head colds. In fact, they took care of each other. They were the best traveling companions—brilliant, energetic, curious, and observant. They had the shared goal, devoid of self-interest, of helping people, curing ills physical and social, David through medicine and Mrs. Roosevelt (on a far more sweeping scale) as a political activist.

Included in their story is my own experience when I entered their lives—first one and then the other, our minuet of changed positions. I have added my recollections of times together during the few but intensive years I knew Mrs. Roosevelt, especially when we shared a New York City house after David and I were married. Affecting to me still are the weekends and holidays we spent in the sprawling Hyde Park cottage that Mrs. Roosevelt really called home, and the exhilarating trips we took as a threesome.

Throughout my writing of this book, I have felt the immediacy of the presence of my husband and Mrs. Roosevelt, and when recollections prompted too sharp pangs of loss, I paused to remember some especially endearing moments. Visions returned of rushing to various airplanes, with Mrs. Roosevelt never relinquishing to anyone her hold upon her heavy briefcase, no matter how hard one tried to wrest it from her; of flight attendants greeting her with the familiarity of old friends; of lines of weary passengers hastily putting down their baggage and brightening to applaud her tall figure as she hurried by; of her self-consciousness when given unsought privileged attention, which would have been impolite to refuse. I recalled the evening when we were seated in the back of a New York City taxicab, returning from the theater, when the driver, excited by his illustrious passenger, half-turned to her and declared, his words tumbling out in reverse order, "Mrs. Roosevelt, I want you to know that your late husband was a great admirer of mine! In fact, your late husband was a great admirer of my *whole family!*" Mrs. Roosevelt charmingly thanked him. A block farther on, David, who had been lost in thought, murmured, "What did he say?" How can I forget my pride in the countless signs of high esteem in which Mrs. Roosevelt was regularly held, and the respect shown to David by his patients? My admiration of the resourcefulness of each of these two fascinating people remains profound.

Armed with purpose and goodwill, Mrs. Roosevelt and David fell into step together at home and abroad. They were creative in solving problems in their respective fields, and they were not afraid to take risks or attempt new approaches in their efforts to do so. Taste and needs were remembered, vulnerabilities perceived and respected. They were entirely at ease with each other, and together, they were a unique pair. They were, in fact, kindred souls. Here, then, is their story—and mine.

· 1 ·

BEGINNINGS

House Call

THE DAY BEGAN LIKE any other in the life of a busy New York City doctor. It was 1944, wartime. Because of David Gurewitsch's boyhood bout with tuberculosis, he had been rejected by the armed services, despite persistent attempts to enlist. That day, on his heavily scheduled medical rounds, he was making a house call on a patient.* He hurried, late as usual, moving quickly and lightly, his long strides reflecting the racewalking championships he'd won as a youth in Berlin. David appeared younger than his forty-two years. A slender, elegant man over six feet tall, he was uncommonly handsome. Dark hair parted to one side revealed a smooth, broad forehead. His blue eyes (the left one with a significant brown spot in its center) were penetrating. He stood impatiently at the door of his patient's home, waiting for someone to answer his ring. To his astonishment, the door was opened by the wife of the president of the United States.

Due to the shortage of civilian nurses, Eleanor Roosevelt had come to help a friend who was ill. David described in his journal: "[She was]

---

*The patient was Trude Lash, wife of Joseph P. Lash, Mrs. Roosevelt's friend and biographer. David had known Trude in Germany, when she had tutored him in Latin as he prepared to enter medical school. He had been twenty-five at the time and was returning to his studies after several years out in the business world.

Mrs. Trude Lash, whom I had known from student days and who had become one of my first patients in New York. I found Mrs. Roosevelt at her bedside at subsequent medical visits."

Mrs. Roosevelt had been impressed by David's quick and thorough examination of Trude, had noticed his head imperceptibly trembling at times with the intensity of his concentration. No one was a keener observer than she. David's quiet dynamism, his alertness to everyone and everything around him, was not lost on her. From his mother, who had studied medicine in London and who was an innovative physical therapist, he had inherited an uncanny ability to sense what lay beneath the surface of the skin. Added to this was his talent for correct diagnosis. Regardless of the demands upon his time, David was never rushed with patients. He gave himself fully to the moment at hand. He spoke gently with patients, thoughtfully weighing his words, occasionally taking long pauses before answering anxious questions in order to be as certain as possible of the completeness and clarity of his reply, always concerned with its effect upon patient and family. He would tell medical students, "A good doctor answers the questions a patient is afraid to ask." And he would add, "Remember, you are not treating a broken leg. You are treating a *person* with a broken leg."

Though his background was in pathology and internal medicine, David had become a pioneer in the new field of physical medicine (later called physical medicine and rehabilitation). In 1939, he had joined the staff of the Neurological Institute of Columbia-Presbyterian Medical Center—his professional home for the next thirty-five years—appointed to its Physical Therapy Service. A poliomyelitis specialist, he was known for achieving outstanding results in the treatment of this paralyzing disease so prevalent at that time among children. He was active in the development of burgeoning physical medicine departments of other hospitals in the early 1940s, and he also looked after his private patients and those of colleagues in the armed forces.

A paralyzed patient once described David Gurewitsch's first visit to his hospital bed:

My favorable impression of him, apart from the fame that had preceded him, was based on three quite unscientific factors — that he was exceedingly handsome, that he finished the examination very quickly, and that my case did not seem to worry him. The first consideration is, of course, irrelevant. . . . But speed in sizing up the situation meant to me perspicacity and long experience. This man could hold a leg in the palm of his hand as if he were divining the muscular strength from a delicate but almost instantaneous appraisal of its weight. No plodding neurologist he. In minutes he had seen everything. When he noticed I was particularly worried about my arm, he flashed it up again . . . then announced, "I guarantee that arm. . . ."*

His compelling need to observe and experience as much as possible enhanced his enjoyment of life and helped him to be the astute physician that he was. With an innate understanding of suffering, his easily sensed compassion made him distinctively appealing. He had struck a chord in Mrs. Roosevelt.

The superbly organized Eleanor Roosevelt had the possessions that the family had accumulated during its twelve-year occupancy of the White House packed and shipped to Hyde Park within a week of the president's death, April 12, 1945. The White House had never been home to her. She had moved into it with trepidation and moved out with alacrity. The family's large house and extensive property at Hyde Park were presented to the government in accordance with the wishes of FDR, and from her husband's estate, Mrs. Roosevelt purchased the nearby Val-Kill cottages and land. Her New York City residence was the apartment that she and the president had shared at 29 Washington Square West, Greenwich

*Edward L. Comte, *The Long Road Back. The Story of My Encounter with Polio* (Boston: Beacon Press, 1957), p. 45.

Village. Estate matters settled, freed of her central position as First Lady, the sixty-one-year-old Eleanor Roosevelt could, for the first time after forty years of marriage, move out of the imposing shadow of FDR and have a life of her own. Her public duties were over, or so she thought, but she was soon persuaded by President Truman to accept an appointment as a delegate to the first session of the United Nations. In April 1946, a year after FDR's death, Mrs. Roosevelt was made chairman of the Commission on Human Rights, but before that appointment, needing a physician in New York, she remembered David and telephoned him.

David wrote, "After the President's death, Mrs. Roosevelt, having settled in her New York apartment, called and asked me whether I would be willing to take her as a patient. She added that she was quite healthy and would probably not take up too much of my time. I readily agreed. Soon afterward a rather voluminous record arrived from the National Naval Medical Center in Bethesda [Maryland], containing her medical data."* The box arrived in David's office in December 1945. His first serious medical encounter with Mrs. Roosevelt occurred on August 14, 1946, when she had a car accident, having fallen asleep at the wheel while driving. He sent her a bill on September 1 for medical care. It was the last time he ever billed her.

Over the course of the next two years, Mrs. Roosevelt made a few telephone calls to David's office, and from time to time, she dropped in to see him, generally for the then-required inoculations before a trip abroad. He was a visitor to Hyde Park only once or twice in those years. That is how it began, the unique friendship between the famous American widow and the cultivated European doctor eighteen years her junior, to whom she would one day write, "You know without my telling you that I love you as I love and have never loved anyone else."** Their story sheds fresh light on her last years, a time of important achievement and a deep new attachment.

---

*A. David Gurewitsch, *Eleanor Roosevelt, Her Day* (New York: Interchange Foundation, 1973).
**Birthday letter to David Gurewitsch from Eleanor Roosevelt, October 31, [1955?].

· 2 ·

FRIENDSHIP ABROAD

Flight to Switzerland

DAVID WROTE IN HIS journal about the plane trip to Switzerland:

On November 29, 1947, I was seated next to Mrs. Roosevelt in an airplane heading for Switzerland, she for Geneva, as Chaiman of the United Nations Commission on Human Rights, and I for Davos, for a tuberculosis cure. This trip to Geneva turned out to be most memorable. The very beginning generated much excitement. As the plane took off, the historic voting at the United Nations General Assembly on the proposed Partition of Palestine had just started. Strongly in favor of Partition [the establishment of an Arab and a Jewish state as two separate entities], Mrs. Roosevelt had exerted considerable energy and all her influence to get the United States to vote for it. A friend had brought a small radio on the plane and our group was listening intensely as one by one, the votes were announced. With great relief our party realized that the necessary two-thirds majority in favor of Partition had been reached. We were elated.

In those days the journey to Geneva in a propeller plane required two refueling stops, usually in Gandor, Newfoundland, and Shannon, Ireland. It was expected to take just short of twenty-four hours. This particular trip, however, took four and a half days. The plane had mechanical trouble in Newfoundland which delayed us, and [when we stopped] in Ireland we were fogged in. In the absence of the normal ties and obligations usually present in our daily lives, the contact which had grown between Mrs. Roosevelt and myself in the course of the last two and a half years developed a different dimension. The many hours in the air, and especially the days in Shannon airport, resulted in a friendship most meaningful to me and one which was to last throughout the remaining fifteen years of Mrs. Roosevelt's life. In the detached and somewhat unreal atmosphere of an airplane, I heard much about Mrs. Roosevelt's life and she, in turn, learned about some of the vicissitudes of mine, of my hopes and ambitions. Mrs. Roosevelt was an extremely avid and sympathetic listener and questioner. I told her about my background, about my extraordinary philosopher-father . . . who, with my mother and their baby, my older brother, had lived in Switzerland. A short time after having found an adequate solution to his philosophic questions involving the relationship between man and God . . . and with the fulfillment of his mission in life, at the age of twenty-six [my father] drowned in a Swiss lake. This was three months before I was born. My mother firmly believed that, at that point, life did not offer him any further challenge and that his death was a suicide.* For her this loss represented a blow from which she never recovered. In her response to a little note I had written her on July seventh, the occasion of the thirty-fifth anniversary of my father's death, she answered: "Don't you know that for me, every day is the seventh of July?"

David spoke to Mrs. Roosevelt about his mother's strength of character, her deeply religious approach to life, and how she had survived the blow

---

*David was never quite convinced of this. He thought it possible that having gone for a swim, as his father usually did on summer Sundays, he might have been caught in a whirlpool and drowned. When his body was recovered from the lake, the serene expression on his face, as shown in a photograph taken by an unknown person, led David to speculate that having been caught in a swirling tide, his father did not struggle against his fate and "lent himself" to it.

of her husband's death, cut off from family (which was in Russia), with a ten-month-old baby and a second child due to be born in three months. He told her that when he was two and his brother three, his mother took them to live with her parents in Russia while she went to study medicine in England and how she returned for them after five years, then settled in Berlin, where she started her practice. He also told Mrs. Roosevelt how his mother had managed to educate her sons, publish her husband's writings, and support her family. He described life and education in Berlin during and after World War I, his family's experiences as aliens in Germany, his determination to be a doctor, and his reluctance to enter medical school because of the financial burden it would place upon his mother. He discussed his seven or eight years in the business world before beginning medical school with his own financial resources, saying that while the time he spent working was largely wasted, the experience had helped him in administering a medical department and a hospital. He explained that he had been educated in German universities and had done his medical training in Switzerland, Israel, Austria, and England before going to the United States on a fellowship. His financial reserve from his premedical years allowed for independent and long-term education, he said.

Although he and Mrs. Roosevelt had come from different parts of the world, from different backgrounds, and were of different ages, it developed, he noted, that they had much in common. They had both grown up fatherless, for example.

> . . . I, searching for the father I never knew, Mrs. Roosevelt for the father she had lost. During our impressionable young years we had both been raised by grandparents. We both had feelings of early deprivation. The sense of "service" had been strongly instilled into us and accomplishment in life was to be measured more in terms of service than happiness. With a completely different upbringing, each of us was shy, felt somewhat "outside" of the established norms, and were essentially lonely.

In spite of having been born into the "establishment," the niece of a President, the wife of a President, Mrs. Roosevelt was basically a deprived person. It began with the separation from her beloved father, was continued by his early death and by the loss of her mother. In her most impressionable years she was brought up a homeless orphan by a stern grandmother. She found her main emotional support in a French teacher in a school in England. Finally, this feeling of homelessness was repeated in the pattern of her marriage, in which her domineering mother-in-law's house never seemed her own. These were the stories we exchanged.

In Shannon at the time, sleeping quarters in the event of flight delays were in barracks located over a mile away from the airport dining room. The distance had to be covered on foot. Mrs. Roosevelt often took it upon herself to provide me with necessary food, when I, ill, remained mostly in the barracks during the three days of our delay there, waiting for the fog to lift. Her interpretation of "help" was overwhelming. . . . Our uninterrupted hours of conversation grew. By the time the plane arrived in Geneva, the doctor-patient relationship we had had before became a real friendship. Throughout my stay in Davos our contact continued. We wrote each other almost daily. Mrs. Roosevelt consistently provided me with thoughtful gifts. She sent me a radio, books, fruit and sweets, the manuscript of the book she was writing,* and I began to learn what it meant to be Mrs. Roosevelt's friend.

Their backgrounds were indeed different. Eleanor Roosevelt was born into an aristocratic American family, her future position in society predetermined. David was the son of Russian-Jewish parents living in Switzerland. Stateless until he was forty-two, having been issued a Nansen passport** (a document identifying those persons who, because of war or

---

*Eleanor Roosevelt, *This I Remember* (New York: Harper & Brothers, 1949).
**The Nansen passport was named for Fridtjof Nansen (Norwegian, 1861–1930), an Arctic explorer, zoologist, and statesman. After World War I, he led the first High Commission for Refugees and won the Nobel Peace Prize in 1922.

for other reasons, were stateless), he spent his youth in the midst of European political upheaval, and he followed no certain course except that which was defined by his mother. Yet he and Mrs. Roosevelt recognized in each other an extraordinary inherited ability to empathize with people, and the fact that they were motivated by compassion to care for those in need. During the long journey, Mrs. Roosevelt found herself increasingly drawn to David. His understanding of his mother's lonely struggles impressed her, as did his resolve to make his life count for something. Reserved manners in an informal man were appealing to Mrs. Roosevelt and helped to establish a rapport between them. He was honest and intense, and his need for support at the time was hard to resist, particularly for a woman so profoundly responsive to frailty. He had many contrasting characteristics that were interesting to her. He was worldly and innocent at the same time. A passionate man, he could be coolly objective. Critical of himself, he was nonjudgmental of others. Highly educated, he was not snobbish. Warmly outgoing, he was a touch elusive. He was aware of the unusual impression he made, of his charisma, which attracted men as well as women. A conventional physician, David was magical. Yet his nomadic formative years in Europe had left him feeling isolated. His vulnerability to the ups and downs of life, a tendency he never quite conquered, and his sense of apartness were felt by everyone to some degree, and deeply by a few.

In 1927, at the age of twenty-five, David had given up his business interests—at nineteen, he'd been a partner in Berlin's first plastics factory, then successfully invested in the newly developing motion-picture industry*—before beginning medical school in Freiburg, Germany. With Nazism on the rise, he transferred to the Basel Medical School in his native Switzerland. He was older than most of the other students. "He kept to himself a good deal," I was told by one of his classmates, Dr. Anna-Marie Weil.** She remembered how handsome and gifted he was and that he

---

*David also produced two films with Elizabeth Bergner, a star of early motion pictures.
**Author's interview with Dr. Anna-Marie Weil, New York, 1992.

was always the subject of romantic stories among the other students. Those who had left German universities for study in Basel knew, of course, that there was no going back. They spent endless hours discussing in which countries they could safely practice medicine once they'd received their degrees. David had arrived in Basel with his decision made. He would go to Palestine.

David discussed these early years with Mrs. Roosevelt. As an idealistic boy he had been a member of the German Zionist Youth Organization. Immediately after his internship at Basel Medical School Hospital, he joined the staff of the Department of Internal Medicine in the small and relatively new Hadassah Hospital in Jerusalem, serving at the same time the settlement (kibbutz) of Degania, near the Lake of Tiberius, an early center for the treatment of arthritis. The life and spirit in Palestine attracted many gifted young Europeans, who responded to the challenge of building a Jewish homeland. But at that time, there were few opportunities for advanced medical training and research. Before David left, a year later, to continue his studies elsewhere, he bought a piece of land jutting out into the Sea of Galilee, south of the Golan Heights. He felt he had roots in Palestine and hoped one day to return. He came to the United States on a fellowship to Mount Sinai Hospital in New York City, first working in pathology, then in hematology. Two years later, in 1938, he joined Mount Sinai's Department of Physical Therapy; he was drawn to this specialty because of his mother's work in the field.

From the time he arrived in New York in 1936, David had been making regular visits to Berlin to see his mother and brother, who was by then a practicing physician, had married, and was the father of two small children. Returning after just such a visit aboard the HMS *Mauritania*, David had a flirtation with a tall, attractive Englishwoman, a musician and singer, Nemone Balfour, who was traveling to the United States for a concert tour. David did not pursue the new friendship after the ship docked, but a chance meeting at the country house of mutual friends brought them together again. Their courtship then began in earnest and continued in long-distance fashion following Nemone's return to London. The hectic pace of New York was so unlike Nemone's gracious English way of life that David was not sure she could adjust to it, and he had misgivings about marrying her. Nevertheless, after deciding to do so, he joined her in London in 1937 for their wedding, then brought her back to settle in Manhattan. Three years later, their daughter, Grania, was born.

From the start, their years together were far from smooth. Nemone was emotionally fragile and had to have special care. That, and being fully responsible for the new baby, placed a considerable strain on David as well as on the marriage. But his professional life was satisfying. He explained to Mrs. Roosevelt how in 1939 he had joined the staff of the Neurological Institute of the Columbia-Presbyterian Medical Center, while at the same time he held the position of attending physician for the Physical Therapy, Polio Service, at Knickerbocker Hospital in New York. His patients were those suffering from different kinds of incapacitating illnesses, such as cerebral palsy, stroke, multiple sclerosis, and spinal-cord injuries, and he was deeply involved as well in the development of special equipment designed to increase patients' independence and improve the quality of life of the physically impaired. In this era before the Salk and Sabin anti-polio vaccines, David's main focus was the treatment of poliomyelitis.

He went on to describe to Mrs. Roosevelt his alarm over the inability of his family to escape from Germany. In 1941, however, a way out had been found for his mother, who had refused to leave without her son Vladimir and his family. He explained how he'd gotten a short leave of absence from the Neurological Institute to go abroad, where his concentrated efforts to rescue the family finally resulted in their being granted asylum in England.*

Now David was on his way to Switzerland to receive treatment for his tuberculosis. He had been to the sanitorium of Dr. Alfred Maurer in the Schaltzalp before. Until the discovery of antituberculosis drugs, the usual prescribed treatment was a year of bedrest in a clear, high altitude. His

---

*Five years later, they emigrated to the United States. Vladimir Gurewitsch practiced medicine as an internist in New York City and in Woods Hole, Massachusetts.

emotional withdrawal from his troubling marriage was now made more poignant by the prospect of his physical removal to a Swiss mountaintop.

This was the gist of the account he gave to Mrs. Roosevelt. Her instincts had already told her that he was a man to be trusted. His disquiet spirit evoked her own. Engulfed by fog in the bleak Shannon airport, Mrs. Roosevelt told him something about herself and her childhood and described what her father had meant to her. David asked about her husband's polio. She answered his questions, knowing that he understood the things she left unsaid. I am sure the fact that his field was the treatment of infantile paralysis had to have connected them from the start. Not only was he attentive and sympathetic, he was also a person who thoroughly understood the nature and complexities of this grim illness and her ordeal in coping with it. He was a compassionate doctor, accustomed to listening and to honoring confidences. She felt she could unburden herself. This was a rare experience for the reserved Eleanor Roosevelt. I believe she felt she had found someone she had long been seeking. By the time she stepped into David Gurewitsch's life, she had already transformed herself through determined self-discipline, patient self-analysis, and constant self-improvement, turning from a pathetically shy and insecure young girl into a woman who knew the convincing power of her personality and her capacity to assume responsibilities. She also knew that if all else failed, she could rely upon herself.* Now sixty-three years old, she had been a widow for two years. An important United Nations mission awaited her. On her own, she faced other challenges, as well. David was not only someone in whom she felt she could confide; he was a sensitive, sophisticated, insightful man, one who saw problems from different points of view and was accustomed to giving advice. This new friendship had much to offer.

---

*David described her: "An orphan, a poorly-dressed, unattractive child with a minimal education, who never recovered from the loss of her father, Eleanor Roosevelt was left with a deep core of loneliness which was incurable. . . . I do not think she ever overcame these childhood problems, the time when most of a person's characteristics are formed, but she surmounted them to the degree that her blend of strengths and weaknesses made her the rich personality that she was."

By the time their plane landed in Switzerland and they went their separate ways, he to Davos, she to Geneva, the professional doctor-patient relationship had changed and a deep bond had begun. "May your strength grow and with it our friendship," Mrs. Roosevelt wrote him soon afterward. Throughout her stay in Geneva, their close contact continued by telephone and almost daily correspondence.

David's bedrest cure at the TB sanitorium in the Alps had begun. When the nights were not too frosty, he slept wrapped in blankets on a balcony under the stars. One day followed the next in a similar, monotonous pattern. In their secluded community, patients read, wrote letters, socialized, flirted, and occupied themselves in such gentle ways as limited physical activity would allow as they anxiously waited for the results of their frequent laboratory tests, which tracked the progress of their illness. Most of all, they waited for time to pass in the pure, healing mountain air. Each day, David wrote his daughter, Grania, recording an ongoing story on sheets peeled from birch bark. To alleviate boredom and because he always needed patients to care for, he took on Dr. Maurer, the head of the hospital, who consulted him about his neurological problem, as well as attending to one or two other people.

Mrs. Roosevelt was serving as both chairman of the Commission on Human Rights* and of its selected Drafting Committee. She was determined that the draft for an international document incorporating the civil rights and liberties and the social and economic rights due to individuals everywhere be in a form acceptable to all the then fifty-eight member governments of the United Nations. Despite the enormous task of completing this project, David was never far from her thoughts. In his letters to her, he revealed his need for the emotional nurturing that he'd lacked

*The Commission on Human Rights, composed of eighteen governmental representatives chosen by the Economic and Social Council of the United Nations, had begun its deliberations in January 1947. Mrs. Roosevelt, as the United States representative to the commission, having been appointed by President Truman to a four-year term, was elected its chairman.

in his first years, spent apart from his mother, and which his marriage evidently had not—perhaps could not—satisfy. Anxiety about his illness opened a Pandora's box of hypochondriacal fears. Mrs. Roosevelt dealt with them. Her concern for his health and morale certainly steadied him, and her calls and letters, solicitous and comforting, brought a warm response. She also wrote him about her activities and the people she saw, bringing the outside world to his isolated place, and he was grateful.

In December 1947, the draft of the Declaration of Human Rights* was finally approved by the commission, ending a two-year period of intensive work. With this accomplished, Mrs. Roosevelt made preparations to leave for home. She wrote David:

> *Geneva, December 12*
> ... Somehow I shall not like leaving and feeling so far away. It has been so good to talk to you—don't tear up any more [of your] letters for I am going to want to hear whenever you can write and feel that I am not really far away from your thoughts at least. Do plan to come home soon enough to take a holiday with us at Hyde Park or Campobello, and do bring your little girl. Sometimes little girls get on well with old ladies and there will be some children about. ...

She flew back to New York December 18, in time for Christmas.

Reunion in Zurich

From Hyde Park Mrs. Roosevelt sent David chapters of the manuscript of her new book, *This I Remember*, for his opinion. She told David to

---

*The Declaration of Human Rights is based on the premise that all human beings are born with equal and inalienable rights and fundamental freedoms. It was what U Thant, the future secretary general of the United Nations, would later call the "Magna Carta of Mankind."

expect her call, and she took steps to make David's reunion with his young daughter easier when he returned home by contacting Nemone and Grania and inviting them to Val-Kill. She mentioned Grania's visit to him: "What a charming and fascinating little thing she is." Another letter from Val-Kill Cottage read:

Sunday, December 28th
David dear,

    Many thanks for your cable. It was nice to get it Xmas day. I called your little girl and she sounded very happy and I talked to your wife also and she said they would come over for a weekend sometime this coming month.

It ended: "My thoughts are with you constantly."

In the early part of 1948, political battle lines were forming for the presidential election. President Truman had troubles enough in his own party without the prospect of the tough contest he would face with Governor Thomas E. Dewey, for whom the Republicans had high hopes. Threatening the president's bid for reelection were the serious "Draft Eisenhower" movement among Democrats, of which Franklin D. Roosevelt, Jr., was a leader, and the declared candidacy of Henry Wallace, who was heading the Progressive party. Mrs. Roosevelt had not been happy with Mr. Truman and would not openly endorse him, despite pressure to do so. He was leaning toward a conservative policy; he had, in her opinion, made some poor cabinet appointments,* and his vacillation on the subject of Palestine—the right of the Jewish people to a homeland—had angered and exasperated her. Standing firm against powerful State Department forces still opposed to the recognition of Israel, she worked persistently and unyieldingly for the United Nations Palestine resolution,

---

*Joseph P. Lash, *Eleanor: The Years Alone* (New York: W. W. Norton, 1972), p. 130, pp. 140–143.

threatening to resign her UN post if the United States betrayed its obligation to recognize the Jewish state. Her considerable influence in the country, as well as on Mr. Truman, counted for a good deal, and in the end, the president came around and the United States was the first nation to recognize the new state of Israel. But Mrs. Roosevelt wanted to stay aloof from national politics that year. Her time was heavily committed to the UN. She was as publicly engaged as she wished to be. Privately, meanwhile, familiarity between Mrs. Roosevelt and David continued to grow. By February 1, she wrote him: "I think of you every day especially when the snow is deep and the air clear and the sky blue and I wish you were in my guest cottage and I could run over and see you!" That same month, David was beginning to feel well enough to have thoughts about a short leave from the sanitorium in preparation for his eventual medical discharge. Informed by Mrs. Roosevelt that she was returning to Europe in April and that she would like to visit him in the short time she had available, he wrote her on February 16 urging her to extend her visit: "Please if you can only do it, add a little more time." Although she could not, she did write him an enthusiastic letter on March 7: "I am looking forward to seeing you David. It is the one personal and entirely happy time that I count on during this trip!" Similarly, on March 30, she wrote, ". . . I look forward to the 15th more than I can say, it is the only real pleasure part of my trip with no official duties attached. Just seeing you is one of the nicest things I can think about so I think about it a great deal!" David suggested that they meet somewhere more convenient to her than Davos. She replied:

> . . . If you can come to Zurich [and know a quiet hotel] please do so. I don't think there need be publicity or to-do! It would just mean more time to see you and talk and as I wrote you I can't make it longer because I have to speak in Brussels the night after the 17th. The 19th–21st I'll be in Holland with [Queen] Juliana and sail the 22nd. I wish I could be longer with you but the Human Rights drafting committee begins May 3d and I must do some preparation and some personal business.

Zurich it was. The reunion, their first meeting since parting four months earlier, linked them still closer. David took rooms at the Dolder Grand Hotel, whose location above the town offered some seclusion. Respecting Mrs. Roosevelt's wish to be incognito for the visit with him, he made her reservation in the name of her secretary, Miss Thompson, who was accompanying her, believing this would provide the desired privacy. He was elated at the prospect of being able to leave the sanitorium even temporarily and of seeing Mrs. Roosevelt again. Arriving at the airport to meet her, he found, to his surprise, an official Swiss welcoming party already on the scene and the airport humming with the news that the plane about to land was bearing Mrs. Franklin D. Roosevelt. David stood at a little distance, wondering how he could best approach her. He watched her enter the reception area and realized she had spotted him. He admired how she quickly acknowledged the group of waiting dignitaries. In her experienced, gracious manner, she greeted them with a smile, accepted flowers, shook hands, sent Miss Thompson and their baggage off in one of their official limousines, thanked them warmly, and then eased her way past the crowd to David, with whom she rapidly walked to his small rental car. Time together at last after months of letters and calls was pleasure for both of them and certainly a relief to David. He wrote in his notes: "Until now we had often talked by telephone and had exchanged innumerable letters. Mrs. Roosevelt had kept me informed about her activities, a wonderful relief from the tedium of sanitorium life. She also sent me for my comments on the manuscript chapters of a book she was writing as she finished them. This visit provided a leisurely time for us to discuss many things, family and professional concerns."

Mrs. Roosevelt and David were free of interruptions on their long rambles along the private tree-shaded paths of the sprawling old-fashioned Swiss hotel. It was early spring, and the air was filled with the scent of new blossoms. It was David's first taste of freedom in months. Seclusion had produced a yearning in him to talk to someone. Solitary reflection in the sanitorium on the pros and cons of a divorce from Nemone and its possible effects upon Grania had not brought him closer to a resolution. The decision was his, they both knew, but Mrs. Roosevelt would be his sounding board. She responded with warmth and understanding. Accustomed to finding her way out of difficult situations, Mrs. Roosevelt spared no effort to help those she loved do the same.

She aired her own problems; her daughter, Anna, and John Boettiger's broken marriage particularly concerned her at the time. But not only worries were exchanged. Strolling together—an unusual occupation for two such rapid-motion people—stopping at intervals to take in the breathtaking views surrounding them, Mrs. Roosevelt told David that she liked the new statue of her husband, which had just been unveiled in London, and believed that Franklin would have been pleased that he was represented standing. They chatted about their work and plans, agreeing on many subjects, including politics and policies of liberal reform. The United States presidential campaign was in full swing, and with her hesitations about Mr. Truman's leadership, Mrs. Roosevelt was glad to be out of reach of demands by her party. About Mr. Henry Wallace's third party, of which she disapproved, she voiced her often-repeated conviction that needed reform should be made *within* an organization—in this case, the Democratic party—that "splintering off" never counted for much.

All his life, David had been absorbed by history and politics. In the sanitorium, he had kept current on contemporary affairs, and his discussions with Mrs. Roosevelt were stimulating and effortless. They found there was a great deal of equanimity between them. They could be quiet together and were free to be themselves, as if their friendship were an old, established one. But this friendship was new and exciting. David had never before experienced the degree of acceptance and support now offered by Mrs. Roosevelt, particularly welcome in this critical period of illness and marital uncertainty. Mrs. Roosevelt received from David the true companionship she craved, the sense of being emotionally connected to someone worthy, someone she could count on, a man who also loved intimate friendship and was willing and able to share his thoughts and feelings. They had felt before that closeness was possible between them, and the concentrated days together in Switzerland confirmed it. They each left Zurich jubilant.

On April 17, the day they parted, Mrs. Roosevelt wrote David from Brussels. In expressing joy in newfound feelings, she was moved to explain the motivation for her life.

EMBASSY OF THE UNITED STATES OF AMERICA
Brussels, April 17 [1948]
David dear,

It is late but I cannot go to bed without saying goodnight on paper since I can't say it in person. It would be impossible for me to tell you how happy I was to see you at the airport. I thought about you so much but you looked better and happier and I wanted to forget everyone else and hug you there and then. Will you do me a favor and have a photograph taken if you haven't one and let me have one? It is not that I can't see your face before me because thinking of you so much that is quite easy but I'd like something tangible to hold in my hands and look at now and then! You will laugh but I would like it all the same so please do it. Being with you was a little island of self-indulgence and pure happiness for me and I'm so grateful that you let me come and that you came to Zurich so that we could have a little longer time together. I hope you will be none the worse for the visit and that it will help to drive away the "blue devils" that make you feel lost. I'm going to cling to you very closely dear, if it helps, until you have someone of your own to cling [to] even more closely. The only trouble is that I was very sad to leave you, the people I love mean more to me than all the public things even if you do think that public affairs should be my vocation. I only do the public things be-cause I really love all people and I only love all people because there are a few close people whom I love dearly and who matter to me above everything else. There are not so many of them and you are now one of them and I shall just have to try not to bother you too much! . . .

Goodnight dear boy. Bless you take good care of yourself. I love you very much and feel close to you in spite of the distance.

Devotedly,

E. R.*

David was no less thrilled with their meeting, and he replied to her warmly in a letter he began on April 23 and finished on the twenty-fifth:

. . . You have been in Zurich, I got your wonderful letter from Brussels and you reached me from the boat. You are on the high seas, recovering I hope from all the to-do, and I am back on my back, but quite differently, peacefully and comfortably. Like everything connected with you, Zurich was a surprise. It was so much more than I had anticipated. It was more intense and more intimate. . . .

Mrs. Roosevelt's next letter to him was dated April 22, the day she boarded the *Queen Elizabeth*, homeward-bound. She continued the letter on April 24, and on reaching her apartment on April 27, she did not go to bed that night before finishing it.

It is not unusual for a vigorous older woman to be attracted to a handsome younger man. It makes her feel alive, womanly. Women were attracted to David and he to them. Apart from his romantic appearance, he had an interesting mixture of qualities to which they were drawn. There was nothing jaded or cynical about him, and though he was a worldly man, he had a genuine air of innocence, which can be touching to a woman. His shyness made him somewhat elusive, adding to his appeal. He liked women, enjoyed their company, admired their style, and understood the claims upon them in their varied and complicated roles in life. They felt this. Mrs. Roosevelt was no exception.

Their transatlantic correspondence continued. On May 3, Mrs. Roo-

*This letter to David was included in an exhibition the Smithsonian Institution circulated around the country in 1984, Mrs. Roosevelt's centennial year.

sevelt confided her worries about her son James, whose wife at the time (his former nurse, Romaine, or "Romelle," who had cared for him when he'd been ill) had attempted suicide. "On their wedding anniversary," she wrote David, "she took an overdose of sleeping tablets and then woke him up and told him." Her letter nine days later repeated the reference to Romelle's suicide attempt. In it, Mrs. Roosevelt coolly observed, "She was a nurse and knew what she was doing." Other letters to David, who was still recuperating in Switzerland, spoke of her interest in the spring visit he was expecting from Nemone and eight-year-old Grania. He had written Mrs. Roosevelt on May 26:

... After some looking and thinking I took two rooms in a chalet 10 minutes walk above Schaltzalp. I can visit them [Nemone and Grania] there mornings and evenings. It is most beautifully located, no patients around, no contacts with Davos. Only more lovely for Grania than Klosters. If Grania should not be happy or if Nemone becomes too tense having to look after Grania [Nemone was given to bouts of depression], we still can go to Klosters. Does this sound reasonable? . . .

Would you not have more peace for writing in Campobello? People can get less at you [there]. . . . To have to say "no" so often is also an effort and you will not be able to say "no" all the time.

The British seem to have lost their instinct to determine what is good and what is bad for them. They used to adore Baldwin* in the face of flagrant blindness leading them into disaster. Now the only man who is really popular is Bevin.** The abrupt liquidation of India without preparation or safeguards occurred under him and I do not think that later on the British will be declared free of responsibility in the calamity which followed. And now it is being repeated in Palestine. The spirit behind the British Palestine policy

*Stanley Baldwin, British prime minister for three terms: 1923–1924, 1924–1929, and 1935–1937.
**Ernest Bevin, British labor leader; foreign minister, 1941–1951.

was quite clear before, but now they no longer have to disguise it. . . . The Jews in Palestine are no Communists. A quick show of support in the form of money, arms and quick release and transportation of suitable D.P.s [displaced persons] has to be organized if Palestine is not to become a Czechoslovakia in the middle of the English-American sphere. . . .

My thoughts, my affection, my devotion go to you.

She gave him practical advice on how to conserve his energy when he returned to work. She wrote about various family situations confronting her and sent him a copy of the draft of the Declaration of Human Rights. Aware of how deeply the survival of Israel concerned David, Mrs. Roosevelt gave him her news on the subject:

May 26th [1948]
Henry Morgenthau brought a Mrs. Meyerson* from Palestine to breakfast last Tuesday. A woman of great strength and calm and for me she symbolizes the best spirit of Palestine. Evidently at least we mean to follow through on a policy of aid to the Jewish State. The British role seems to me quite stupid, no more greedy and self-interested than ours has been, but at last we seem to be doing better. . . .

Another letter expresses one of Mrs. Roosevelt's most dearly held convictions. Referring to the illness from which David was recovering, she wrote: "Of course you have grown under this experience and everything met and accepted and conquered gives you greater confidence."

---

*Meyerson was the former last name of Golda Meir, who later became prime minister of Israel.

Meeting in Paris

In July, when David was finally pronounced well enough to leave the sanitorium, he decided to remain abroad awhile longer to reorient himself to a more normal routine before returning to a problematic marriage and life and work in New York. With no specific timetable, and traveling lightly, as was his habit, he set off for the Dolomites, the mountains he loved and had climbed years before, heading for the beautiful towns he knew in the lush northern Italian countryside. Mrs. Roosevelt wrote him in care of a General Post Office address he'd given her. The end of August found him in his wife's family's house in London, visiting Nemone and Grania until September 8, when mother and child sailed for New York. That spring and summer, Mrs. Roosevelt was busily engaged in writing her book, her newspaper column, and monthly pieces for the *Ladies' Home Journal*. She hosted a radio program with her daughter; the income from it was meant to help Anna's financial problems. Son Elliott was living in the Top Cottage in Val-Kill, and in addition to his children who came to stay, Mrs. Roosevelt looked after a flow of summer guests. She could not remain entirely aloof from the Democratic National Convention, held in Philadelphia, and looked forward to serving again as a member of the U.S. delegation to the UN General Assembly, which was to open in Paris in the fall of 1948. When David heard on July 19 that she was returning to Europe, he made plans to join her before departing for home. Mrs. Roosevelt was to be accompanied by her eldest grandson, Curtis ("Buzz"), as well as by Miss Thompson, who, though ailing, had wished to accompany them on this trip.

For a while, it appeared that Curtis would have to be left behind. He fell victim to infantile paralysis, and it can be imagined how particularly frightening that diagnosis was to the Roosevelts. David had heard the news abroad and had written at once, frustrated to be too far away to offer his medical help. His letter crossed with Mrs. Roosevelt's to him, in which she described the family's ordeal. David wrote her from London:

29.8.48

My dearest Mrs. Roosevelt,

I just was told about something like infantile paralysis in Anna's boy in the papers two days ago. I sent you a telegram. I just hope that if it should be true, he is a mild case and that he will be entirely well, like the majority [of cases]. That I am not there to help just at such a moment! . . . I know so well the comparative values and merits of the different places and people [of treatment and specialists]. . . . I have the feeling that you have gone out there [to California]. With all your experience in handling a severe case. But most likely it is not too serious—I do so hope that it is so.

A week in London. Now it is time to get out in the country. I shall go in two days with Grania. Nemone is well and obviously happier without me. [Nemone had left to go off on her own for a few days.]

My thoughts are so much with you. How much there was of weariness and trouble for you since you stepped into the plane in Zurich! . . .

September 1, '48

My dearest Mrs. R.,

Your letter came today. Yesterday I had your telegram. It was 4 days later and it was still a mild case. Most cases, specially the mild ones, have shown the worst by then. But the waiting in those first days, the watching of the devastating progress from hour to hour, from day to day, is the one aspect of my association with this disease which I can hardly bear. Poor Anna, and on top of all the rest of it! By now it is all clear. What muscles are affected, and to what extent?

I am glad about your three days on the ocean. But it is not very long for what there was in the way of effort [before leaving] and for what is now ahead! I am afraid that in 20 years our concept of the freedom of the individual has been blotted out in a Russian brain. . . . And it seems so wise that you, with your balance between idealism and reality, have been chosen for this big keynote address [referring to the coming session of the UN]. . . .

Here all goes well. I am going for long walks with Grania and life with Nemone* is much better than I anticipated. . . .

Today I am moving to old grandmother Norman [Nemone's maternal grandmother] till the 8th. She has a large garden and I shall be able to rest and to be with Grania and Nemone till they leave on the 8th. From the 8th–20th I shall stay here in the country and then come to Paris. I think I am getting all the rest required this way. It is finally a matter of self-discipline, not to yield to the temptations of the town. . . .

Mrs. Roosevelt promptly replied:

VAL-KILL COTTAGE
September 2, 1948
Dearest David,

Your dear letter of the 29th was here when I came home from N.Y. late this afternoon. I loved your telegram too, it was a mild case [of polio] and tonight Anna called me to say the quarantine was over [California law required two weeks] and Buzz had had no temperature since he reached the Naval hospital at Colorado, 10 days ago. Nothing more developed than stiffness in his back and in the calf of one leg—They are starting treatments tomorrow— They think he should perhaps go abroad with me as I could make him eat and sleep and watch over him and he would be interested. They will let me know definitely in a few days. Anna sounded so relieved, like a new person, and it seemed to me a miracle that we should be so lucky. My heart was so heavy and now it is light again—

You are right, since I left you in Zurich the problems, mostly psychological ones, have been rather heavy on me. I'll tell you all about them in Paris and you can tell me whether I've been wise or wrong in handling my large and complicated family.

---

*Nemone had rejoined them, and here David refers to Nemone's state of health.

I am glad you and Grania went to the country and I hope you write a little more about yourself before I leave.

Only about 10 days now before I sail and we have much still to do.

You will laugh. I had a wonderful time today doing Xmas shopping! I was afraid I might be late in getting home.

The book is really almost done and I hope to get the first draft in though Tommy [Miss Thompson, Mrs. Roosevelt's secretary] may not find it possible.

A letter from Trude [Lash] says they reach N.Y. September 5 and it has been a good summer. She tells me George [Wenzel, Trude's brother] is to be married but nothing about the lady. . . .

I am really getting excited at the thought of seeing you soon, it will be a real joy for me! Bless you dear for all your thoughts and concern for us and many many thanks.

Affly and devotedly,
E. R.

Curtis was sufficiently well to make the journey with his grandmother after all, and the party left on September 13. The boat docked in France on the twentieth, the same day on which David arrived.

This time, they met in Paris, a city both Mrs. Roosevelt and David loved and knew well. Upon checking into the Crillon Hotel, where Mrs. Roosevelt was stopping, David first examined Curtis,* and then next Miss Thompson, who had been ill. With Mrs. Roosevelt's UN meetings claiming most of her time, and having a grandson on hand to entertain, this reunion was less private and intense than the one in Zurich five months earlier. All the same, Mrs. Roosevelt was happy to have David close by. He attended the speech she gave at the Sorbonne on the twenty-seventh

---

*In a conversation we had together in 1990, Curtis Dall Roosevelt remembered the examination David had given him in the Crillon Hotel. He recalled in particular the gentleness and sensitivity with which David had handled him, for Curtis described himself to me as "a self-conscious adolescent at the time."

and accompanied her to several of her UN meetings, observing her diplomatic skill in achieving compromise among different international delegates regarding the many articles of the Declaration of Human Rights.

David noted:

> Mrs. Roosevelt had to face the question of the plight of the War refugees [those interned in displaced persons' camps after their liberation from concentration camps]. The Russians insisted on having them forcibly repatriated. There were many former Russians in those Displaced Persons Camps, among others. Mrs. Roosevelt was assigned to give the important speech in their behalf and Vishinsky* was to be arguing against her. You never knew how Mrs. Roosevelt worked on a speech; you never saw any evidence of it. She would be thinking about it, turning it over in her mind. Occasionally she would mention a word or two, take in your impression. She did not appear to worry about it, but you knew she was absorbed with it. In her speech, Mrs. Roosevelt discussed her concept of what it meant to be free and what human life represents in a democracy where the State serves the person, as opposed to the concept of the person serving the State. This speech praising freedom was a great success. I believe the *New York Times Magazine* printed it side by side with Vishinsky's speech. It was after this that Mr. Dulles and Mr. Vandenberg, the two Republicans on the American Delegation, stopped her and said that they had originally thought her appointment to the Delegation was a mistake when it was made. They then told her that she had contributed a great deal and they wanted to apologize for their initial attitude . . . words to that effect. This is pretty well documented. She told it to me afterwards. The Russians did all they could to make the debate and

---

*Andrei Vishinsky, Soviet statesman, died in 1954.

speech about the refugees difficult. They dragged it out forever, far into the night. They knew that the later the United States' answer would come in the debate, the fewer the people present listening to it would be, and of course the later the hour, the more tired the speaker would be. It was about 1:30 A.M. when Mrs. Roosevelt finally spoke. They [the Soviets] delayed as much as they could, but they didn't know Mrs. Roosevelt! They didn't know her stamina and her perseverance.

Mrs. Roosevelt was adroit in persuading the recalcitrant Soviets to give up their determination to have displaced persons forcibly repatriated, and to see that they had no choice finally but to agree to majority accord.

Despite her long hours of arduous work for the adoption of the Declaration of Human Rights, she still managed time for sight-seeing jaunts to Versailles and Fontainebleau, among other attractions, accompanied by her grandson and David. She and David arranged private time together, as well. They dined alone as often as possible, usually in small Left Bank restaurants where there was less fuss and some assurance of being undisturbed. David wrote in his notes: "We went many times to the Louvre and walked in the Tuilleries. We saw many art exhibits. In spite of the fact that Mrs. Roosevelt had lots of things to do, there was still time for enjoying just Paris. . . ."

One evening, Mrs. Roosevelt invited two guests to dinner: Gen. George C. Marshall, then secretary of state, and U.S. Ambassador Philip C. Jessup, who had gone to Paris to address the United Nations. She gave David the assignment of finding a good restaurant. Wanting to provide a different atmosphere for diplomats accustomed to the stiffness of formal dinners, David reserved a table in his name at a little-known place in the Latin Quarter, recommended to him by Parisian friends for its excellent cuisine. The entrance of General Marshall and Eleanor Roosevelt caused considerable stir among the diners, not to mention the proprietress, who hardly expected such prominent patrons in her rather modest establishment. But the choice was a great success. Soon afterward, readers of Mrs. Roosevelt's "My Day" newspaper column learned about the delicious meal she and her guests had enjoyed at Le Relais de Porquerolles,* which resulted in traveling Americans as well as curious French rushing for reservations. From then on, out of loyalty to the restaurant she was told she had helped become prosperous, Mrs. Roosevelt never went to Paris without stopping for a meal at the Porquerolles, though each of these visits ended in a hassle between the proprietress, who refused to present a bill, and Mrs. Roosevelt, who insisted upon one.**

David's appearance in Paris had made Mrs. Roosevelt feel less like a public servant and more like a woman. His company was welcome relief in her official life of protocol—meetings, reports, and speeches without end. Although he was there on October 11 to celebrate her birthday, he could not stay abroad much longer. He had already been gone from the United States for eleven months. On October 16, he sailed for home, back to Nemone—the question of the continuation of their marriage still unresolved—and back to the eighth floor of the Neurological Institute, at Columbia-Presbyterian Medical Center, and back to his private medical practice. This time, it was Mrs. Roosevelt who remained behind. After he left, she wrote him: "You know how much I want to be on the same side of the ocean with you. I'm glad you love me. I love you dearly and send you my most devoted thoughts."

Mrs. Roosevelt regretted not being in Hyde Park for Thanksgiving, and she wrote David a letter:

November 25th [1948]
... My thoughts fly off to you so often dear. I hope life is not too difficult and you are well and the troubles will not be all encompassing. I look forward so much to seeing you, do you think you

---

*This restaurant no longer exists.
**The last time David and I were in Paris with Mrs. Roosevelt, the usual debate over the bill took place—David included this time—and was settled surprisingly quickly. Mrs. Roosevelt had come prepared. In moving out toward the door after dinner, accompanied by the restaurant owner, Mrs. Roosevelt pressed into her hand the gold bracelet she had ordered for her at Tiffany's before leaving New York.

can find a little time to sit down and talk or will I have to be ill to get a glimpse of you? I am saying a prayer of Thanksgiving tonight and I send you my love and thanks for being you and letting me know you.

Devotedly your friend,
Eleanor Roosevelt

At 3:00 A.M. on December 10, 1948, at the Palais de Chaillot, delegates to the third session of the United Nations General Assembly adopted by unanimous vote the Universal Declaration of Human Rights, for which Eleanor Roosevelt had so resolutely worked. It was generally thought that only she, who commanded such worldwide respect, could have succeeded in achieving universal consensus. Her mission accomplished, she could hardly wait to get home on December 13.

3

ON THE SAME SIDE
OF THE OCEAN

Mrs. Roosevelt Speaks Her Mind

STEADY CORRESPONDENCE BETWEEN MRS. Roosevelt and David during the entire time he'd been away, together with their overseas calls and meetings in Zurich and Paris, had kept them close. In David's absence, his wife, Nemone, and young daughter had been guests at Hyde Park. David's name began to be mentioned there. In fact, some members of the family were becoming uneasy about him.* Mrs. Roosevelt had seldom referred to David in letters home. To her daughter, Anna, for example, she mentioned him only occasionally and impersonally, referring to him as Dr. Gurewitsch or David Gurewitsch, never by his first name alone. Now, however, with both of them back in New York and David a frequent visitor to Hyde Park, it became increasingly obvious to all that there was a significant new person in Mrs. Roosevelt's life and that this friendship had an undeniable glow. It was soon noticed that a framed photograph of David appeared on Mrs. Roosevelt's desk, and yet another, the one picture on the night table beside her bed in the city apartment. Indeed, she kept his photograph near her at all times, taking one in a green leather traveling picture frame along on her trips. Despite

---

*Author's interview with Curtis Roosevelt, October 1991.

all her comings and goings—the fund-raising speeches she gave for charity organizations, her lectures and meetings, the trips she made as she regularly crisscrossed the country—Mrs. Roosevelt made routine calls to David. Her letters to him were filled with expressions of thoughtfulness, tenderness, and, yes, passion. She kept in touch with David's wife, Nemone, as she later told me, in order to help him maintain contact with his daughter; she also found time to visit his friends in Europe, glad to bring back their news—the young Lady Mendl in Brussels and the widow of a friend from his youth, Pierre Vienot, a French foreign service officer who had been imprisoned and escaped with Pierre Mendès-France during the German occupation. Mrs. Roosevelt's home was open to David at all times, a ready haven if ever he needed it. She understood his preoccupation with work, had endless patience with his indecisiveness, and worried about his stamina and health. David was the first person she telephoned on the mornings she was in New York or in Hyde Park for a few hurried words before they left on their respective rounds of the day. He was the first person she called upon her return from a trip. There were midweek dinners whenever schedules allowed, and birthdays, holidays, and other kinds of occasions were celebrated together. Mrs. Roosevelt's preoccupation with David left little doubt as to his place in her heart. But he had made it clear to her from the start that his privacy was necessary to him, and his candor helped mark the boundary between them.

Despite the closeness of their bond, evidenced in her extremely caring letters to him, Mrs. Roosevelt and David were never lovers. Indeed, the tragedy of this superior woman was that she never had the absolute, intimate love of a man. Franklin Roosevelt had been incapable of a deeply personal, sharing relationship.* It was *that* which she craved. Mrs. Roosevelt generally accepted what she could not change. Long before David came

---

*Conversations with FDR biographer Geoffrey C. Ward (1999), as well as his book *A First-Class Temperament: The Emergence of Franklin Roosevelt* (New York: Harper & Row, 1989), confirmed my understanding, gleaned from my husband, that the president was an extremely private person, unable to confide even in those closest to him.

into her life, she had learned how to create order out of inner chaos. She was able to transform the attraction she felt for David into expressions of tenderness appropriate to an intimate but platonic union.

The nature of the relationship left no room for major disappointments or feelings of abandonment. Before she met David, she had experienced disillusionment and rejection and had had little personal fulfillment. She had given so much, yet had received so little. When she met David, Mrs. Roosevelt must have wanted a more rewarding relationship than those she had had before. She needed to replenish her emotional needs. Although the expectations that a woman ordinarily has regarding a man she loves were never there, Mrs. Roosevelt was ready to embark upon this relationship despite the likelihood that it would satisfy only partial needs. The sadness is that she accepted the partial, that this extraordinary woman had, at that late stage in her life, to accept a relationship that was conditional and incomplete.

She adjusted to the fact that David's romantic life did not include her. She knew that he loved her, that she was important to him, and also that he was not going to change his life to please her. Their love was idealistic on both sides, though David's did not include romantic fantasy. His careful insistence about keeping a private life not only established limits between them; it also enabled him to test her constantly to be sure that she accepted him entirely. She did. She loved him for what he was, for his strengths and weaknesses, seeing and understanding everything. That is, after all, how she loved all people. Mrs. Roosevelt was wise enough to remember that David was wary of possessiveness, and she knew that if she wanted to keep him close, she could not make him feel "claustrophobic" (his word). Carefully, she reminded him, "Don't let anything I ask you to do make you feel hounded. I understand your schedule and never want you to feel you must do something I ask. I only want you to enjoy yourself and get relaxation."

She tactfully accommodated his various romances, befriended one or two of the women involved, when feasible, and, rising above her own longings, unselfishly encouraged him in every way—with rare lapses—to be free and independent, even of her. It is obvious from her letters alone that she accepted the reality of her relationship with David as he defined it, at the same time recognizing the many positive aspects it held for her.

It has been suggested that Mrs. Roosevelt paid heavily in loving David, an unattainable man.* In fact, she received much more than she expected. In his capacity as her physician and as a loving friend, David was the one person who watched over her, who could and did deal with her forthrightly when she neglected herself, or when she was tense from overwork or complications in the family. He gave Mrs. Roosevelt loyalty and affection. He respected and honored her, which was very important to her. She entrusted him with her innermost thoughts and feelings and appreciated his genuine and lively interest in her work. He had a profound admiration for her accomplishments and was fascinated by her inside news of politics and world events. That he had the broad outlook of an educated, sophisticated man and deep insight into human behavior, an important element in his everyday work, intrigued her. She listened avidly to his information about medical practice, patient care, and public health issues worldwide; she put this knowledge to good use whenever it could be helpful, as was her custom. She identified with David's devotion to the welfare of others and admired his achievements as a doctor.

Having faith in him, she came to him with problems of all sorts, consulted him on family illnesses and upheavals, and on her own professional activities, as well. Indeed, in his capacity as her doctor, David had the power to take care of Mrs. Roosevelt. Certainly in her day, physicians were regarded as authority figures. It is not unlikely that in seeking David's advice, she looked to him as a father figure, a role similar to that of a doctor: to comfort and to heal. Here was a man who felt responsible for her health and well-being, someone who literally took care of her—the only one who did. For this, she was very grateful. She related to David on different levels. To her, he encompassed the qualities she had missed in her husband, her sons, and, above all, in that one father she needed to "replace": steadfastness, loyalty, and the capacity to relieve her deeply

---

*Joseph P. Lash, A World of Love: Eleanor Roosevelt and Her Friends, 1943–1962 (Garden City: Doubleday, 1984), p. 269.

rooted loneliness. Her letters reveal thoughts of David as a lover; she revered him at times as a father, and protected him as a son. David was a refuge for Mrs. Roosevelt. Her belief in his work and her understanding of his compassion as a physician were fundamental to her respect and love for him. The longer she knew him, the more her trust was reinforced. An excerpt from a letter to him defined their relationship:

> I came across a nice description today. "To see a face unfold to all its subtle shades of meaning and of softness, and know one had moved that face to such expression, is to feel like God." Perhaps that is what doctors sometimes feel, or friends who find a deep and enduring bond of understanding which does not run dry! . . . I miss having you near. God bless and keep you. My love to you.
>
> E. R.

To a man who had been rootless and had not been eligible for any passport until the age of forty-two, friendship with this powerful, world-renowned figure gave David a sense of stability he had not known before. It was inspiring and immensely pleasurable for someone whose own mother had constant high expectations of him, and who was so self-demanding, to win approbation from such an admired woman. He didn't have to earn Mrs. Roosevelt's love. He had it. In June 1953, this "ideal mother" had written him, "Do you mind if I tell you now and then how much you mean to me? I love you dearly and respect and admire you deeply but the loving is the most important because that will be there no matter what you do. Goodnight and bless you."

What woman could be more symbolic of authority than the wife of a president of the United States? This had special appeal for a man who remembered that in his Berlin boyhood he had been required to make humiliating visits to a German police station on a regular basis because his family were Russian aliens. Indeed, by the time he was seven years old, Germany was the third country in which David had lived. Aside from his commitment to his work, which was a constant element in his life, he had always considered himself a person apart, an outsider, more of a spectator of the mainstream of society than the participant he yearned to be. Closeness to Eleanor Roosevelt imbued him with some longed-for sense of inclusion. As a physician, David had private recognition, but he craved public approval. Mrs. Roosevelt had public recognition, but she craved intimacy. Each satisfied the other's hunger for acceptance. It was a fair exchange.

When David returned from Europe in November 1948, he plunged into work at the Neurological Institute. To treat those suffering from incapacitating illnesses and disabilities, those working in the physical rehabilitation specialty needed to possess both diagnostic skill and knowledge of modern therapeutic equipment and treatment: hydrotherapy tanks, a well-supplied gymnasium, properly fitted prostheses, diathermy, ultrasound, specially designed tables to enable therapists to practice techniques of muscle reeducation and other procedures. To return patients to living as independently and productively as possible, teams of doctors, physical and occupational therapists, nurses and social workers had to be educated and trained to work together. In addition, a homelike atmosphere was required in the hospital, and disabled patients had to be motivated to help themselves.

David was one of the pivotal figures in the field and was totally committed to all aspects of his specialty.* He was keenly sensitive to his patients' feelings. An old-time hospital secretary remembered how unusual it was for a doctor to ask the families of his patients, as David did, if and how they thought he could better serve them.** "Dr. Gurewitsch gave all the time to a patient that he and his family wanted. He *listened* to them and encouraged their suggestions. Above all, he gave his patients hope, realistic hope, that they could improve and get well." In the 1940s,

*Author's interviews with Dr. John A. Downey and Dr. Stanley J. Myers, A. David Gurewitsch Professor of Rehabilitation Medicine, 1991–92.
**Author's interview with Ann Reusch, secretary, Department of Rehabilitation Medicine, Neurological Institute, Columbia-Presbyterian Medical Center, November 1992.

treating the "whole patient," rather than only the physical complaint, was a new concept. From the time he first began to teach, David emphasized to medical students and therapists the importance of a compassionate approach to a patient's recovery. He also told them that "a doctor carries a bag of tricks. If one doesn't work, then another must be tried. You adapt your skills to the patient, not the other way around." His hands-on treatment and psychological insight produced outstanding results.

By this time Mrs. Roosevelt had moved out of her Washington Square apartment to a suite in the midtown New York Park Sheraton Hotel. The management had given her son Elliott a special reduced rate when he had stayed there on an earlier occasion, and Mrs. Roosevelt, not forgetting a favor to one of her children, chose the hotel as an act of loyalty. While her "My Day" columns were ongoing and she managed to finish her book *This Is My Story* (1949), as well as fulfill countless other obligations, the main thrust of her work continued to be her duties at the United Nations.

She also stood guard over her large brood of often-unruly children. Mrs. Roosevelt worried about James's health and marital problems, as well as Anna's difficulties resulting from her second disappointing marriage. Elliott and his wife, the actress Faye Emerson, were living at the time in his father's retreat, Top Cottage, situated on a hill on the Val-Kill property. Mrs. Roosevelt and Elliott had formed a partnership to farm Val-Kill. She would have done anything to keep him there. When the farming plan didn't work out, Elliott, after his divorce in 1949, stayed on, but he did not make a success of his other various Hyde Park projects, either. In 1952, he married Minnewa Bell Ross, a friend of Johnny and Anne Roosevelt, who were then living in Stone Cottage. Their mother's happiness in having two of her sons settled in Val-Kill was short-lived. Before Elliott and Minnewa moved away, to Mrs. Roosevelt's keen disappointment, Elliott sold Top Cottage.*

Meanwhile, David took on the added part-time position of first

---

*Funds have been raised by the Franklin and Eleanor Roosevelt Institute to buy back and restore Top Cottage.

medical officer of the United Nations. Because of his ability to organize care, his interest in foreign affairs, and his facility with several languages, the prospect of setting up an infirmary and a system providing health services to UN personnel greatly interested him. At the end of 1951, when he felt he had accomplished all he had set out to do in the three years he supervised these endeavors, he left. His plans had changed.

In the summer of 1949, Mrs. Roosevelt wanted to take David to Campobello so they could be together and she could share with him the place she loved—the big red Victorian "cottage" that held so much of her family history and where she felt he could have a needed rest. Choosing to go his own way, he declined, preferring to vacation on Cape Cod with friends. She wrote him:

PARK SHERATON HOTEL
Monday night
David dear,

I've wanted to talk to you but kept to my resolve not to pressure you! I think I should try to tell you why I wanted you so much to go to Campo and spend your 3 weeks with us. I've never felt sure that you enjoyed being with me enough so you would be willing to relax and be without other people and not be bored and when you accepted another offer with such alacrity I realized that I had been right not to be sure and even though I saw your reasons were right and your instinct probably correct, I couldn't help being a little sad for as one gets older the joy of real companionableness is rarer and rarer especially with the young and one cares for fewer and fewer people. Most people are an effort and the hope of finding a mutual pleasure in enjoying any extended, quiet time together is not a hope often entertained. Then too I was not and am not sure what you are doing will give you comfort and rest and no worry but I do hope so now with all my heart for I want you to be well and happy and return to the work you love fully refreshed.

In a letter whose envelope was marked, "For Dr. Gurewitsch only to read, personal and private," Mrs. Roosevelt wrote:

WESTBROOK
Thursday night
David dear,

Since our talk today I have thought much of what you plan and I am not happy. First to be worthy of you it seems to me 2 things must be considered. The decision must be clear with Nemone. Next, because a woman offers to go on a holiday with you and you want to find out if you can stop thinking of Nemone does not to me seem good enough. If you told me you were in love [and] the decision [to divorce] was taken between you and Nemone, and you wanted to be sure for you and a new love if this was a real and deep love that would be clear, but going off for a 3 week holiday cannot be casual and if on your side there is no real love, well, one may forget a night now and then but 3 weeks of constant companionship either is very good or no good it seems to me.

Does there come into your plan any thought that you don't want to beholden to me or to put me out? I think I will take Tommy [Malvina Thompson] to Campo in any case. I can leave the 15th or you and Tommy can go up ahead and stay after I leave or leave with me. I realize I cannot give you what a young woman can but til you are fairly sure of what you want, do you really want what you are now planning? It worries me for you, and I think just now the care and love that it would be a joy to me . . . to give might make you happier with yourself in making your final decision.

I do not want to interfere in your life for of course I have no right to do so but I do not want you to do something you may regret. May God help and bless you.

E. R.

P.S. Perhaps one basic thing that bothers me is that you are letting an offer of this kind be made *to you* rather than making it yourself to a woman because you really love her. From all you tell me you have always been pursued and I think it is time for you to do the pursuing if any real good is to come to you. You are spoiled by pursuit and you are perhaps too sensitive to go out and get what you really want.

I imagine I am 20 or so years older than you are and I have lived many emotions and observed many and I am sure happy marriages develop when the man shows his desire to the woman and she responds fully and happily. Even at your age, tho' some physical satisfaction is essential, you must be even surer of mental interests and sympathetic understanding which will lead to complete and happy companionship.

E. R.

Another time, she wrote:

... I used to love Campobello, the air, the woods and sea and sunsets, very much, but people matter to me more than places. It would have been fun to show it to you and hope that it would give you some of the lift it used to give me. Tommy will enjoy it and I will try to give her a good time but our contacts are best in the field of work and not much good otherwise tho' we love each other dearly! She likes to play cards in the evening and I find it dull but I have to play! I'll decide with Elliott on what needs to be done and get contracts and Elliott and David [his son] will leave us and I think we'll start home with Linaka [Campobello housekeeper] on the 24th for nowadays unless I have someone I really want to be with up there it is not a good place to be. There are good and bad memories there but the bad get the better of me when I'm there alone. I'll read a lot and practice typing and the lamps aren't too good for night reading and there the night has a thousand eyes— So I'll be home the 25th or 26th. God bless you! and my love to you.

E. R.

As usual, Mrs. Roosevelt overcame her disappointment when David went elsewhere. It wasn't until twelve years later that he made the trip to Campobello with her.

Martha Gellhorn

For four years, David and Nemone's marriage had been on the brink of dissolution. Though both were aware of its temporary nature, they nevertheless continued to live together, connected by a kind of familiar, friendly interdependence, although they led separate lives. This arrangement gave David maximum social freedom and the added advantage of continued contact with Grania. Then the inevitable happened. When it did, it took Mrs. Roosevelt by surprise, though she had known all along it was in the offing. David fell in love. His choice was Martha Gellhorn, a gifted writer and former war correspondent, best known for her earlier marriage to Ernest Hemingway. Born in St. Louis, she was a bright, attractive, ambitious young woman who knew her way around the world. David's feelings were reciprocated. Years later, Martha Gellhorn wrote her friend Bernard Berenson that David had been the only true love of her life.* I never thought to ask David how they'd met when he told me about her, but I imagine it was through Mrs. Roosevelt.

Mrs. Roosevelt was acquainted with Martha's mother, who had been active in Democratic party politics in Missouri, and came to know Martha herself in 1934, when she was a young New Dealer briefly working as an investigative reporter for the Federal Emergency Relief Administration in Washington. At that time, Lorena Hickok, Mrs. Roosevelt's close friend, who was also employed by the agency headed by presidential assistant Harry Hopkins, brought Martha ("Marty") to the First Lady's attention as

---

*Correspondence with the art historian Bernard Berenson, the Harvard University Center for Italian Renaissance Studies, Berenson Archive, Villa I Tatti, Florence, Italy.

someone whose reports would interest her. In the following years, a friendship developed between the two women. Martha had been invited to the White House and to Hyde Park. Mrs. Roosevelt was familiar with Martha's romance with Ernest Hemingway, from whom she parted bitterly after a few years of marriage, and knew her work as a foreign correspondent, especially her firsthand observations of the civil war in Spain and postwar Germany.

Restless, and having a kind of chronic discontent, Martha was happiest on the move, an unpromising outlook for David, who was seeking an anchor. But he didn't seem to care—at least in the beginning. For most of their love affair, which lasted about two years, Martha Gellhorn lived in Mexico, not the most geographically convenient place for a busy New York doctor to go courting, but passion prevailed and go he did—mostly weekends. Back and forth. In considering remarriage (the matter of settling divorce details with Nemone had yet to be resolved), David and Martha had more than the ordinary complications facing them. For one thing, Martha had a decided aversion to all things American. She disliked the United States in general and New York in particular, the very places David had chosen to live. If David wanted to marry her, he would have to live and work in Mexico. Martha could not be persuaded to move east, nor, I suspect, was she sure that the role of doctor's wife would suit her. But David was carried away and willing to risk all, and he began to make plans to reestablish himself south of the border, buoyed by the hope that the move would bring them both the happiness they had long sought. He was granted a professorship in the Mexico City Medical School, and he opened a bank account in Mexico.

From the start, Mrs. Roosevelt felt it would be a mistake for David to move to Mexico, to uproot himself yet again and to relocate a medical practice he had worked so hard to establish. While he discussed the pros and cons in New York, little by little Martha began to have second thoughts. Her doubts became contagious, and the weekend flights to and from Mexico seemed more grueling to him. Despite the fact that David placed his passport and a DO NOT DISTURB sign on his chest so he could sleep, undisturbed by customs officials, as his plane crossed the Mexican border, the trips were strenuous. As months passed, uncertainty, so easily stirred in David, began to surface, and he contemplated his and Martha's future together with somewhat diminished delight.

Referring to one of his sojourns in Mexico, Mrs. Roosevelt wrote him rather listlessly in the spring of 1951:

HOTEL DES BERGUES
GENEVE SUISSE
May—
Dearest David,

It was good to find your two letters on getting back from London today. I had worried a little for fear you were not feeling well — Now I quite understand playing with fire is rather exciting, isn't it? Joking aside it must have been a nice change and I hope all the "papers" go well. Sometime I'd like to hear you give one. I'm sure you make the dryest subject sound interesting!

Geneva is beautiful in Spring and I am enjoying it, the lake and the flowers and the mountains, how could one do other than drink in the beauty. The hours of work are long and it is every bit as frustrating as I expected and the U.S. Senate will never ratify [the Universal Declaration of Human Rights] but so far we've not accepted anything we can't honestly fight for.

The weekends for work on radio and television do leave one no time free but I loved the day in Paris. The chestnut trees are just beginning to blossom. I dined at Les Porquerolles, and wished you were there with me.

London twice but now I'm through there.

I'm quite well again and what is even better I think Tommy is getting a rest and isn't overworked! Elliott and Minnewa arrived last Thursday and go home next Sunday. It is nice to have them but they keep me very busy.

I hope you gave my love to Martha. If she is depressed you will help her. It helps to talk out one's troubles to an understanding and sympathetic person.

My love to you, take care of yourself—and send me a line when you can. Love to Nemone and Grania.

Devotedly,

E. R.

Mrs. Roosevelt had been drawn into this love affair by the confidences of both parties. I can well imagine how disconsolate she must have been over the prospect of no longer having David near, of "not catching a glimpse" of him nor of "having the joy of hearing his voice," as she put it. Still, she transcended her own feelings, as usual, and thought only of David's happiness. She could not bear to see him disappointed again. She knew Martha, and felt quite strongly, as she once told me in a burst of confidence, that it was unfair and self-centered of her to ask David to sacrifice all that he had built up in New York, since, as Mrs. Roosevelt said emphatically (and from her own experience), "a writer can write anywhere." Also, she held the traditional belief that a woman adjusts her life to the man's. Although David's welfare was her main concern and she could not deny her misgivings about Martha's ability to make him happy, Mrs. Roosevelt was nevertheless prepared to love whom he loved, not to risk losing him. And if the marriage was inevitable, she wanted to be on good terms with Martha. She did everything possible to uphold whatever and whoever brought David fulfillment, even when she questioned its wisdom for him. Her birthday letter to him that year had an undertone of farewell: "I am grateful to have known you . . ." Across its envelope were the words "To read now or on 31st, as you wish. E. R."

PARK SHERATON HOTEL
October 31 [1951]
David dearest,

This is a birthday letter whenever you read it. I fear it will not be a happy day this year but I will be thinking of you *every* day and wishing you greater happiness in the future than in the past. I shall be deeply sad when you go away but if you are happy I shall be glad for you. Remember always please that wherever I am open arms await you. My home *anywhere* is yours when you need it whether you are alone or whether you want to bring those you love. If you forget this I will never see you and that would leave me bereft. I cherish every moment we are together these last days that I am here for I realize that there [may] not be many more. You know I think that I would rather be with you than with anyone else, whether we are alone or whether I am just watching you from afar. I am grateful to have known you and hope that we may keep close even though you establish a new life far away.

God bless and keep you and bring you satisfaction and happiness in your life, that is my daily prayer.

I wish I did not have to be away these coming weeks.

All my love David, dearest friend, and happy days to you always.

E. R.

That fall, Mrs. Roosevelt was in Geneva and Paris for United Nations meetings. In Paris, she enclosed a four-leaf clover for good luck in an anxious letter she left behind for David, who was going to Cuernavaca to spend his vacation with Martha.

David dear,

I must give you this little line to wish you luck and wisdom and ultimate happiness. I hate to have you go because I don't want you hurt and yet you can't be content unless you do so you must go. Remember dear marriages are two-way streets and when they are happy *both* must be willing to adjust. *Both must* love.

My love to Marty and her mother.

My thoughts and my love will be with you and please wire when you leave. God bless and help you my dear.

E. R.

She wrote again from Holland, where she was visiting Queen Juliana:

[November 1951]
Dearest David,

So, you left last night for Mexico and I never spoke to you. I should have tried to get you even tho' I wasn't sure of the best time. Now I feel sad because I deprived myself of a great pleasure! You will be gone 4 weeks and you will have your divorce on your return? Please go to the apartment in the hotel on your return [in the event that he had left Nemone] so I find you settled there on my return for whatever time you spend in New York now or in the future alone.

I am glad all was well with Nemone. You say nothing of Grania? Does she know? I am glad you are no longer frantic, settled things are always easier than uncertainties. Marty will be alright now you are with her.

Your plan for the fellowship sounds very good and I think it is wise to keep some ties to the [New York] hospital and your courses until all is settled and you are sure what you want to do.

Our committee met Friday morning and I left in the afternoon for Holland. . . .

By maintaining his professional connections in New York, David had kept his options open. Feelings were shifting. Now Martha was more inclined to the idea of marriage than David was. Ever cautious about committing himself intimately to someone, he was gripped by his demons of indecision. His letter to Mrs. Roosevelt read:

CUERNAVACA
Wednesday, November 28, '51
Dearest Mrs. R.,

It is sunny here and peaceful. All is well except for a little digestive upset, the first one on all the Mexican trips so far and seems to be on the mend.

I have two patients and the lectures seem to be coming off. I am still not thinking though. There is an apprehension deep inside, unexpressed and without reason, but it is there, an apprehension against starting life here. But I arrived only yesterday one week ago and I have the right to a little more time. Marty is well. She does not press and she is in no hurry. . . .

CUERNAVACA

Sunday [December 2, 1951]

Dearest Mrs. R.,

Your good letter written mostly in Holland came. . . . I just cannot help feeling that in spite of the explosive spots around the globe, increasing in numbers and intensity, in spite of the world's seemingly reaching new heights of violence, that the danger for a big-scale conflagration is continuously becoming smaller, in favor of many smaller-scale wars which will probably go on here and there and in new places for some time. (My present source of information is an English language Mexican paper mostly concerned with Mexican news, "society" and crime.) No, Grania does not know [referring to a legal separation between Nemone and himself], and I am having nightmares about it. I am still not thinking, but still I am much less relieved than I expected. It is beautiful here and filled with vacation spirit, in spite of a little work and beginning lectures. And I still cannot write. Cannot commit myself to an expression of how I feel, not even to you — I imagine this is because I do not know myself. Martha understands that her gift (for organization) and her inclination to make plans have to be held back just a little at the moment.

My love to you and many thoughts.

Your

David

Mrs. Roosevelt had been in Europe for the meeting of the United Nations General Assembly, which was preoccupied with the Korean War. Indeed, she crossed the Atlantic frequently in 1950, 1951, and 1952 for Human Rights Commission meetings in Geneva and Paris. The "declaration of basic principles" needed covenants from individual governments to give it legal weight. It was this which absorbed Mrs. Roosevelt, though, unfortunately, she was correct in feeling pessimistic about the outcome.*

She wrote a letter to David on December 4, 1951, from Paris, while he was still vacationing with Martha in Mexico. It read in part: "Everything I do here makes me wish for you, to talk and consult with, to enjoy things and feel them with you would add a great deal. I wonder if we will take a trip together! Bless you and take care of yourself. My love to you."

When shortly after his Cuernavaca visit David left his job as first medical officer at the UN and accepted the coveted part-time position of medical director of what is now Blythedale Children's Hospital** in Valhalla, New York, it signified the end of his relationship with Martha. Although she later pretended to have forgotten David's name,† she confidentially wrote to a friend that "He will always have a magic no one else can have."‡

---

*The covenants have still not been ratified by the United States Senate.
**At that time, Blythedale was a children's convalescent home. In the last years of David's tenure, he, together with the executive director, Robert Stone, helped to transform it into what is known as the best children's hospital on the East Coast— certainly one of the best facilities in the country for treating children with long-term disabilities.
†Martha Gellhorn, "Oral History, Eleanor Roosevelt," Franklin D. Roosevelt Library, Hyde Park, New York.
‡Letter from Martha Gellhorn to Bernard Berenson, the Harvard University Center for Italian Renaissance Studies, Berenson Archive, Villa I Tatti, Florence, Italy, July 27, 1953.

"I Don't Suppose You Feel Like Going to India?"

Mrs. Roosevelt had kept up with the unruly progress of Martha and David's love affair. She had asked the two to join her in Paris on the last day of 1951, before she left on a long trip scheduled after the sixth General Assembly adjourned. David already knew about her plan to visit India and had been very tempted to accompany her. He noted in his journal:

> This trip had really begun with a discussion of our going to India. I remember a walk with Mrs. Roosevelt in the woods behind her Hyde Park cottage on an autumn day in 1951. It was shortly before noon, the time when Mrs. Roosevelt, her day's mail having been read and answered, liked to go walking. As usual, she was wearing her old tweed coat and sturdy brown rubber-soled shoes. I remember the exact spot, thick with fallen oak leaves, where we stopped to talk about this. Prime Minister Nehru had been in Hyde Park the year before and had invited Mrs. Roosevelt to visit India. Earlier and independently, I had been asked to lecture in Bombay, where they had started a hospital for Infantile Paralysis, and we thought, couldn't we join forces and make the trip together? Typically she worried, "There will be protocol to observe and lots of official duties and you won't enjoy that." "Don't worry," I said, "I'm sure I will enjoy it. And there will be so much to see." The Nehru invitation was still valid and she accepted it.

Learning of the India trip, her good friend and UN colleague Dr. Charles Malik urged her to include some Arab countries, particularly his own, Lebanon. Mrs. Roosevelt believed that it was time to focus on the needs of people of the East and Middle East, who were so dependent upon outside help. She decided she would first visit the Arab countries of Lebanon, Syria, and Jordan before going to Israel and then to Pakistan and India.

On the flight to Paris and for the month or so she worked there, Mrs. Roosevelt had with her in place of Miss Thompson, who was not well enough for the strenuous journey that lay ahead, her young second secretary, Maureen Corr, who was to make the entire trip with her. Anna's daughter, Eleanor ("Sisty"), and her husband, Van Seagraves, were already abroad waiting for them. The young couple planned to remain in Europe for a while after Mrs. Roosevelt and Maureen left Paris. It was Maureen's first experience in traveling with her boss, and the real beginning of their eleven-year association. Meanwhile, Mrs. Roosevelt heard from David that he had decided to join her in the last free time he had before his directorship of Blythedale Hospital in Westchester began, but— stunning news—he would be traveling to Paris alone. The breakup with Martha seemed definite, but with mercurial David, anything could happen. Dare Mrs. Roosevelt believe him? She wrote him on January 5, 1952: "Mme. [Léon] Blum* came to tea and when you come (if you do) I hope you will have time to meet her and hear her ideas. . . . I love you dear and I know how hard these days are for you and my thoughts are with you much of the time. God keep you." And then Mrs. Roosevelt began to count on David's arrival.

PARIS, HOTEL DE CRILLON
Jan. 10th, 1952
Dear dearest,

Thanks for the card [yellow inoculation form necessary for re-entry into the United States] which I will take to Dr. Tolstoi next Monday and get him to fill out. My passport is being visaed and when it returns I'll put the card and your letter on yellow fever into it.

Henry Morgenthau told me they got on well in Israel but you will be there longer than I will. I will ask Mr. Ziades, who came to see me about our trip from the Israel delegation and he'll tell

---

*Léon Blum, former premier of France.

me whether it is necessary and what hotel you would use as head-quarters. I saw Trygvie [sic] Lie* and he feels we may end the 9th or 10th but I don't think we can leave for Israel till Feb. 20th so you can plan when you want to leave N.Y. and then leave here for Israel. I will tell T.W.A. here to make arrangements for the day you wish to leave here but you arrange in N.Y. and get your visas there.

Please what do I give you for vaccines? I'd like to send a check before you leave. I think I can arrange to come in thro' Jerusalem so you will meet me there.

We are all invited, as I feared, to stay and be the guests of top people in Pakistan but I've written you've wanted to make a study of present-day medicine and I've said what I wanted to see. You won't have to do any parties or meetings that I do unless you find them interesting. They do plan to let us go a way into the Khyber Pass and I've always thought that would be beautiful.

Be sure to let me know the day you get here so I have your room and can meet you at airport or if I have meetings can send car.

Your letter makes me feel you are really coming and yet I can't help worrying about all your uncertainties. Not to have Martha come and not to see her, not to have anything definite with Nemone, you must feel sad and in some ways lost. I feel happy at the thought of seeing you and yet I want you to do what will bring you real happiness in the long run. I hope Nemone is not resentful against you or me when she is less unhappy. I wrote her and I hope I said the right thing. I wrote Marty too and thanked her for her Xmas wire and said little else.

I am very busy too but I keep the evenings free the first days of Feb. tho' I may be in Luxembourg from the 1st–3d but even if you get here the 2d I'd know you want to see old friends probably, nevertheless if I *know* you are coming I will probably stay here as

*Trygve Lie, Norwegian statesman and secretary general of the United Nations, 1953.

I long to see you and won't be able to wait a day if I know you are really here!

Take care of yourself and keep well. I know these weeks are a strain and you suffer in many ways. I wish I could really help but I love you and when you come I hope I can make you feel what it means to me to have you near.

Bless you,

E. R.

The General Assembly session ended on February 6, the day on which David arrived in Paris. He and Mrs. Roosevelt had little time together until the ninth, when she and Maureen left for Lebanon. He waited in Paris for the time he could join Mrs. Roosevelt in Israel, visiting friends and seeing patients in the meantime. He wrote in his journal: "Mrs. Roosevelt planned to fly directly to Beirut from Paris. . . . Because of my being Jewish, the United States Minister in Lebanon, Mr. Harold B. Minor, advised Mrs. Roosevelt that it would be 'politically most unwise if not impossible' for me to enter Lebanon or other Arab countries. [Mrs. Roosevelt and I] agreed that after her visit to the Arab countries, she would cross from the Arab to the Jewish side of Jerusalem, and that we would meet at the Mandelbaum gate."

Mrs. Roosevelt began her book *India and the Awakening East** by describing her brief trip to Lebanon, Syria, and Jordan, her sympathy with the plight of Arab refugees, their frustrations and bitterness against Israel, and their expressions of mistrust of Western nations, particularly the United States.

"But," she wrote, "memories are short when people suffer, and today most of the people in the camps, thinking only of what they have lost,

---

*Eleanor Roosevelt, *India and the Awakening East* (New York: Harper & Brothers, 1953). She inscribed David's copy: "To David, Without you this book would never have been written. With love and gratitude, Eleanor Roosevelt."

put the blame for their wretched plight on Israel and the United States rather than on their own leaders and the British." The people responded to Mrs. Roosevelt's compassion, aware that she was a woman with a purpose, someone with the power to help. Despite anti-American sentiment, she experienced warm hospitality from her Arab hosts and guides.

Mrs. Roosevelt and Maureen Corr drove from Amman, Jordan, to Jerusalem. David wrote about the trip in his journal:

> I was waiting there [at the Mandelbaum Gate] when she crossed over [into Israel] at a given time. It was an emotional moment for Mrs. Roosevelt. She had fought for Partition and was intensely and passionately pro-Israel. It certainly was an emotional moment for me. I was returning after an absence of seventeen years. I originally had gone to Israel in 1934 and had worked for a year in Tiberias for the unions' medical organization, called the "Sick Fund."* . . .
> On this return visit, I could see the growth, the progress made in the intervening years. No one who goes there escapes being caught up in the current of vitality — and Mrs. Roosevelt was no exception. The people who live there are politically fragmented. For example, they have twenty or thirty different political parties. But out of this melange comes a potency, and enormous dynamism. For a person of Mrs. Roosevelt's sensibilities and acute political antennae, being embraced by this drive and energy was inescapable. The boundary between the Arabs and the Jews was a winding, artificial, wayward-seeming line. From an airplane and from our rooms in the King David Hotel one could easily discern the border; the Israeli side was green, the Arab side brown and arid. Mrs. Roosevelt noted the remarkable spirit of a people who had made the desert bloom through irrigation and an unquenchable personal resolve. "This country teems with life and purpose," she said.

---

*The majority of Israelis were unionized. The "Sick Fund" was the name of the service that provided medical care to all union members, similar to present-day health-insurance plans.

Her own life had been devoted to solving human problems. . . . At home she knew what could be solved and what remained insoluble. In Israel she found a society where nothing seemed impossible. No problem was beyond solution by these determined people. They could not afford the luxury of postponement. . . .

Of all the world figures she met, I think she found Prime Minister Ben-Gurion the most intriguing. . . . She once remarked that whether he was speaking or listening, his eyes were always sparkling and alert. . . . In Beersheba, once a small communications center for Arab caravans, we noted how the training given to a newly arrived group of beggars helped them to help themselves to [achieve] self-sufficiency. . . . By 1952, we saw a town with wide, tree-shaded streets and 50,000 inhabitants. . . . Tourists visiting there are almost invariably sent to meet an Arab chieftain in Israeli territory who has remained neutral and rather friendly to the Israelis through the years of Arab-Israeli conflict. We were also directed to him. It was common knowledge that the gentleman kept a large harem. When the tall, handsome chieftain met Mrs. Roosevelt, he rather quickly proposed marriage to her. She immediately inquired, jokingly, "And what number wife would I be?" Hearing the high number, she declined the offer with mock regrets.

After six days of intensive travel throughout Israel, Mrs. Roosevelt, Maureen, and David flew on to Karachi, the capital of Pakistan. As their plane was descending, David pointed to the window, from which could be seen masses of people waiting on the airfield below. "Look!" he exclaimed to Mrs. Roosevelt. Among the crowd were thousands of brightly clad, flag-waving schoolchildren; as they later learned, the city had declared the day a school holiday in honor of the famous American visitor. "This welcome must be for you," David told Mrs. Roosevelt. "Oh no," she replied. "Someone important must be on this flight." David later noted, "That was a characteristic response of Mrs. Roosevelt."

When traveling, they followed David's proposal. Instead of accepting

the many invitations extended to Mrs. Roosevelt to see a wide variety of
things, he felt they would gain broader information by concentrating on
their specific interests. It was the procedure they followed on subsequent
travels, as well. Mrs. Roosevelt provided David with opportunities to observe people and activities to which he might not otherwise have had
access. Some, she herself might have bypassed had he not been with her.
Before the trip began, Mrs. Roosevelt had asked to see different kinds of
medical facilities and to speak with varying levels of caregivers. While she
had always been interested in the subject of public health, on this, her
first trip with David, she wanted to be especially sure that his main interest, was incorporated into their schedule. This worked to her advantage
as well, for through his expertise she learned a good deal about medical
education and the care being given the sick. They traveled to village and
mobile dispensaries, where David examined patients together with local
medical teams. He lectured on his specialty and spoke to groups about
hospital and departmental organization. As often as possible during the
brief snatches of privacy amid their daily activities, and customarily at the
end of each day, David and Mrs. Roosevelt talked things over and traded
impressions, helping to clarify each other's views. And they recorded what
they saw, Mrs. Roosevelt in her ongoing newspaper column, magazine
articles, and, in this case, a book, as well as in reports for United States
and United Nations officials for whom certain information might be
useful.

David wrote in his journal: "The night before going up the Khyber
Pass was spent in Government House in Peshawar, preceded by a dinner
given by the Provincial Governor, which was followed by a colorful open-
air show. . . . Visiting the Khyber Pass—the gateway to the plains of India—for Mrs. Roosevelt was 'a sentimental journey.' "* She and her party
took the same route her father had taken while on a hunting trip seventy-
two years before; he had told her many tantalizing stories about this trip
when she was a child. David recorded what happened at the Khyber Pass:

*See Roosevelt, *India and the Awakening East*, p. 92.

"Elder Afridi tribesmen had gathered at the mouth of the Khyber Pass to meet Mrs. Roosevelt, bringing to present to her a huge, flat, round loaf of bread and three large sheep as a gift. There was an awkward moment after the presentation. . . . to my relief I heard her first graciously accept the bread and animals and then ask the donors to slaughter the sheep and have a feast in her honor."

Mrs. Roosevelt, David, and Maureen left Pakistan on February 27, flying from the airport in Lahore to India. David's journal entries describe various highlights of their time in India:

In India, we stayed in the Prime Minister's house. His official hostess was his daughter, Indira Gandhi [later to be prime minister herself]. Mme. Pandit, Nehru's sister, was also there in the house. At the time she headed India's delegation to the United Nations and was, naturally, well known to Mrs. Roosevelt. . . . Shortly after our arrival, Mrs. Roosevelt was scheduled to address members of the Indian Parliament, many of whom harbored bitter anti-American feelings in their struggle to be a neutral Third World force. Having gotten rid of British rule, they were determined not to be controlled by either the U.S.S.R. or the U.S. It was the moment in post-war history when there was growing distrust of foreigners. The United States was offering foreign aid and the Russians were trying to dissuade countries from accepting it. . . . I listened to Ambassador [Chester] Bowles brief Mrs. Roosevelt for her appearance before Parliament. He produced a list of questions and problems, which he advised her not to mention. The list seemed endless. Finally Mrs. Roosevelt asked him, "Then what am I allowed to speak about?" To this, Ambassador Bowles smiled [and said], "Oh, you will know." Then I heard Mrs. Roosevelt ask Prime Minister Nehru how long he thought her speech should be. "This is your occasion," he replied. "As long as you like."

Mrs. Roosevelt was the first foreign woman to address the Indian Parliament. The atmosphere was icy. I sat in the audience and watched her walk onto the platform. Wearing a simple dress, comfortable walking shoes, and a little flowery hat, she stood at the edge of the platform, holding her handbag, a microphone in front of her. She was so unpretentious and charming as to begin to disarm them. She carried no notes, not a single sheet of paper. She never used notes or read a prepared speech. She would rehearse it in her mind. She "read" her audience, adapting her words to them. Mrs. Roosevelt's shy, nervous smile caught the audience's attention at the outset. She began to talk, not as an orator might, but in the most informal, chatty manner. The Indians were accustomed to formal speeches from foreign dignitaries. But Mrs. Roosevelt was herself and spoke her mind directly. The audience obviously felt the strength of her personality and quickly sensed that here was a friend come to share her thoughts, not to lecture them. She did not defend the United States nor attempt to persuade her listeners to act or think differently. She said she understood their position of aloofness. After all, who could understand them better than Americans? We were once in the same position, she said. We had wanted to stay out of other people's squabbles and troubles; we had been a young country. Originally we also had had to get rid of the British. After some five or so minutes, there was a scattered applause. After a few more minutes the applause became more widespread and after twenty minutes, Mrs. Roosevelt had the audience in the palm of her hand. She had told me that she planned to give a thirty-minute talk, and without having written a single note, much less a draft of a speech, she stopped promptly after a half hour.

I felt that no one else standing before the Indian Parliament could have eased the tensions between the two countries [India and the United States] as well as she had done. . . . The reaction to the speech was enthusiastic. The next day the front pages of papers I saw were covered with a verbatim record of it.

At formal dinners everywhere, the "Star-Spangled Banner" was played, not always entirely recognizable but always with enthusiasm.

Mrs. Roosevelt deeply appreciated this gesture, believing it to be a tribute to her husband and country, not to herself.

Writing about their time in Bombay, David explained in his journal why he had changed the subject of his talks from rehabilitation medicine to the more pressing problem of containing India's exploding population, and the importance of organizing mobile medical units to travel to women out in the hinterlands to dispense birth-control information and devices.

I came to the conclusion that in improving the beggar's crippling condition, you took away his livelihood. I began to be interested in a completely different problem, that of population control. Any progress India would make today would become nullified by the constantly increasing population. I discussed this thoroughly with Mrs. Roosevelt, who very much agreed, and together we worked out a plan. I proposed to her the idea of dividing India into a thousand districts with a thousand ambulances to disperse and deliver not only birth control education to women in the vastly spread areas of the country, but the actual birth control devices as well. [They got support from the Ford Foundation.] . . . Back in New Delhi [after traveling around the country], we suggested to Mr. Nehru, when we had a formal appointment with him for the purpose, that the question of birth control be treated as one treats an epidemic of cholera, as if it were an utter emergency measure. Mr. Nehru was quite impressed, or expressed himself to be, and referred me to the Ministry of Health. The Minister of Health, Lady Rama Rao, was a converted Roman Catholic spinster who believed in the methods acceptable to the Pope: the rhythm method and abstinence. . . . Nothing came of our plan.* That means however much

*When David and I were in India in 1966, the population was estimated to be around 550 million. When he first proposed his plan in 1952, the population numbered 350 million. Fourteen years later, India had a birth-control plan in motion, but instead of a thousand ambulances and teams, they had fifty of each.

they increase their food supply, there is always a race against starvation. . . . I didn't like Nehru. . . . He was so agreeable and then he referred me to such a health minister, knowing perfectly well what that would mean. . . .

We had often spoken, as we traveled, how in India all problems were magnified by the huge size of this subcontinent. She [Mrs. Roosevelt] had said at one point that Indian problems resemble Mount Everest. You look up towards its height and you see how un-climbable it is. The result is that it paralyzes you to take even the first step. . . .

Mrs. Roosevelt's father had written her when she was a little girl that when she grew up she must see the Taj Mahal in moonlight. We planned our visit there to coincide with the full moon. Mrs. Roosevelt had, of course, seen photographs of that memorial to a beloved wife by a Mogal emperor many times. [She] had prepared herself to be disappointed by the sight, thinking it could not possibly live up to her father's excited reaction to it. She was wonderfully surprised. . . . She sat contemplatively on the bench described by her father, looking at the Taj Mahal by the light of the full moon, seemingly lost in memories.

Before leaving New Delhi, Mrs. Roosevelt had a long talk with Prime Minister Nehru about her impressions of all that she had seen, and she attended a formal farewell garden party given for her by the President. We then took a plane for Calcutta, our pilot flying as close to the Himalayas as he dared. I left Mrs. Roosevelt in Calcutta. . . . She and Maureen traveled home after short stops in Rangoon, Djakarta, the Philippines, and Honolulu. I went to Italy, to Capri. We all arrived in New York around the same time, about ten days after we had parted. She frequently said that while she loved traveling, once she came to the end of her journey, she couldn't wait to get home. Her trip was considered by officials to have been a great success. She brought with her much information and many messages. She spoke with Secretary of State Dean Acheson on her return, as well as with members of Congress, who invited her to give them her impressions of that newly developing part of the world from which she had just returned. As always, she had been a most wonderful and admired representative of her country.

On Home Ground

David was deeply committed to Blythedale Children's Hospital for the seventeen years he was medical director there. Immediately after his return to New York, he immersed himself in its operation. In 1952, it was still a convalescent home, a children's country nursing home, to which major New York City hospitals transferred children suffering mainly from tuberculosis of the hip and spine, conditions requiring long-term care. To reorganize the facility, thus improving and expanding its services, was the kind of challenge David relished. With his appointment, the emphasis was changed from the then-dominant speciality of orthopedics to physical rehabilitation medicine. Under David's directorship and later, with the help of Blythedale's executive director, Robert Stone,* and the industrious board of trustees, mostly women, Blythedale evolved into a fully accredited teaching hospital, which concentrated on children and adolescents with a wide range of disabilities, including polio and Legge-Perthes disease.**

Nineteen fifty-two was a significant year in Mrs. Roosevelt's personal life. Besides Elliott's marriage to Minnewa, Anna also married again, to

---

*Robert Stone spearheaded the drive for hospital accreditization for Blythedale. He played a significant role in the development of the hospital during David's last few years there, and he continues to this day to be its executive director.

**In his once-weekly visits to Blythedale, where he spent the entire day, and in countless midweek consultations, "David guided Blythedale to being what is generally considered the best children's rehabilitation hospital on the East Coast," reported a younger colleague and close friend, Dr. John A. Downey. "It is the only hospital in New York State devoted exclusively to pediatric rehabilitation." Author's interview with Dr. Downey, who continues to serve on the Blythedale Hospital staff as attending physician in the Department of Rehabilitation Medicine.

a doctor named James Halsted. Several months later Mrs. Roosevelt was off to Norway with Elliott and two of his children, Chandler and Tony, to unveil a statue of FDR in Oslo. Franklin, Jr., married Susan Perrin, a lovely Long Island girl. At the end of the year, Mrs. Roosevelt represented President Truman at the inauguration of the president of Chile.

That year, her birthday letter to David read:

[postmarked October 31, 1952]
Dearest David,

This little gift I hope you will find useful but what I really give you is my deep love and devotion. Each year I want to tell you how much I admire the qualities of mind and heart which you possess and which I hope I grow to understand and appreciate more fully. Bless you, for all you do for me and so many others, the ready sympathy and your forgetfulness of self make you a very rare and treasured friend.

Forgive me if I am selfish and demanding and try to remember that I really love you and seeing you is one of my great joys.

May the years bring you many birthdays and may your happiness increase.

E. R.

Mrs. Roosevelt was not particularly involved in the Adlai Stevenson campaign for the presidency in 1952, although in July she did appear at the Democratic National Convention, at which he was nominated. After Dwight Eisenhower defeated Stevenson in the election, Mrs. Roosevelt wrote him, resigning from the United Nations Commission on Human Rights. This was customary for officials of the outgoing party and Mr. Eisenhower accepted her resignation in December 1952, as she knew he would, and named Mrs. Oswald B. (Mary) Lord in her place. David was not alone in believing that an exception should have been made in Mrs. Roosevelt's case. Certainly her UN colleagues had hoped so. A tireless and effective advocate for that body, Mrs. Roosevelt had been regarded as being "above politics," and many thought that the esteem in which she was universally held and her unique diplomatic experience should have overridden party politics. David spoke of her leaving as "such a waste of extraordinary talent." Experienced politician that she was, however, Mrs. Roosevelt accepted matter-of-factly what David called her "firing," and she joined the American Association for the United Nations,* a private educational organization, in which she remained active for the rest of her life. She always missed her participation in the "real" U.N., as she occasionally remarked, where she felt she had held her own among the most skilled international professionals, and where she believed she was doing "useful" work in line with her husband's vision, work that had brought her the most satisfaction.

By 1952 David and Nemone were separated at long last. He moved into the Delmonico Hotel on Fifty-ninth Street and Park Avenue in New York City, and the following year he took an apartment in a brownstone building on East Sixty-first Street. His office, in which he saw private patients during certain specified hours during the week, was conveniently located across the street.

Apart from Hyde Park, Mrs. Roosevelt did not take the surroundings in which she lived too seriously. It was always the work that came first and the comfort she could offer others that counted. To her small, cramped apartment in the Park Sheraton Hotel, there flocked, as usual, friends and family, former United Nations colleagues, past and present politicians, teachers, writers, police commissioners, heads of state, concert artists, and folksingers, active, thoughtful people from all over. Mrs. Roosevelt wrote out menus for her cook and enjoyed the animated discussions of the mixture of guests around her table. David was, of course, frequently present. He also escorted her to charity balls, concerts, and a variety of

*Presently known as the United Nations Association of the U.S.A.

evening events around New York. When I first came to know Mrs. Roosevelt, I was somewhat surprised to note that such a formidable, independent woman still felt that she needed a male escort for evening social events, even when out with a noncoupled group. But then, she was such a "man's woman" in every way. I recognized from the start that she was happiest functioning politically and socially in the company of men. Although after David and I were married she seemed content to go to places with just the two of us, without us she did not prefer being the third person. She felt similarly comfortable joining Joe and Trude Lash for an evening event. There was a small pool of unattached men from which she drew escorts, such as Harry Hooker, FDR's former law partner; the financier Bernard Baruch; the theatrical producer John Golden; the progressive Catholic priest Father George Ford; and a few others. In this regard, Mrs. Roosevelt's old-fashioned upbringing asserted itself: Ladies did not go out into society unaccompanied after dark.

The devoted and incorruptible Tommy — Malvina Thompson — Mrs. Roosevelt's secretary and standby of thirty years, who had been ailing for some time, died on April 12, the same day that President Roosevelt had died, though eight years later. She had been the guardian at Mrs. Roosevelt's gate and certainly one of her best friends. They had been inseparable, and David said that it was with Tommy's death that Mrs. Roosevelt was truly alone. She felt the loss so deeply that she vowed at the time never again to form such a close working attachment. David remarked, "Maureen [who took Miss Thompson's place] knew that and was the ideal person to respect Mrs. Roosevelt's feelings."

In the spring of 1953, under the auspices of Columbia University, Mrs. Roosevelt was invited to be one of a group of people from the United States to go to Japan, their hosts being the International House of Japan and the Committee for Cultural Exchange. She chose to travel with her daughter-in-law, Minnewa, as Mrs. Roosevelt thought it would be a good opportunity for them both to get to know each other better. She had specifically asked that Hiroshima be included in her itinerary. Seeing the place where the atom bomb had exploded, devastating the city and its population, was a highly emotional experience, and she wrote about it in her autobiography.*

Before leaving for Japan, Mrs. Roosevelt had invited David to join her for part of her trip—in July, the month in which he had scheduled a vacation. The plan was to have a short, purely sight-seeing holiday in Greece before going to Yugoslavia. They met in Athens on June 29, briefly toured Greece, and then flew to Belgrade. "Yugoslavia was the first Iron Curtain country that Mrs. Roosevelt visited," David noted in his journal. "She was curious to learn first-hand how it worked. . . . It was understood that Mrs. Roosevelt would see Marshal Tito (president of Yugoslavia). That was the purpose of her visit. But it was suggested that the interview with him should occur at the end of her stay rather than at the beginning. Mr. Tito had wanted her to have first gotten her own impressions of things before discussing with him whatever questions she had."

David reported on their visit with Marshal Tito:

The task to unify the country, to keep it together, was a tremendous one. There was a tradition of enmity and war between one part and another. Languages were quite different in different provinces. Customs varied enormously. Yet the strong personality of Marshal Tito was able to hold down the continuous tensions, quarrels, and jealousies. . . . In the summer Marshal Tito lived on Brioni. By now we had driven all over Yugoslavia and visited with Tito at the end [of the trip]. We went to Brioni by boat, flying from Zagreb and driving down the Istrian coast to the place where we were fetched. Mrs. Roosevelt, Maureen Corr, and I stayed in a villa that had

---

*"We know that they [the American leaders] thought first of the welfare of our own people, that they believed the [atom] bomb might end the war quickly with less loss of life everywhere than if it had not been dropped. In spite of this conviction, one cannot see a city and be shown the area that was destroyed by blast and fire and be told of the people who died or were injured without deep sadness . . . it seems to me that the only helpful thing we can do . . . is to pledge ourselves to work to eliminate the causes of war through action that is possible only by using the machinery of the United Nations." Eleanor Roosevelt, *On My Own* (New York: Harper & Brothers, 1958), pp. 340–341.

once belonged to the German industrialist Krupp, the one that Tito had occupied while his own house on the island was being completed.

When I first met him I was struck by how immaculately tailored he was, looking similar to how one would expect an important United States executive to look. Extensive security . . . measures were enforced on Brioni. On our second day Mrs. Roosevelt had a private meeting with Marshal Tito. While the island of Brioni was an official residence of the head of state, a small island close by was given to him personally. He took us by boat on an excursion to this island and we enjoyed a day on the beautiful beach. We all went swimming, including Mrs. Roosevelt. On our way, there was an armed ship in front of us and one behind us. Just for that little pleasure outing. Nothing was *said* about these vessels, but they were certainly in view. Mrs. Tito was with us. [The] small lodge on his island . . . remained cool through the hot summer because of the thick stone walls. It was there, where Tito showed us how he stored his wine, that Mrs. Roosevelt interviewed him further. In addition to a number of motorboats and a yacht, Tito had very light speedboats, and he prided himself on being a good racer. He challenged me to such a race and invited Mrs. Roosevelt to ride with him. With her usual steadfastness and courage she stepped into the light, narrow craft with its powerful Ford motor, certainly not too happy about it. I felt unequal to his prowess, but I raced him as best I could. Of course the winner . . . was a foregone conclusion. I would have let him win even if I had been the most experienced speedboat racer in the world. . . .

On another occasion Tito challenged me to see which of the two of us could stand on our heads under water the longest. I declined the invitation, but chose instead to shoot a photograph of him doing that. It seemed pretty clear to me that he was 'showing off' in front of Mrs. Roosevelt. . . . As it was the middle of the summer there were many vacationing children on the beach and word had evidently gotten out that their President was on his boat. From the distance we could see the children, hundreds of them lined up at the water's edge, shouting TITO, TITO! I stood next to him and I asked him, "What does it feel like to be Tito?" He gave a little shrug [and said] "Oh, one gets used to it."

The Next Move

Mrs. Roosevelt had not seen her new apartment on East Sixty-second Street before the lease was signed. Her friend Esther Lape had found it for her in her absence. She moved into it in the fall of 1953, on her return from Europe. It was a garden apartment, a small duplex in a red-brick town house. To the left of the entrance foyer, in which a winding staircase led to bedrooms and office above, there was a large kitchen. A spacious and cheerful living room to the right had French doors leading out to a pleasant expanse of garden. Mrs. Roosevelt liked the garden, especially for her Scottish terriers. She adapted to the fact that the apartment had no dining room by having the large living room serve a dual purpose. There were deep easy chairs before the fireplace, on either side of which were handsome glass-enclosed built-in bookshelves. Along the opposite wall above the blue silk damask sofa hung a dramatically beautiful many-paneled eighteenth-century Japanese screen. Four watercolors of views of Venice, which Franklin Roosevelt had purchased on their wedding trip, were close together on a wall, two above two, while in another place, there hung an excellent etched portrait of FDR by Frederick Stoessel.

Comfortable chairs, a spinet piano, and some round drop-leaf tables with big old-fashioned lamps completed the decor. Fresh flowers in abundance were a clear sign that Mrs. Roosevelt was in town. Sun-filled during the day and softly lighted at night, it was an attractive and personal living room. For meals, however, it had to be transformed. When Mrs. Roosevelt had a few people in for luncheon or dinner, one or two of the tables were opened and set. Dining arrangements for larger numbers, though, were a bit more complicated. After drinks and hors d'oeuvres were served before a dinner party, for example, very small, precariously balanced black folding tables for two were swiftly brought out by the cook and a waitress, opened, and placed in front of the sofa and the other seating areas. Except for Mrs. Roosevelt, who chose her partner for some specific reason, guests took their places rather casually. When the meal ended, the tables were efficiently whisked away and coffee trays passed.

As all the world then knew—if not firsthand, then from published reports—Mrs. Roosevelt's residences were always the most hospitable of places, centers for the comings and goings of her children, friends, and people from everywhere. One could count on the most interesting mixture of guests of all ages, cultures, occupations, and degrees of importance in life. It was, however, the birthday and anniversary parties she arranged for family and friends that were closest to her heart. Those and the small, intimate meals with people she loved. Busy though she was, she allowed enough time to plan thoughtful gatherings at home and painstakingly organize their details. She did not intend to dominate the company, but she inevitably did. It was her strength and authenticity that made her such a magnet.

David was a frequent guest. Despite the long hours of his medical practice, he could put aside his work to enjoy lively occasions. "A day without pleasure is a day lost" was a favorite saying. Glamour and gaiety had always attracted him, and he made the most of his limited time to pursue them. Friends from abroad made a point of calling when they were in town. Russian gatherings, with their bohemian flavor—big crushes of multilingual people, with more than a sprinkling of artists and members of ballet troupes past and present—intrigued him. He had a circle of French friends living in New York, some of whom he had known in Europe and others from his United Nations days.

While he loved music and books, contact with people was his main stimulus, the thing that revived him. Food did not interest him. His preoccupied professional mother had had an aversion to the kitchen, and he had been raised to share her view that food was only fuel for the body and not something worth dawdling over. He was a teetotaler besides.

"People are my champagne," he often said, and it was true. Enjoying people as he did, and being forever curious, David loved conversing and was fascinated by people's stories. Having a phenomenal memory, he never forgot what others told him, often remembering their tales long after they'd forgotten them themselves. Although he was open to all aspects of pleasure, there was still never any doubt that David valued most the seriously afflicted people with whom he spent his days. He was their healer, confessor, and friend. For fulfillment, he needed them, as well. Nevertheless, though he spent a good part of his professional and private life independently of Mrs. Roosevelt, there was no denying that by now he had quite willingly accepted that their friendship was an important part of his life.

By 1954, her friendship with Adlai Stevenson had grown, and Mrs. Roosevelt thought well of his prospects for a second run for the presidency. She became increasingly involved in his future campaign plans, holding press conferences to support him and writing and speaking out for him as she traveled around the country. As usual, family affairs occupied her. Her son James's turbulent divorce from Romelle Schneider was in the news. Against her better judgment, James ran for Congress and won, while Franklin, Jr., a congressman of five years' standing, was defeated in his bid for New York State attorney general, an event his mother saw as a betrayal of her son by Tammany Hall's omnipotent boss, Carmine DeSapio. She never forgave Mr. DeSapio for what she considered his deliberate sabotaging of Franklin's chances. In 1961, with Senator Herbert Lehman and Thomas Finletter, she was one of a small group of New York Democrats who began a reform movement that forced DeSapio from power. There was a touch of motherly revenge added to the satisfaction of political success.

In July, David had taken fourteen-year-old Grania to Europe and shown her Brussels, Paris, Switzerland, and Venice, hoping to ease her concern about the approaching divorce, which became final in the same year that Mrs. Roosevelt reluctantly celebrated her seventieth birthday at a great party given her by Americans for Democratic Action. Birthdays had an unsettling effect on Mrs. Roosevelt. She hated them. She was vain enough not to want to be considered "old," her effectiveness diminished. She loathed the idea of physical limitations, the lessening of that enormous vitality on which she depended to get things done. David smilingly answered her occasional outburst of "I am getting *old!*" with the admonition "Don't be impressed by numbers!" She continued tours around the country, and in March 1955 she made another visit to Israel, on this occasion with Maureen Corr and Trude Lash. Maureen remembers how shocked she was by Mrs. Roosevelt's fresh appearance when she walked into the apartment shortly after their return from Israel. "She had slimmed down considerably, was dressed in a chic black Paris suit and a becoming hat. She was so elegant, I hardly recognized her."* Had David's recent divorce something to do with it?

David and Mrs. Roosevelt traveled together the following May, a journey initiated by David. He had been asked by a medical colleague whether he would be interested in being a delegate of the American Association for the United Nations (of which he was a member) to the World Federation of United Nations Associations at its annual meeting in Bangkok. Yes, he was interested, he said, and when he saw Mrs. Roosevelt a day or so later, he asked her how she would feel about being a delegate. He wrote in his journal, "Her immediate reaction was, 'Why should they make me a delegate? I have no connection with the WFUNA.' " David replied: "If *I* am to be a delegate why on earth should they not want *you?* May I ask them?"

David wrote in his journal about the first leg of their trip:

She was a good sport to go. While the work of private organizations supporting the U.N. had real value, it had not the significance and professionalism to which Mrs. Roosevelt was accustomed in the United Nations. We started the first part of our journey with Grania

---

*Author's interview, 1990, with Maureen Corr, who repeated her impression several times thereafter.

at Elliott and Minnewa's Colorado ranch. Senator and Mrs. William Fulbright were their house guests, as well as two of Elliott's children, William [Bill] and Chandler.* To encourage Grania, who had not been on horseback for some time and was reticent to go out on rides, Mrs. Roosevelt overcame her own reluctance to spend hours in the saddle and stayed close to Grania, encouraging and reassuring her. Though she hadn't ridden in years, Mrs. Roosevelt was still an excellent horsewoman, having forgotten nothing of her former skill.

Returning to Denver, Grania flew home to New York, and David and Mrs. Roosevelt went on to San Francisco, where they enplaned for Japan. Stops at Hong Kong, Jakarta, and Bali preceded Bangkok. David wrote, "The Bangkok meeting of the WFUNA took on a completely different standing with the presence of Mrs. Roosevelt. Instead of being one of many international meetings there . . . ours was regarded with distinction. Because of Mrs. Roosevelt, we were met at the airport by the dictator himself and his wife."

Years of closeness and mature friendship prompted this unusual love letter from Mrs. Roosevelt to David on his birthday in 1955. How wonderfully free she had to have felt to express herself in this way:

October 31st

David dearest,

I would like to telephone you Wednesday morning but I may not have time between train and plane so I leave this as a greeting on your birthday morning. May it be a happy day from beginning to end and may you have many, many more. I am thankful every

---

*David wrote, "Bill Roosevelt was not on close terms with his father. Bill's coming to his [Elliott's] ranch was an important gesture for Elliott, and Mrs. Roosevelt was helpful, as usual, in reconciling any difficulties between children and grandchildren."

day that you were born and I pray for your health and happiness daily.

You know without my telling you that I love you as I love and have never loved anyone else, and I am grateful for the privilege of loving you and thankful for every chance to be of help. God bless you and keep you and give you joy and every wish now and always.

E. R.

"You Give Me All My Real Happiness"

VAL-KILL COTTAGE
July 22d [1956]
David dearest,

No news so you must have landed safely in Paris and I fear the day will have been hard and left you sad and I know it will be hard to leave Yvonne [Mendl, a patient and friend who was very ill]. I only hope you found her better. . . .

Little things to do here like putting linen away, seeing Jimmy and Irene's [James's new wife] room was ready and that there were flowers for them when they arrived. We dined at 7 and I left at 10 minutes before 8 and drove alone to Vassar. Spoke and answered questions til 9:45 and drove home, and went over to Johnny and Anne's where Ellie [Mrs. Roosevelt's niece] and Jimmy and Irene had gone after dinner. All went very well, no quarrels, and Anne and Johnny were sweet and kind to Irene. This afternoon, Sunday, after having Leila Delano to meet Irene at lunch I took them to tea at Franklin Jr. and Sue's. They were nice too, no strain, and they look well and had a happy time on their cruise. . . .

I lay in bed last night and again early this morning, thinking how lucky I am to have met you 11 years ago and how grateful I am that you have allowed me to be your friend when youth and beauty and more interesting people are constantly at hand and claiming what little time you have to give. I never cease being surprised and grateful but I love you very much and I hope you know it and you give me all my real happiness.

Bless you and my love.

E. R.

The end of July 1956 found Grania en route to France with David. Mrs. Roosevelt wrote David from the Sheraton Blackstone Hotel, in Chicago, where she had gone for the Democratic National Convention:

Monday night
August 11th, 1956
David dearest,

This goes to you in Paris and I hope you return there in the hope of finding Yvonne better, so you can enjoy your time there.

I left Hyde Park Saturday evening. . . . Sisty left Friday and I put her on the train with the three children and thought how much harder this generation works, but how much happier the children are and in a way the parents are too. The house seemed very quiet after the last children were gone and I felt sad for Joanie [John and Anne's youngest daughter] left all alone and for Duffy [Mrs. Roosevelt's Scottie], who looked so sad when we left. I wish one could explain to animals.

I left to come here at 8 a.m. Sunday and it has been hectic as it always is. Truman's decision to support Harriman threw Adlai's people into gloom but I'm not sure (the ball pen just gave out) it is all bad. He himself knows now that if he wins he is free and owes no allegiances to Truman. The latter is using all his influence and much Harriman money to defeat Stevenson but it does not seem hopeless to me. They are making me stay over till Tuesday evening but I hope I can get away then. I enclose an account of my press conference which went well. My speech to-night was *very* bad.

I hope your time in the South of France has been wonderful. Goodnight dear, and bless you. My love to you.

E. R.

And a penciled letter, written en route, followed.

ON PLANE
August 17th, '56
Dearest,

. . . I had a hope, I didn't dare even acknowledge that you might be at the airport tomorrow morning but I know now that you won't be and I am somehow sad. I wanted just a glimpse of you more than I realized I guess!

Well, Stevenson was nominated and they've just told us Kefauver wants the vice-presidency. They'll make a good team for the campaign but I'm not so sure how they will work together afterwards. I think they can win but it will be a hard fight. I've brought some clippings, too personal to me to give you much idea of what went on, but it may give you a little. It was all exciting and I wished for you so often. This would have been a most interesting convention for you to see and so often I wanted to know what your judgment would be. I may have been very wrong in my stand on the platform and I still want to talk to you about it.* You, forgiving soul that you are, would like Stevenson's attitude on Truman.** I'll tell you the whole story when we meet, if our young ones give us any time to talk! You won't consider coming with us on the 5 day motor trip in France, will you? . . .

---

*She had influenced the Platform Committee to adopt a more conservative stand with regard to its civil rights plank. Opting for the moderate approach in enforcing the Supreme Court's desegregation decisions in order to hold the support of the South, Mrs. Roosevelt opposed the position of black leaders pressing for a stronger plank which would include federal military action, if necessary, to enforce desegregation.
**Stevenson did not bear a grudge against Truman, who had aggressively supported Averell Harriman at the convention.

There has been little sleep for the past nights and ever since I
left Chicago I've been hours on the telephone. (I dread to see my
telephone bill next month!) I am completely drained, but well and
not especially tired, just glad it is over.

Bless you and all my love. I need you.

E. R.

Mrs. Roosevelt had gone to the Democratic National Convention to
discuss the party platform — in particular, to support a more moderate civil
rights plank, which would hold the support of the South and which Stevenson would enforce — to address the delegates, and to exert her considerable influence to support Adlai Stevenson as the standard-bearer of the
party. Despite the fast-approaching U.S. presidential election, she interrupted her intensive campaigning for Stevenson for two weeks in August
to join David and Grania in Paris, and to meet there two of her grandsons,
who were close in age to Grania: John's son Haven, and Johnny Boettiger,
Anna's boy. Her arrival gave David some freedom to go out socially without Grania. Looking after teenagers gave Mrs. Roosevelt some anxious
hours. Against her advice, David had permitted the exquisite sixteen-year-
old Grania to attend a friend's costume ball without setting a curfew for
her. Mrs. Roosevelt was appalled at his leniency, but her words had no
effect. Grania recently recalled that upon her return to the hotel well
after midnight, she found a stern (and completely dressed) Mrs. Roosevelt
waiting up for her. The cosmopolitan woman of the world could be quite
old-fashioned where youngsters in her charge were concerned.

Sacks of mail requiring decisions to be made for the busy political
autumn, to which she was soon to return, helped divert Mrs. Roosevelt's
attention from adolescent antics. David described her work habits:

She was very punctual. That was one of her time-saving, energy-
saving ways. Running late would have made her tense, and tension
is a big energy-consumer. She arranged for having sufficient time
for whatever needed doing. She was able to finish the business
before her in the time that was allotted to it. She could make a

82

visitor comfortable, have in-depth discussions, answer questions, and be free when she was meant to be free for the next business without the visitor having felt rushed. That was an art of the first order. There was no wasting of time. She wouldn't do unnecessary things. She was concentrated and disciplined.

Returning to New York in early September, Mrs. Roosevelt was in the thick of the campaign for the Democratic ticket.

Adlai Stevenson's run for the presidency made 1956 a significant year for him. It was a special one for me as well, but for a totally different reason. It was the year in which I met David.

4

"MAY I BRING A LADY?"

Art

I VIVIDLY REMEMBER THE first time I saw David. He is standing clearly before my eyes, tall and graceful in his dark gray English coat. We had been invited, independently, by mutual Canadian friends visiting New York to attend a performance of the Pirandello play *Six Characters in Search of an Author.* David and his guest, a chic and striking young woman, arrived after us and a bit late. Since we could not all be seated together, it wasn't until the first intermission that introductions could be made. Shy, I thought as we shook hands. Our hosts, Sam and Ayala Zacks, prominent art collectors,* had asked another friend to join them that evening as well, a witty and brilliant lawyer, also a great collector and connoisseur, Louis E. Stern,** with whom I was well acquainted. Conversation among us was animated. I was an art dealer, my field primarily old master paintings, and my hosts and Mr. Stern collected French Impressionist paintings and classical antiquities, giving us a broad spectrum of news to exchange of the then small, exciting New York art world. David and his lady friend stood somewhat apart from our foursome, quiet amid the general chatter of an intermission audience. His quietness did not

---

*The major part of the Zackses' art collection forms an important part of the permanent collection of the Art Gallery of Ontario.
**The Louis E. Stern collections of Impressionist paintings and rare books are in the Philadelphia Museum of Art.

make David seem remote. I felt he was an engaged member of our circle because of his lively interest in listening to us, an attitude to which I was to grow very accustomed and which had a sparkle I always enjoyed. And yet the graying hair at his temples marked David as off-limits to me, a young woman, to whom an older man offered no romantic challenge— or so I thought. Besides, he was with a glamorous fashion model, who appeared to be a close companion. Thus I had two reasons not to give him second thoughts, despite how charming he looked, and how quickly his warm and radiant smile surfaced. When the six characters onstage concluded their search for an author, we six sought a pleasant end to our evening with a post-theater supper in a nearby Greenwich Village restaurant. There our spirited talk continued. David was interested in art and asked perceptive questions. He never mentioned his work or said anything about himself. More than once, I made an effort to bring David's young lady into our conversation, but without much success. As I later learned, her distant air was due more to the impending breakup of her relationship with David than to any feelings of exclusion from us. It was quite late when the party was over and we went our separate ways.

Our accidental second meeting occurred a short time later that autumn, again when I was in the company of Sam and Ayala Zacks. The three of us were at a preview of an exhibition at the Museum of Modern Art, when David, looking particularly handsome in a perfect dinner jacket and certainly ten years younger than his fifty-three years, suddenly appeared. "We will see you in Canada next week," Ayala reminded him. The Zackses were lending their collection to the Toronto Art Gallery* and had invited a number of New York friends to fly up for the weekend to attend the opening and other art-related events. David turned to me and asked, "Will you be going?" When I replied that I would, he said, referring to the flight to Toronto, "I will save a seat for you."

When I boarded the plane, I had forgotten his kind offer and settled myself elsewhere. He walked slowly up the aisle and softly announced,

---

*Now named the Art Gallery of Ontario.

"I have your seat." I gathered up my various belongings and moved into the window seat he had reserved beside him. From New York to Toronto, he chatted away. He described his school days, pranks he and friends had played, bicycle trips he'd taken in Italy, and other juvenile expeditions. He spoke of the close call he'd had when his group, climbing the Dolomites, had had to cling overnight to a narrow mountain ledge and recounted their relief upon seeing, at the break of dawn, in the distance below, the thin ribbon of lights of the rescue party in its slow ascent to them. He did not lack for topics to discuss. He told me about a Pablo Casals concert in Berlin that he'd attended during one of his visits home from Basel when he was a medical student. The renowned cellist had had a fainting spell during the performance. "Do you have any idea of how many doctors attended a Casals concert in Berlin?" he asked me. "Though I was one of the first to jump onstage when someone called, 'Is there a doctor in the house?' I was soon outnumbered by 'real' doctors rushing to attend to him." He recalled a special comrade of his youth, a French foreign service officer, Pierre Vienot, who had been imprisoned by the Nazis.

I had the feeling that few, if any, comments from me were expected during David's monologue. He spoke English very well in a pleasing foreign accent not exactly identifiable. Although German had been his main language, his accent was more Russian than German, with British traces. If he meant to entertain and impress me, he succeeded. I was beginning to be fascinated. And not only by his stories. Truth to tell, I had not been listening too intently the whole time. His personality and refinement attracted me. And he was an exceptionally handsome man. Over my left shoulder, the still bright early-autumn light filtered in through the plane window and was reflected in his eyes.

It was late that Friday night, after the splendid museum dinner and exhibition preview had ended, when we and other guests returned to the hotel where our rooms had been reserved. It was one of those sprawling old "palace" hotels built back when there was more space than people. "May I take you to your room?" David inquired. A nagging thought bothered me as we went alone down the long carpeted corridor, an occasional word passing between us. When we reach my room, I thought to myself, this lovely man will ask to come in. What will I answer him? A quick decision was essential. Honest. I will be honest with him. I will say, Dr. Gurewitsch, you are an appealing and interesting man. But you are much too worldly for me, and I don't believe in starting something that I can't finish.

My stiff resolution in place, we arrived at my door. "May I come in?" David asked. "Yes," I replied. It was about one o'clock in the morning. I seated myself at the dressing table. He drew up an easy chair and began to speak, this time not to entertain but to inform me. He was serious and wanted me to know as much as possible about himself. "I want to tell you everything, including all my sins," he began. Now he had my close attention. He began his story with the lives of his grandparents in Russia and his parents in Switzerland. Mainly, he described his mother, the person who had most profoundly influenced his and his brother's life. I recall thinking, How proud a mother must be to have such a son, and I asked him if indeed she was. He shook his head. "I missed being a genius," he replied unsmilingly. Two hours later, dazed with fatigue, I interrupted him. Assuring him of my interest, I asked whether his life story could be continued the next day. He rose and, European-style, raised my hand to his lips. At the door, he smiled at me, pausing a long moment to say "Good night" in his soft and graceful way. He lingered, nodding good night twice more. I remember it well.

Until now, David had given me little chance to speak at all, and so I seized the opportunity to assert myself when he called the following morning. Before he could resume his chronicle I plunged in. "Wouldn't you like to know something about me?" I asked. "You?" he replied. "I know all about you." And he proceeded at once to tell me in general terms about the life I'd had, the kind of person I was, and something about my hopes and dreams. He was surprisingly on the mark. It proved to me how experienced and intuitive he was and how finely tuned was his understanding of human nature.

A day of visiting the very few private art collections that existed in Toronto at the time and our hosts' dinner party on Saturday night allowed

us no further time alone. Before David and I boarded the plane for our
return flight to New York on Sunday, he bought many bars of chocolate
from vending machines just in case Air Canada did not produce a meal
on time. (I later learned that worrying about a delay in having something
to eat was a residual anxiety from boyhood, when food was scarce in post–
World War I Berlin.) David's pensive mood en route home was, I thought,
a natural reaction to our socially hectic weekend. We were, in fact, both
subdued. Suddenly, he turned to me. Spreading thumb and forefinger
about an inch apart before my eyes, he declared with great emphasis,
"You and I have this much chance." "For what?" I asked. "For marriage,"
he replied. That inch between his fingers looked awesome. What he'd
begun as an interesting flirtation had unexpectedly taken on a serious
aspect, something he had not bargained for. (Served him right!)

For the past seven years, ever since I had left the Institute of Fine Arts,
New York University's graduate school of art history, I had been associated
with the E. and A. Silberman Galleries of New York, an old, well-
established firm of art dealers. They had gradually been expanding their
impressive collection of old masters to include modern works of art. My
first assignment there had involved research on the gallery's collection of
mainly fourteenth- to seventeenth-century pictures, and their extensive art
history reference library had been at my disposal. The walls of my office
were hung with paintings by Sassetta, Bosch, and Cranach the Elder,
while paintings by Frans Hals and Goya, oil sketches by Rubens, and
other gems filled the stockrooms. At that time, important works of art
were available, private collectors relatively few in number, and the international art community small. Although slowly but surely purchases by
public galleries forever removed significant pieces from the art market,
choices to buy and sell were still abundant. Stockrooms of established
dealers bulged with treasures they could afford to purchase, accumulate,
and exchange with one another at a time when art was primarily acquired
privately by clients and museums and not, as today, bought and sold at
public auction. The Silberman Galleries, in expanding its collection, ac-

quired a large Monet *Water Lilies*, pastels and bronzes by Degas, a Manet portrait and still lifes, Renoirs, Pissarro snow scenes, Gauguins of Brittany and Tahiti, Cubist Picassos, and other important nineteenth- and twentieth-century sculpture and paintings.

When I became vice president of the firm, I began to buy and sell works of art at home and abroad. I loved my job. Seven months before David's surprise pronouncement to me in the plane from Toronto to New York, I had been encouraged by a friend, Sir John Rothenstein, director of the Tate Gallery in London, to buy the art of contemporary British artists for exhibition and sale in New York. Living English artists (with few exceptions) were not well known or sought in the United States at the time, but I agreed to take a look. I stayed in London's Brown's Hotel for more than a month, visiting English artists' studios and acquiring for the Silberman Galleries paintings and sculpture for the first major exhibition of contemporary British art to be shown in a private gallery in New York. I spent a day with Henry Moore in Hertfordshire, where he was proud to show me the new studio he had just been able to build, one with a removable roof to allow his tall sculptures to be moved out onto the lawn. From him, I purchased a bronze and two wonderful drawings. Sir Philip Hendy, director of the National Gallery, invited me to tea with Mr. and Mrs. Jacob Epstein. At the conclusion of our visit, I bought the sculptor's bronze *Ann*, which had stared back at me from their piano. By springtime, our shipment had arrived at our Madison Avenue premises: works by Graham Sutherland, Francis Bacon, Ben Nicholson, John Piper, William Scott, Lynn Chadwick, and many others. The gala evening preview, a charity event for the benefit of the British Council Fine Arts Collection, was scheduled for October 11, soon after my Toronto trip.

When our Toronto flight landed, David and I took a taxi into Manhattan. David asked me if he might attend the preview of British art, which had been discussed during the past weekend in Canada. "Of course," I replied, very pleased. His next question was perplexing. "May I bring a lady?" he asked. My heart sank. "I will call you on Thursday and let you know whether the lady will come," he said. My interest in having David at our opening had suddenly crumbled and I couldn't have cared less if the lady came or not. But, true to his word, on Thursday, David telephoned to say she had agreed to attend but that they both would arrive late. "I am bringing Eleanor Roosevelt. October eleventh is her birthday and I am taking her to the theater. We will come to your exhibition directly afterward." This was the first I had heard of a connection between Eleanor Roosevelt and David Gurewitsch. There is apparently never a dull moment with him, I thought.

A little before eleven o'clock on the appointed evening, with champagne flowing and the pitch of voices in the large gathering at its height, a door opened to admit Mrs. Roosevelt and David. They looked very distinguished, Mrs. Roosevelt in a long evening dress covered by a brilliantly embroidered Japanese coat, and David, tall, graceful, and very handsome, in a dinner jacket, a small yellow rose in his lapel. Slowly, the crowd spotted her. Her presence was imposing. A hush replaced the din in the large main room. I walked forward to welcome them. Her appearance, as I later learned, was not as casual as it appeared. (David had already told Mrs. Roosevelt about our meeting, for in a letter dated about three weeks earlier, she had referred to the possibility of the three of us going out together that evening.) After introducing us, David asked me to give Mrs. Roosevelt a tour of the exhibition. While I did so, he and everyone else stood in a half circle around us. If this was David's way of giving Mrs. Roosevelt a good first impression of me, he had to have been disappointed. I commented as best I could with so many eyes upon us as we moved at a measured pace from picture to picture. I did not know that Mrs. Roosevelt was hard-of-hearing, and I, consumed by self-consciousness, spoke more and more softly as Mrs. Roosevelt bent her almost six-foot frame close to my five-foot-two one to catch my barely audible words. She was so polite that she managed to seem genuinely interested, but I don't think she heard much of what I was saying.

She and David did not stay long. Though she was gracious, I doubted then that she relished this ending to her birthday celebration. She had come only to oblige David. I did not think there was anything special about their relationship, other than the few facts I learned—that David was Mrs. Roosevelt's physician and they were friends. Returning to the gallery the following day to take me to lunch, David bought a picture, a lovely fifteenth-century Flemish miniature, with only the briefest glance at it and a question to me: "Do you like it?" He presented it to me there and then, a thoughtful gesture.

Early in 1956, before David and I met, Mrs. Roosevelt wrote David this remarkable letter, which shows her view of their relationship at that time:

Feb. 8th [1956]
David my dearest,
   I've been sitting here thinking of you to-night and wondering why I make you feel shy. I want you to feel at home with me as you would with a member of your family and I can't achieve it! Something wrong with me! I'd love to hear you call me by my first name but you can't. Perhaps it is my age! I do love you and you are always in my thoughts and if that bothers you I could hide it. I'm good at that.
   You read me a lecture and I thought you really cared and so I'm being very careful, but it is a good deal of bother, anyway I'll see if I can go on for awhile. In the meantime love me a little and show it if you can and remember to take care of yourself for you are the most precious person in the world. All my love.
                                                                 E. R.

After the art exhibition, David's and my meetings became frequent. We saw the memorable film *La Strada*, went to a performance of *Romeo and Juliet*, attended concerts, and lunched and dined together. He told me a good deal about his medical specialty, his daily hospital and office routine. He continued to describe his past life to me—his marriage, his love affairs. He spoke warmly about his daughter, Grania, and of his worries that she would develop the strain of depression that was prevalent in her mother's side of the family.

I soon gleaned many clues concerning David's ties to Mrs. Roosevelt. One evening as he explored the meager contents of his refrigerator for our dinner, he produced two forgotten meat loaves now turned to stone. They had, he assumed, been put there by Mrs. Roosevelt's cook, who had the key to his apartment. The relationship became even clearer the evening I was invited to dinner in Mrs. Roosevelt's apartment, a short walk from David's. Only we three were present. She was kind, if reserved, addressing me as "Miss Perkel." We sat at a small round table in the living room, near an upright piano, on which there was a photograph of President Roosevelt. In its frame on the piano, the photograph lost its historic significance and was simply a family picture—someone's distinguished husband, father, or grandfather. The atmosphere of the large, comfortably furnished room was cozy, having a simplicity that I later came to recognize as Mrs. Roosevelt's own. She had placed a number of papers and letters to one side for discussion with David during the early course of the meal, asking how he thought certain questions in them should be handled concerning friends they had made on a recent trip. She did not mean to exclude me. The subjects were quickly dealt with and conversation became more general. Her openness in airing some of her opinions in the presence of a newcomer surprised me, and I wondered how she could have spoken so freely before someone she hardly knew. At first, I concluded that she trusted David's judgment that I would be discreet. While that was an element, I think her candor showed her wish to treat someone who was becoming important to David as naturally as possible. I sensed all this, rather than actually knowing it. She had understood the significance of David's request that she invite me to an intimate dinner. It was a rare step for him and a declaration of sorts to her, of which I was unaware. To me the most revealing and startling part of the dinner was their familiarity with each other. They were utterly frank, open, and completely at ease together. Yet I took the nature of their relationship at face value; it was so natural, so matter-of-fact. I completely understood why each enjoyed the other's company. I did not have the insight then to assess how much she loved him. And I was too self-absorbed.

On a summer day years later, when Mrs. Roosevelt and I were sitting alone on the back porch of Val-Kill Cottage having tea, that dinner came to mind. I confided, "You know, Mrs. Roosevelt, being in your presence in your living room the first time we had dinner together was so exciting, I could barely eat anything at all." I received a typical Mrs. Roosevelt reply: "That was foolish of you, dear," she said, "you are much too thin."

The limousine taking Mrs. Roosevelt, Joe and Trude Lash, and David and me moved swiftly uptown to Yankee Stadium on a cloudy Sunday afternoon. There in the wintry baseball park, empty of players on Salute to Israel Day, Mrs. Roosevelt was scheduled to address a crowd of thousands. Israeli general Moshe Dayan and Ambassador Abba Eban were to share the platform with her. At no time during the half-hour drive to the Bronx did she refer to the speech she was about to give. Other issues were on her mind and conversation in the car centered upon them. When we arrived at the ballpark, we separated; the Lashes, David, and I went to seats in the grandstand, and Mrs. Roosevelt headed to her wooden chair, set out among several others on the baseball diamond. The threatening sky sent down a gentle rain just as the program began. Some in the large audience sought cover. No attention was paid to the weather by the general or the ambassador, even as the rain fell more heavily. Mrs. Roosevelt, however, reached into her handbag; I assumed she was retrieving the notes for her speech. Instead, she drew out a packaged plastic raincoat and hood. Donning them, she sat entirely unruffled, waiting for her turn to speak. Her words were eloquent and exuberantly received. All in a day's work. For me, it was an early glimpse into Mrs. Roosevelt's unmatched professionalism. Soon after, I had another.

On a night just before the 1956 presidential election, a giant Democratic party rally was to be held in New York's Madison Square Garden.

An hour before the event, some dozen or so Democratic party officials, the Lashes, David and I, and several others had been milling around on the pavement in front of Mrs. Roosevelt's apartment. Having given us all dinner, Mrs. Roosevelt had energetically ushered us out to the street to be sure we arrived promptly for the coming event. There we stood, eyeing the row of rented limousines for the short drive to the Garden. If you've ever seen a general commanding his troops to advance, you will have a picture of Mrs. Roosevelt in action. In her long evening dress with its usual (and unwelcome) orchid corsage in place on her shoulder, she emerged from the house last, a list of guests' names in hand to assign us to our car seats. There were carefully thought-out reasons for placing us as she did, and if you knew her, it would be clear that no one was to make changes, lag, or be left behind. Mrs. Roosevelt always looked strained when she had to move groups from place to place, and this evening was no exception. She kept to timetables. I slid into my assigned seat beside Trude without a word and without delay. Agile David was quick to find the jump seat, his usual and preferred spot in a large car. Directed to their places, several of the other men demurred for gentle-manly reasons and, deferring to their hostess, held back, exclaiming, "After you, Mrs. Roosevelt!" A mistake. Impatiently making it clear that they were not to alter her plan, she induced them to yield by giving one or two gentle shoves in the right direction, and yield they did. Car doors were slammed shut and we were off in ample time for Mrs. Roosevelt to introduce Adlai Stevenson to the thousands already gathered in the Garden.

Though all signs pointed to an Eisenhower reelection, the excited audience filling the hall that night was alive with hope that the intelligent, witty, and civilized Illinois governor would somehow slide through to victory. Mrs. Roosevelt had worked hard for him. The usual rousing speeches by party leaders, with their exhortations to get out the vote, were planned to lead to Mr. Stevenson's climactic entrance. The timing of the governor's dramatic introduction and speech was to be coordinated with his appearance on national prime-time television. All major television channels were set to cover him.

Mrs. Roosevelt entered the hall briskly. Our group dispersed, but she kept the Lashes and David and me close to her, especially looking out for us as a crowd delightedly bore down on her. Spirits were high and rose to unmitigated joy at the sight of Mrs. Roosevelt, whom people loved and respected and whose name was synonymous with victory. Impatient to address the audience briefly in order to leave as much television time as possible to Mr. Stevenson, she never took a seat at all, but stood waiting with us off to one side in the wings of the immense stage on which were seated famous local and national politicians. To Mrs. Roosevelt's chagrin, it was her political foe, Carmine DeSapio, the boss of Tammany Hall, who had contrived to introduce her. Mr. DeSapio's choice for the presidential nomination had been Averell Harriman; he'd reluctantly given minimal support to Mr. Stevenson, and that night, as he prolonged his introduction of Mrs. Roosevelt, purposely keeping her waiting in the wings, she was furious. The longer he spoke, the more time he took from her address to the audience, thereby reducing her time to introduce the nominee. Both were fully conscious of the fact that his dragged-out oratory would give Mr. Stevenson only moments to make his grand entrance at the rally if his entire speech were to be carried on television. Steely-eyed and upset, she continued to whisper to us, "He is not leaving me any time!"

No longer able to monopolize the microphone, Mr. DeSapio concluded his remarks. He had barely announced her name, when Mrs. Roosevelt strode out to the center-stage podium. To a standing ovation, which she wasted no time to acknowledge, she waved the crowd to silence and twice firmly emphasized, "Please sit down! I have been given only two minutes!" The minutes were used to best advantage for Mr. Stevenson, and precisely at their conclusion, she introduced him to the cheers and chants of the crowd. Spotlights dancing around him and band blaring, the candidate made his way down the middle of the vast interior to the stage, waving left and right, responding unhurriedly and with great charm to the roar that greeted him. He was, after all, a gracious and genial man. In the glare of television lights and with cameras focused upon him, Mr. Stevenson spoke eloquently. He had a good deal to say and was an effective speaker, displaying the quickness of mind and fine command of language that made his speeches famous. As his talk went on and on, either he could not or would not take notice of the various emphatic signals being made to him by the television crews to wrap it up, if he did not want to be cut off to accommodate the TV program scheduled to follow. Neither did he respond to the anxious gesturing of his staff to do the same. According to broadcast protocol of the time, a televised program, even with presidential candidates, had to adhere to preestablished schedules. Mr. Stevenson was unable to adjust his carefully formulated speech to time limits. He was unceremoniously cut off in the middle of a sentence, his thoughts unfinished, his last words to the American people close to the end of his campaign left hanging in midair. There was something sadly absurd about it. A very disappointing performance. Mrs. Roosevelt had worried about this right along. Mr. Stevenson's eventual defeat at the polls left her feeling utterly discouraged and in a dark mood, David later told me. He said that her response to his probing was that in the country's rejection of Adlai Stevenson, for whom she had campaigned so diligently, the people had turned their backs on her, as well. The defeat had been her fault, she believed, and she felt useless.

When David's English friend Louis Kentner, a well-known pianist in Europe, came to New York to make his belated Carnegie Hall debut, David invited Mrs. Roosevelt to join us. During the intermission, Nemone, who had come independently, became part of our circle, which included Lou's wife, Griselda, Yehudi Menuhin's sister-in-law. It was my first meeting with David's tall, good-looking ex-wife. While he appeared somewhat ill at ease, my curiosity overcame my self-consciousness. So, apparently, did hers, and whenever possible, we stole glances at each other.

The backstage area of Carnegie Hall reserved for artists to receive friends and admirers at the conclusion of a performance was small, overcrowded, and overheated on this wintry night. The long line of well-wishers in which we were standing parted for Mrs. Roosevelt to go forward. After her greeting to the artist, she moved off to one side to wait for David and me. Lou Kentner was aglow with the excitement of the enthusiastic response to his brilliant American debut and flushed by his recent musical exertions, not to mention the very effective backstage heating system. That he was also fatigued was obvious. With a quick whisper to David, I left the line and went to stand with Mrs. Roosevelt. She looked at me questioningly. I told her that Lou Kentner seemed exhausted and would not miss one fewer hand to shake. Mrs. Roosevelt knew better. Taking my coat, a thick scarf bulging in its pocket, she gently urged me back, saying that an artist is never too tired or too uncomfortable to be told he is appreciated. It was her first piece of advice to me.

When I returned to her, she helped me into my coat, which she had held folded over her arm. She then wound the scarf tenderly, it seemed to me, about me. She was leaning down. Our faces were close. She did it all so simply, so modestly. I was quite touched. We had shared an intimate moment. David joined us and we left.

It is not unusual that a father's comments about his daughter are lovingly understated. David's softly spoken "Grania is nice" implied every paternal superlative. He had not, however, prepared me for her breathtaking beauty. Grania was sixteen when I first met her at lunch in the Russian Tea Room with the Kentners on the Sunday following Lou's concert. It took several moments of looking into those serious large green eyes in that perfect delicate face before I could murmur a greeting. Being the teenage daughter of a handsome father, she was not predisposed to be impressed by me. But she was polite. By this time, David and I had been seeing each other steadily. I'd met his daughter, his ex-wife, several of his friends, had learned something about his medical specialty, and had heard a good deal about his family and his past. As for Mrs. Roosevelt, I saw her, I think, one more time, at a formal dinner party she gave at Christmastime, before David vanished from my life. He vanished with the same speed with which he had entered it.

He was supposed to telephone me on a Sunday afternoon after seeing hospital patients so that he could tell me the time we were to meet. He did not call. I dialed his number twice. The first time, I left my name with his answering service. The second time, some hours later, I inquired whether he had been given my message. He had. I was baffled and miserable. What had happened? David was gone — and without a word. It was not at all like him. We had had an exhilarating time together and I was by now quite smitten. Hopes for our growing attachment were as yet fragile, but they had been real — or so I believed. Although a blow to me, David's flight was not altogether a surprise. There had been signs that the original spontaneity of feeling he'd had for me, which was so engaging — that burst of insight or premonition or something from the heart so genuine and contagious — was replaced by a touch of restraint, a subtle hesitancy here and there, a backing off. I was in a quandary and had to decide what, if anything, to do about his flight, so sudden and painful. I longed to see him. David was a responsible man and I knew he did not act lightly. Perplexed, and with a heavy heart, I decided to respect whatever reasons he felt he had to end our relationship. Feeling that I had no choice, I would learn to do without him. Mrs. Roosevelt evaporated from my thoughts.

In time, I missed David less and less. Though we had been very close, I had, after all, known him only a matter of months. Sometime in February, Sam Zacks, my Canadian friend, who was once again in New York, dropped into the gallery to take me to lunch. "Do you mind if I ask David Gurewitsch to join us?" he asked, reaching across my desk for the telephone. With a casualness I certainly did not feel, I replied, "What a nice idea." Longchamps was just across the street from our Madison Avenue art gallery, and it was there that the three of us met. Miraculously, David was not too late, considering the last-minute invitation and his having had to drive down from the hospital, where Sam had located him. It was a delightful lunch. As it ended, I silently complimented myself. I had behaved miraculously well. I had been properly conversational and had appeared, I thought, sufficiently relaxed to mask my fluttering heart. Alas, my self-satisfaction was premature! As we were saying our good-byes on the street, I turned and walked straight into a lamppost!

The next day, Saturday, brought the long-awaited call. Another invitation to lunch, but this time from David. Our meeting in the same restaurant was much happier than the previous one. The moment we were seated, he demanded, "Why didn't you call me during these past six weeks?" Startled, and suppressing my indignation, I managed to reply that while it had been tempting, I just did not have the nervous system to undertake that kind of initiative with a man. It would have been too uncomfortable for me to pursue him, somewhat demeaning and too much like work. "But didn't you realize how difficult it was for me to telephone you?" he asked. I was incredulous. "Difficult?" I replied. "Because," he said, "you are the type one marries, and I had to be sure that if I called you, I was ready for marriage and babies. I could never deny a woman the right to have a baby if she wanted one. The longer I put off calling you, the harder it was for me to do it." He was not arrogant in assuming he would be accepted, merely matter-of-fact. He spoke without pretense. I was quiet. It *sounded* like a marriage proposal, but was it? Events had certainly taken a sudden and surprising turn, and I had to absorb them. Though not exactly sure of his intention, I finally told him that I was too excited to mind that he had taken my future for granted. Had we touched our food that day? I don't think so. Still, it was the most memorable lunch I've ever had.

There was very little commonplace about David's past, which he resumed describing to me, except his so-called sins. He told me more about his mistakes and shortcomings, and about his first marriage, to which he referred with no rancor and as though it had existed in some distant time and place. His words flowed like a stream of consciousness. He traced the years of his medical training in Freiburg, Basel, Jerusalem, Vienna, London, and New York. He told stories about special teachers under whom he had worked and scientific experiments in which he had participated. He explained a good deal about the nature of rehabilitation medicine, stating that his mother's work had influenced his choice of the specialty. He described its newness and the low esteem in which it was regarded by many orthopedists and surgeons who did not appreciate the use of physical modalities and treatments necessitating the laying on of hands. He never indicated that in this new and complex specialty, he was a pioneer. Fascinated, I rarely interrupted him. He wanted me, he said, to see all his sides. It was typical of David to be thorough and honest and eager to confide. All this talk was meant to clear the air for a fresh start for us—probably also to test me—and to lay the groundwork on which to build a marriage of closeness and trust. As young-looking and dashing as David was at fifty-four, he took great pains to remind me of the more than two decades' difference in our ages, repeating periodically that he had reached the time when "I can already see my horizon and yours is not yet in sight. Are you *sure* you understand what that means?" It was irrelevent to me, but I didn't admit it.

What David's marriage proposal would mean to Mrs. Roosevelt never entered my mind.

I visited Mrs. Roosevelt's apartment more frequently, lunching and dining there when she was in town, but never without David. Though she still called me "Miss Perkel," maintaining formality between us, I was always comfortable in her presence. Her behavior toward me was thoughtful, consistent, and gracious. I very much enjoyed her company, totally unaware that my increasingly steady appearance was a complicated issue for her to accept, and that my being in David's life was a serious intrusion into hers. Without knowing anything other than that David loved and admired the lady he called "Mrs. Roosevelt," and that she was extremely devoted to him, it did not occur to me that I was in any way a threat to the former First Lady. Nor did she betray such feelings. Besides, David's happiness came first. But, human as she was and yearning for love, Mrs. Roosevelt did occasionally succumb to attacks of frustration at his elusiveness.

Only once in an undated letter, which I surmise was written around 1956, shortly after David and I met, did she expose how vulnerable she was to what she considered David's lack of attention to her. It was triggered by a casual incident, which took on exaggerated importance. He had slighted her. She had apparently just returned home from an eleven-day trip and had looked forward to seeing him with a kind of euphoric anticipation that surprised her. In the letter, she wrote that she had waited and worried as the night grew late, wondering where he was and whether an accident might have befallen him. When there was still no word from him, she tried, unsuccessfully, to reach him. Finally, he called at midnight, explaining that his lateness was due to the fact that he had escorted a lady home. Such a casual response to such anticipation and anxiety was not acceptable. In her letter, she openly reproached herself for needing him and she berated him for disappointing her. The emotional outburst was quickly repressed. By the end of the letter, Mrs. Roosevelt managed to regain her perspective and self-esteem. Magnanimously, she reminds herself that "love must be given freely and not look for any return, it is only pride that makes one crave a return." She apologized for making unwarrented demands.

Yet she had not entirely forgiven him, for it is the only letter to David that ends simply "E. R."

The profound contrast between Mrs. Roosevelt's dependence upon receiving love and her considerable awareness of the power of her capabilities—the bottomless neediness that coexisted with her enormous strength—never ceases to amaze me.

To Morocco

Toward the end of March 1957, David traveled with Mrs. Roosevelt, Grania—on her spring school break—and Elliott and his wife to Morocco at the invitation of Sultan Mohammed V. The fact that Elliott and Minnewa were bringing three of their friends along caused Mrs. Roosevelt to view the two weeks with apprehension. Elliott's penchant for good times made her nervous, and she never liked unwieldy additions to her party. The prospect of revisiting Morocco pleased Elliott enormously, since his air force unit had been stationed there during World War II and he'd been assigned as aide to his father for the Casablanca Conference.

The rather large party stayed at the Hotel Anfa, where President Roosevelt and Prime Minister Churchill had held their conferences; in general, Mrs. Roosevelt followed her husband's itinerary while they were there. David noted, "In Rabat Mrs. Roosevelt had an audience with the Sultan. Its only importance was that she pleaded with him for the plight of the Moroccan Jews, who were particularly badly off.* The audience was all very formal, with lots of ceremony." As anticipated, there was dissension between Elliott and his mother. Grania told me there had been friction between them and that at one point Mrs. Roosevelt had wanted to give up and go home. The two groups with different interests soon went their separate ways. En route back to the United States, Mrs. Roosevelt and Grania stopped off in Paris. David had by then returned to New York. I had not figured in this trip to Morocco at all and did not resent it, as matters were not yet clearly defined between David and me.

For most of our weekends that summer, we went to Bridgehampton, Long Island, where we often sailed with friends, Genia Delarova and Henri Doll. Other times, David drove to Hyde Park to be with Grania. Through Mrs. Roosevelt's intervention, Grania had been given a job in summer stock at the Hyde Park Playhouse. While it turned out to be a worthwhile experience for her, the idea had come from Mrs. Roosevelt, perhaps partly to ensure David's visits to Val-Kill Cottage, where Grania was staying with her. Mrs. Roosevelt was on the go, as usual, in and out of Hyde Park, and as I did not expect to be invited there, I was not disappointed when no invitation came. I still had not grasped how deeply important this friendship was to both David and Mrs. Roosevelt, and she was scarcely in my thoughts at the time. I never thought of Eleanor Roosevelt as being part of my private life at all. In my mind, she was in a class by herself and this had little to do with me. David rarely referred to her when we were alone. I do not recall ever feeling that she cast a shadow over us. As it turned out, she more than justified my instinctive trust in her, but of course I had no way of knowing it at the time. Meanwhile, as I realize in hindsight, there was indeed a part of David's existence unknown to me. He did not confide that he was preparing Mrs. Roosevelt (and himself) for his remarriage.

---

*Her plea to the sultan and a follow-up letter to him produced results, in that many Moroccan Jews were subsequently allowed to emigrate to Israel.

While Mrs. Roosevelt remained his "ideal mother" and perfect friend, they both knew that some time ago he had stopped needing her in the deep, hungry sense he had earlier. He understood her worries that his marrying might create a barrier between them, that their ideal companionship would change, and that assurances to the contrary would not help to assuage her fears. He knew for certain that he would never lose Mrs. Roosevelt's love, no matter how the situation between them might be altered. That had been tested before. Still, care had to be taken. With sinking heart, Mrs. Roosevelt regarded a future where she would probably play a very diminished role in David's life. Nevertheless, she stood ready to support him when the time came.

To the Soviet Union

One August evening in 1957, when David and I were dining together, he told me that Mrs. Roosevelt had invited him to accompany her on a monthlong trip to the Soviet Union on the first of September. She intended to report on conditions there both for her "My Day" newspaper column and magazine articles. Though he asked me how I felt about it, it was clear he had already decided to go. I was hurt that he could so easily leave me behind, but I couldn't be angry. Clearly, it was not yet appropriate for me to be included in such a trip, and I would have been uncomfortable had I gone along. He told me that he had at first refused Mrs. Roosevelt. Mainly, he was afraid that his going would worry his Russian-born mother, who feared he might be detained there.

David had left Russia at the age of seven, after a five-year stay with his grandparents, and the idea of revisiting his parents' native land was almost irresistible to him. He was intensely curious about how life was lived in that vast area of the world, a place that so few outsiders had access to, and was anxious to learn about Communist medicine, its level of education, practice, and organization. Having been in Russia only as a child, he read and wrote Russian painstakingly, but he spoke the language quite fluently and was eager to meet with Soviet colleagues. He wanted to be shown their hospitals and research centers, which had been seen by few in the Western world at that time. To go behind the Iron Curtain would be a real adventure. He spoke excitedly about it. Mrs. Roosevelt had offered a final temptation: "Didn't you ever dream of going to Samarkand?" she had asked, referring to the capital of an ancient empire that had been sacked by Genghis Khan and rebuilt by Tamerlane, the Mongol conqueror. He was amused at how well Mrs. Roosevelt knew his weaknesses. "She certainly knows how to appeal to me," he acknowledged with a smile (I unsmilingly agreed). He had finally consented to go, hoping I would understand. In my heart, I didn't reproach Mrs. Roosevelt for enticing him away, but I was disappointed in him for not wanting to share such an experience with me. She had not invited me—why should she?—and he had not asked her to. It was to be one of their customary journeys together. But he sensed that he had let me down, for before our dinner was over, David volunteered that we would set our wedding date on his return. I did not care for such appeasement, although I believed him to be sincere.

He later pledged to his mother, who was convinced that he would not be allowed to return, that Mrs. Roosevelt would see to it that the Soviets would not keep him. She was not consoled, and her alarm never lessened until she set eyes on him again. Sometime before they left, David informed me that he had discussed our marriage with Mrs. Roosevelt. He explained to her, he said, that if he did not marry me, he would never marry again. "Mrs. Roosevelt encouraged me," he continued. "She said she would not live forever." Now *there* was a revelation if I'd ever heard one. For the first time, a statement had been made that underscored the depth of their attachment to each other, making it outstandingly clear to me. I was aware all along that David felt that he, more than anyone else, was accountable for Mrs. Roosevelt's well-being. That she felt equally responsible for his was news to me.

This was their last trip à deux. I did not yet know that, but I believe she did.

By now a seasoned amateur photographer, David added a portable dictaphone to his various cameras, lenses, and boxes of film. Maureen Corr accompanied them to the Soviet Union and worked with Mrs. Roosevelt on her "My Day" news column for United Feature Syndicate, Inc., which had to be written within the limits set by Soviet censors. Once back in the United States, however, she freely described what she had seen and done. In his Russian journal, David wrote:

> On the way to the Soviet Union we stopped in Berlin. We stayed in the Kempinski Hotel. . . . The main synagogue is also on that street—or was. Now it is a ruin behind a wooden fence, and I knew that ruin was not produced by Allied bombings but was the result of the so-called "Kristalnacht" [Crystal Night] which was November tenth, 1938 [sic].* Before the war started the Nazis had destroyed many synagogues and this particular one, before it became a massive rubble, was the symbol of German Jews. We were now twelve years after the war, and the Germans were meant to be democratic, meant to be sorry for what they had done and there it was, with the same fence they had put around it after '38. Not one plaque, no identification, no gesture of regret for their inhuman deeds appeared on the ruin. I went through the fence. The remaining mass with holes in it had been a very large building. I went back to the hotel and asked Mrs. Roosevelt if she would mind coming back with me inside that former synagogue and letting me take a picture of her there. I told her my feelings about it. She came and we took the picture and she wrote about it in her column. Within a few weeks the Germans made plans to erect a community house on the site with acknowledgment of its history. The Germans were aroused and did something about it.

---

*So-named for the destruction of windowed synagogues and Jewish-owned shops caused by a German anti-Semitic rampage on the night of November 9.

David and Mrs. Roosevelt arrived in the Soviet Union on Wednesday, September 4. Her first column bore the dateline "Moscow, September 6, 1957." David began his travel diary by noting:

Going to the Soviet Union it was clear that it would be more productive to study one or two subjects in depth rather than butterflying to whatever the authorities would be willing to show you. So Mrs. Roosevelt and I concentrated on education and medicine and I think we got more out of it in that way than if we had just run around to see things in general. . . . Mrs. Roosevelt looked at places of education, including medical schools. She explored all levels, from children's schools to the university. . . . It is all different than how it is done in the United States. The Soviets copied a good deal from the Germans, both in medicine and in general education. The professorial system, typically German, is maintained in Russia, which means that the professor, the authority, cannot be wrong, he can never be challenged. This system is dangerous for advanced learning. . . .

We did not want to be led to the various "showplaces" they are eager for the visitor to see. We went prepared. Our party traveled as private citizens, organized by the Soviet Intourist Office. Mrs. Roosevelt had her own Intourist guide [translator] assigned to her, a fine woman, a senior person, Anna Lavrova, who had served President Roosevelt at the Yalta Conference. I was also assigned a guide whose job was, as far as I could make out, to dog my footsteps and frustrate my requests for information. We listed hospitals and medical schools, primary and secondary schools and universities and included the hope to meet government officials responsible for activities in them. We had also said that we wanted to see as much of the Soviet Union as could be crowded into a thirty-day visit, in Moscow, other cities, and the distant Soviet Republics.

The Mausoleum in the middle of Red Square in front of the Kremlin wall wherein lie the bodies of Lenin and Stalin is probably the prime sight-seeing object in the whole of the Soviet Union. A line more than a mile long forms daily before and during visiting hours, wending its way across the Square, down towards the neighboring square and park. As a matter of course the Intourist guides wanted to take Mrs. Roosevelt directly into the Mausoleum. However, she insisted upon waiting her turn in line. Only rarely was she recognized.

Mrs. Roosevelt and I were shown Lenin's small apartment in the Kremlin. It is being preserved exactly as he used it; the calendar on his desk shows the last day he sat there. Both for Mrs. Roosevelt and for me this modest apartment represented the most impressive sight in the Soviet Union. On our twelve thousand miles of travel, crisscrossing this huge country, whatever we saw emanated from this little apartment. . . .

In visiting nurseries, kindergartens, and institutions of higher learning, one principle could be traced throughout. It was Pavlov's "conditioned reflex." . . . The system aims at creating a human being whose natural reactions are entirely controlled. . . . The discipline is claustrophobic. Mrs. Roosevelt doubted that basic human reactions could be altered by conditioning reflexes. She felt that the basic drive toward freedom would win out once a certain level of material wealth and well-being had been reached.

Mrs. Roosevelt and David occasionally separated. David was worried that she might be bored by too much concentration on his medical agenda. But it does not seem so from the talks she later gave and the newspaper columns she wrote on the subject. David returned stimulated by the important news he'd learned about Soviet medicine, details of which he recorded in his journal:

Most interesting to me was the work in [organ] transplants which I heard about just as Mrs. Roosevelt and I were to leave the medical school after many hours there — hours which I worried had produced too many details for Mrs. Roosevelt. The Director . . . was accompanying us to the car after a long, most interesting visit which had just come to an end. Mrs. Roosevelt had gone on a little ahead and had already seated herself comfortably in the car. I was thanking the Director for all the time he had given us and added, "You have shown us what so many people are doing, but you have not told us about your work." His answer was: "I am your host and it would not be polite to talk about myself." I persisted. "What are you doing?" "I am an experimental surgeon." "What are you experimenting on?" "On transplants." "What are you transplanting?" "Hearts and heads." I was taken aback and repeated my question: "Transplanting *what*?" He gave the same answer as before. "Can one see this?" I asked. "Of course. My institute is over there," he said, pointing towards a roof not too far away. This was 1957. No such transplants that I knew of had been heard of or written about in the medical literature. By then we had approached the car in which Mrs. Roosevelt was sitting and I explained to her what we had missed on our visit and asked whether she would be willing to see some of these transplants. Somewhat reluctantly, she got out of the car. . . . We were shown a dog with two hearts, the second heart having been transplanted thirty-six hours previously. The dog showed two different pulses and was very lively. We were also shown a dog with two heads. . . . This surgery was meant to be an exercise to perfect the technique of suturing blood vessels in human beings. We were taken around the cardiology department by a highly respected heart specialist, well known, in addition to his work, for having been involved in the so-called "doctors' plot"* which was fabricated by Stalin. The doctor had spent some time in prison and then was completely vindicated and freed. He told us that his specialty at present was to evaluate effort spent during different types of work. I asked him whether they had evaluated the work stress of switchboard operators.

---

*Shortly before his death in 1953, Soviet leader Joseph Stalin—in an alleged attempt to purge the Soviet leadership—accused nine doctors (six of them Jewish) of plotting to poison and kill high Communist party officials. The trial and rumored purge were deterred by Stalin's death on March 5. All doctors were subjected to torture, and by the time they were exonerated, two had died.

Mr. and Mrs. Khrushchev visit the Roosevelt family home in Hyde Park, New York.

David when he was known by his first name, "Arno," Berlin.

The photograph of David that Mrs. Roosevelt kept on her bedside table. The picture is presently on view in the Franklin D. Roosevelt Library, Hyde Park, New York.

Apartment 15-A
29 Washington Square, West
New York City 11

November 26, 1946

Dear Dr. Gurewitsch:

        The daughter of one of the
elevator men in this apartment house
by the name of Lillie Heller, has
just had a brain operation at the
Medical Center.

        If you are not too busy, I
thought perhaps you might inquire
about her. The operation was a
success, the final outcome is still
in doubt.

        Very cordially yours,

        Eleanor Roosevelt

A 1946 letter
from Mrs.
Roosevelt
to David
Gurewitsch.

Top: David's first wife, Nemone Balfour, with their daughter, Grania, Cape Cod, Massachusetts.

Left: David.

Top: Mrs. Roosevelt on the move, Washington, D.C.

Left: My mother-in-law, Maria Gurewitsch, and Mrs. Roosevelt.

Right: Mrs. Roosevelt with Israeli prime minister David Ben-Gurion and his wife, Paula, in their house in Tel-Aviv, 1952.

Bottom: Mrs. Roosevelt at a children's settlement in Israel.

THIS PAGE

Left: Schedule of a typical day for Mrs. Roosevelt when she traveled. This day was spent in Pakistan.

Bottom: Prime Minister Nehru and his sister, Mme. Pandit, with Mrs. Roosevelt in New Delhi.

OPPOSITE PAGE

Top: David and Mrs. Roosevelt with unnamed official. Mrs. Roosevelt wrote on the back of the photograph, "Taken in Nikko."

Bottom: Mrs. Roosevelt being welcomed in Greece. David (in dark glasses) is at left.

Eleanor Roosevelt

David and Mrs. Roosevelt being shown the sights, Dubrovnik, Yugoslavia, 1953.

Mrs. Roosevelt meeting Marshal Tito on the island of Brioni, Yugoslavia, 1954.

David and Mrs. Roosevelt on Marshal Tito's yacht off the island of Brioni.

David and Marshal Tito watching the crowd on shore.

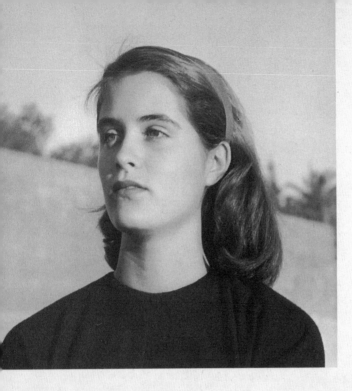

Left: David's daughter, Grania, Morocco, 1956.

Bottom: Mrs. Roosevelt standing in the ruins of a synagogue, Berlin, 1957.

Mrs. Roosevelt and
I in the living room of
her East Sixty-second
Street apartment, 1958.

I am speaking
to a guest at a
Silberman Galleries
art preview. It was
on just such an
occasion that I met
Mrs. Roosevelt for
the first time.

Nikita Khrushchev showing Mrs. Roosevelt and Anna Lavrova his gardens in Yalta, September 1957.

Mrs. Roosevelt interviewing Khrushchev on the porch of his Yalta summer house. David's recording device is on the table.

Mrs. Roosevelt and
I at the Brussels
World's Fair,
September 1958.
I am carrying one
of David's cameras
and a lens.

Interpreter Anna
Lavrova, Mrs.
Roosevelt, and
I entering a Soviet
ministry, on a return
visit, September 1958.

Top: Mrs. Roosevelt and I seated in her sleek silver convertible Fiat in front of the children's playhouse, Val-Kill, Hyde Park. Her son Franklin, Jr., had a Fiat automobile agency.

Right: I love this photograph of Mrs. Roosevelt standing in her Val-Kill garden. I feel that it conveys a true impression of her.

Thanksgiving dinner, Val-Kill Cottage, 1958. Standing, left to right: granddaughter Nina, Mrs. Roosevelt, Joe Lash, and grandson Haven Roosevelt. Seated, facing the camera: me, Ruth Roosevelt (Curtis's wife), Henry Osthagen (friend of Malvina Thompson), Anne Roosevelt, Lorena Hickok, grandson Curtis Roosevelt, two unidentified people, and Grania Gurewitsch.

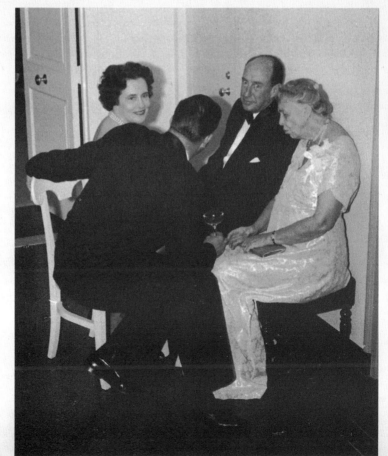

A conversational corner at Grania Gurewitsch's debutante party in New York, December 1958: Franklin D. Roosevelt, Jr. (back to camera), Mary Lasker, Adlai Stevenson, and Mrs. Roosevelt.

Top: Lunching at the pool, Stone Cottage.

Bottom: Fourth of July picnic lunch at the pool, Stone Cottage. James Roosevelt reading aloud from the Declaration of Independence. Also standing: Anne and John Roosevelt. Seated at back table: sons of Mrs. Roosevelt's niece, Eleanor Elliott Roach (she has since resumed using her maiden name, Eleanor Roosevelt), and a friend of Grania's. Table at left: Grania, Mrs. Roosevelt, and me. Mrs. Roosevelt's Scottie, Duffy, is at her feet. Foreground table: Ellie Roach and Curtis Roosevelt.

Before leaving Moscow, they had some time for social activities, which included a reception by our ambassador to the Soviet Union, Mr. Llewellyn Thompson, and his wife, with several members of the American and foreign press corps, and a lavish production of *Swan Lake*. A Russian-built jet carried them to Tashkent, a two-thousand-mile flight. On the morning of their arrival at Tashkent, David visited hospitals while Mrs. Roosevelt called on the ministers of culture and education. Samarkand was a highlight of the journey and lived up to all intriguing expectations.

Interview with Nikita Khrushchev

In making arrangements for her visit to the Soviet Union, Mrs. Roosevelt had asked if there was a possibility she could see the prime minister, Nikita Khrushchev. David's journal continued:

> When we arrived she repeated this wish but never seemed to get a direct reply. Only after we landed at the Moscow airport from Sochi was Mrs. Roosevelt told that Mr. Khrushchev was ready to see her the next day. . . . Just coming from the Black Sea, we turned and took the next flight back to Yalta. We spent the night there in a hotel and went very early the next morning to see the Divadia Palace, where the Yalta Conference had taken place. It was now being used as a convalescent home. Maureen did not come along. With us, as usual, was Anna Lavrova, Mrs. Roosevelt's Intourist guide. Driving to the Khrushchev villa, his vacation house, there were many security checks. At one point our driver stopped the car in the woods for several minutes without explanation. This delay made the punctual Mrs. Roosevelt quite nervous. It was a poor moment for motor trouble, she thought. But we soon learned that the pause was made to be sure we would arrive exactly at the appointed time. The villa was completely isolated and surrounded by fences.
>
> Mr. and Mrs. Khrushchev, their daughter and son-in-law were

gathered on the front steps of the house, expecting and welcoming Mrs. Roosevelt. The cordiality and warm hospitality cannot be imagined. We were shown their beautifully kept garden and the spectacular view of the city of Yalta before we were finally led into the house and invited into the sitting room. We were alone with Mr. Khrushchev. Mrs. Roosevelt knew that I was anxious to take photographs. The room was comparatively dark. She therefore suggested to have the conversation on the porch. Mr. Khrushchev kindly agreed, concerned only that it might be too cold there. Mrs. Roosevelt kept her coat. He wore a woolen shirt. As long as it was comfortable for her, it was all right with him. [The result was a good many photographs.] The two were seated at a table opposite each other, with Anna Lavrova seated beside Mrs. Roosevelt. My tape recorder was on the table. When he saw that I would from time to time rise from my place at the end of the table to take pictures, Mr. Khrushchev would move his hand away from his face or otherwise adjust his posture obligingly during the interview to give me a clearer view of him to photograph. It was most considerate of him. I tried to be as quick and quiet as possible.

The interview was long.* It lasted over three hours and covered a great deal of ground. It began with our host's remarks of appreciation of President Roosevelt. Each one said something of comparative length and then the interpreter would translate it, necessitating a considerable pause between question and answer. I took advantage of some of these pauses to comment directly to Mr. Khrushchev. . . . The two countered as to which side broke the Yalta agreement, and in general terms talked about the two different philosophies of their respective countries, each convinced that their side would be victorious in the world. Peace was also stressed, the necessity of making and keeping it. His powerful personality impressed Mrs. Roosevelt. During the interview Mr. Khrushchev

---

*David later added, "After her return to New York, Mrs. Roosevelt reported this interview in five lengthy *My Day* columns."

was amiable, but he would not budge on any point. Mrs. Roosevelt later told me that throughout the interview she tried to think who, on the Western side, could be a match for him, and she did not find an answer. I, as a listener, felt that Mrs. Roosevelt had been quite a match for him herself. The interview was followed by a relaxed family lunch. . . . In parting, Mr. Khrushchev asked me to ask Mrs. Roosevelt whether he could tell the newspapers that they had had a friendly conversation. I translated the question to her and she replied, "You can say that we had a friendly conversation but that we differed." When I repeated this to Mr. Khrushchev, he grinned. "At least we didn't shoot at each other," he said.

When the time came to leave the Soviet Union, they headed home via Copenhagen, heartily appreciating the marked contrast between that lovely, open city and the oppressive atmosphere they'd just left behind.

Meanwhile, back at home, I had followed their journey with thousands of others through Mrs. Roosevelt's informative columns in the *New York Post*—and David was a faithful correspondent. On their stop in Frankfurt, Germany, en route to Moscow, he had mailed his first letter, which ended with "A kiss and be well. And don't forget me." I did not. For me, the month of his absence passed slowly. I could hardly wait for it to end. Fortunately, September is a time of major activity in art galleries after summer doldrums, and I was in the middle of preparations for our large annual exhibition, scheduled to open in December, and the publication of its catalog. Almost from the moment of David's telephone call from the arrival building of Idlewild Airport (the former name of the John F. Kennedy Airport), Mrs. Roosevelt reentered my life, with more regularity and less formality than before.

Immediately upon his return, David had his daily dictation about the trip transcribed. Medical colleagues were keen to hear his firsthand observations, and many scientific groups and various hospital departments invited him to speak. It is a tribute to his diligence and excellent memory that he never gave the same medical lecture twice, directing his commentary to the specialty of the audience he was addressing. I know, because I attended all of his talks, generally given in the evening, after his day's work. The long walks taken with Russian colleagues proved an excellent source of information for David, walks in the open air, where conversations could not be overheard or monitored, where knowledge could be freely asked for and given on both sides. Probing, patient questioner that he was, understanding the Russian mentality as he did, David got the responses he sought. Naturally, wherever he traveled, he followed developments in his own fields of interest—neurology and rehabilitation medicine—and asked if and how Soviet physical-rehabilitation apparatus functioned. Indeed, he came home with an extraordinarily flexible multijointed artificial hand, the best prosthesis of its kind that he had seen to date, but as yet unavailable to Soviet patients in need of it. To his lectures, David added slides made from photographs he had taken, among them shots of certain surgical procedures, and of medical work in progress in specific clinics and hospitals, until then not generally known. In a widely circulated article, he wrote:

I have seen ten research institutes in Leningrad, Moscow, Tashkent, Sochi. . . . What impressed me was the emphasis on the team approach. Specialists in many fields were brought together to tackle a given problem. In the Institute of Experimental Surgery in Moscow, engineers specializing in precision tools worked together with the surgeons, seeing and perfecting surgical instruments in use. . . . The first emphasis of the Soviet planners was quantity. . . . Gradually the quality is also improving.*

David believed that Soviet accomplishment in science should not be underestimated. When the Soviet Union surprised the world with the launching of *Sputnik I* on October 14, 1957, David's audience broadened

---

*A. David Gurewitsch, "Proceedings of the Rudolph Virchow Medical Society," *Report on Organization of Medicine in the Soviet Union* 17 (1958).

to include United States military personnel and foreign-policy professionals suddenly awakened to Soviet scientific achievement and eager for
information. Mrs. Roosevelt's lecture agent, W. Colston Leigh, received
more requests for her to speak than she could possibly handle.

It was on an evening when David showed some slides he had made
from his photographs of the Soviet trip to several of Mrs. Roosevelt's
friends and family gathered for the occasion in her living room that I first
met Mrs. Roosevelt's primary secretary. From her slim, delicate good
looks, it was not at once apparent that Maureen Corr was the sturdy
trooper who kept pace at home and on the road with the indefatigable
Eleanor Roosevelt. She was conscientious and able, and the essence of
discretion, as I later learned, and had hosts of other admirable character
traits besides. Among the group in Mrs. Roosevelt's apartment, Maureen
was effervescent, bantering with David and relaxed with her boss, though
highly respectful of her. I liked her at once.

From October 1957, when they returned, until almost the year's end,
Mrs. Roosevelt and David gave talks on the Soviet Union together whenever possible; that is, when she was in town and his lectures were not
scheduled specifically for medical groups. Their sharing a platform began
by chance when Mrs. Roosevelt was invited to address a New York
women's club of which she was a member. The three of us were going
out elsewhere to dinner after the talk. Mrs. Roosevelt was speaking on
the stage of the ballroom, in which members and guests were gathered,
when she asked David, seated with me in the audience, to substantiate
some facts. He did, and then she urged him to join her. Each comple-
mented the other's views on various subjects in much the same way and
spirit that they reached conclusions in private discussion. They worked
so effectively together that to repeat the procedure in public seemed a
natural step. Addressing other interested groups—in colleges, city agencies, civic organizations, and settlement houses—with David's slides pro-
jected onto a screen, they described the significance of all they had seen.

Before setting out, Mrs. Roosevelt, David, and I would generally have
a quick early dinner. I always enjoyed these excursions, especially the
lively prelecture give-and-take between the two, which took place as we

drove to the evening's destination in David's car, where I sat between the
two of them in the front seat. "Remember, dear," Mrs. Roosevelt once
gently reminded David, reaching over to tap his knee, "a speech has to
have a beginning, a middle, and an end." As Mrs. Roosevelt became more
familiar with me, I grew more and more comfortable with her. It happened so naturally, I was hardly aware that we were becoming a trio on
a somewhat regular basis. Thus the month of October passed. Still no
wedding date.

Invitation to Hyde Park

I was invited to Hyde Park for Thanksgiving. "If your family can spare
you," Mrs. Roosevelt had said. Of course I welcomed the invitation, but
more for the reason that David and I could be together than because of
the invitation's possible significance. He usually spent holidays there, often with Grania, but this year a snowstorm in Vermont prevented her
from leaving school. On Wednesday night, Thanksgiving eve, around ten
o'clock, David and I drove into the long, narrow dirt lane, crossed the
pond over the little bridge, whose wood planks rattled under the weight
of the car's rolling wheels, to Val-Kill Cottage. The moment the car
stopped before the house, Mrs. Roosevelt appeared almost magically out
of the darkness to greet us. She was coatless in the crisp November air,
smiling, saying that we must be hungry and that she'd had a plate of
sandwiches prepared for us. Had she been outside waiting for us? I wondered. We'd taken the trouble to arrive quietly. But I did not realize that
the clatter of the little bridge's timbers announced all visitors. Mrs. Roosevelt welcomed me with a warm embrace and for the first time called
me by my given name, Edna. This sudden new familiarity sounded deliberate. I interpreted it as a new acceptance, an acknowledgment that I
belonged with David, and only that night did I understand it as a recent
development with her.

The fire was lighted in Val-Kill's pine-paneled study, its walls covered
with photographs of people Mrs. Roosevelt knew and loved. Papers were

piled high on the sturdy desk, next to which stood a manuscript-laden small table. Two couches of a soft blue cottony fabric edged with white piping faced each other on either side of the fireplace, one of them directly in front of Mrs. Roosevelt's desk. A floral chintz armchair stood next to a side table at the end of one couch. I learned that most of the simple, beautifully designed American country furniture in the house had been made right there in the Val-Kill factory by local craftsmen. Originally, the study had been the sitting room of Miss Thompson's apartment after Mrs. Roosevelt transformed the furniture factory into a house. It could not have been a more inviting room. (It amused me to notice that here, too, the lamp shades were tilted at the same slightly crooked angles as those in Mrs. Roosevelt's city apartment, probably hurriedly brushed against by the very same people.) There was a bedroom and bath behind the study—a guest room at present—and a door to the far right as one entered led to a kitchen, now a potting and flower-arranging room. Seated at her desk, Mrs. Roosevelt could look out onto a large glass-enclosed veranda, dark that night, and empty in winter, but, as I later learned, with the screens in, easily converted into an outdoor warm-weather dining room.

Now the lady of the house sat cheerfully close to David and me as we enjoyed the sandwiches thoughtfully provided. The atmosphere was so harmonious that I felt the three of us were becoming quite accustomed to being together. I was oblivious to the effort Mrs. Roosevelt was making to cause it to appear so. We went up to the second floor. She showed me to the first room on the right at the top of the stairs. It was David's usual bedroom, so he was given another. When we came down early the following morning for breakfast, several guests were already at the table. In her customary place at its head, Mrs. Roosevelt was manning the toaster and teapot, filling requests, her head bent and, literally, her tongue in her cheek, her habit when she was struggling with a task. Ample dishes were brought through the swinging door from the kitchen on her left by Marge Entrup, the extraordinary cook, who, together with her husband, Les, was in charge of running Mrs. Roosevelt's cottage. Son John came in with forced brightness to boom, "Hello, Mummy," his usual morning greeting whenever his mother was at home. He and his wife, Anne, and their four lovely children, Nina, Haven, Sally (Sara), and Joan spent summers and holidays in Stone Cottage, their residence on the Val-Kill property. After breakfast, David and I, together with Mrs. Roosevelt, who was dressed in her ancient brown-and-tan tweed "Hyde Park coat," with her Scottish terrier, Duffy, a Fala look-alike, trotting beside us, took a long, leisurely walk in the woods behind the cottage. There was a chill in the air that gray day as we crunched along the gently winding footpaths, stopping now and then as Duffy darted out of view to retrieve the objects David randomly tossed out for him along the way. I surmise now that it was on similar outings that Mrs. Roosevelt confided her problems to David.

On our return to the cottage, we found the place bustling with arriving guests and Thanksgiving dinner preparations; enticing aromas from the kitchen permeated the house. By one o'clock, about twenty-four were gathered in the study for drinks. In addition to David and me, they included John and Anne and their children; the Lash family; Curtis, Anna's son, and his wife, Ruth; Lorena Hickok; Margaret Cutter, a former wife of Mrs. Roosevelt's late brother, Hall, their daughter, Ellie, and her four children, "Little Nell," Stewart, Teddy and Lauren. Franklin and his wife, Sue, came from their farm in nearby Poughquag. Present, too, were distant cousins Marie Morgan and her daughter and son, Barbara and Forbes (among those who had spent the night).

Mrs. Roosevelt continued to read and sign letters at her desk as we milled around her until two o'clock dinner was announced. Val-Kill's laden table, very festive in its variety and abundance of decoration, gifts, and food, was always extended to its full length in Mrs. Roosevelt's lifetime. Whenever I visit Val-Kill now, seeing the table without its extension leaves is startling, as is the silence surrounding it.

Thanksgiving was a holiday Mrs. Roosevelt loved, and it showed. She had found time to select place cards suitable for each person. (David was frequently given different drawings of a "wise owl.") Gifts on the children's table were appropriate for their different ages. Chocolate turkeys and other sweets and small mementos crowded ours. The massive silver candelabra on either end of the long table framed a wonderful center-piece. Brought out annually on this holiday, the horn of plenty was a cornucopia of colorfully cascading autumn leaves, yellow-and-orange corn, red apples, and chestnuts. Standing at the sideboard behind their seated mother, John and Franklin carved the huge ham and turkey for plates held out by Marge and the waitress, Becky, who handed them in turn to Mrs. Roosevelt. She added to them from the many serving dishes beside her on a table to her right, and the plates were passed one by one around the table to their recipients; a very efficient system—so many served so well by so few.

Everyone passed plates and conversed simultaneously, except our host-ess, who barely looked up or said a word until her job was done. Heaping portions were typical fare for the Roosevelts, and second helpings not unusual. Curtis was in charge of keeping glasses brimming with cider and/or wine. Mrs. Roosevelt had seated me, the newcomer, close to her on her left. It was not difficult to feel at home in the spirited and friendly circle. For me and others, the presence of Mrs. Roosevelt gave unique meaning to a wonderful American celebration. When the table was cleared before dessert and glasses filled with champagne, everyone grew expectantly quiet. It was the first time I was to hear Mrs. Roosevelt's memorable three-part toast. She rose and, lifting her glass, soberly said, "To the United States of America." I could not have been more touched. A sip of champagne and a pause as she continued: "To the president." Lastly, she said, "To those we love who are not with us today."* In that atmosphere, who could not have proud thoughts of the best that America could be?

It had been arranged between us that David would leave Hyde Park late that afternoon to drive to see Grania at the Putney School in Ver-mont. Learning that I had not yet visited the presidential Library and home, Mrs. Roosevelt made arrangements with the curator and the

---

*David took a photograph of Mrs. Roosevelt giving her toast, and in her centennial year, 1984, the United States Postal Service made a commemorative postage stamp from this portrait photograph.

United States Park Service people on duty to show me around the National Historic Site before I took the train back to the city. At the last minute, however, she decided that she herself would be my guide. She still had a houseful of guests and looked worn-out after the demanding day. Clearly, it was on David's behalf that she extended herself, and I suspect, too, that she wanted to compensate me for his departure. Her subtle, understanding ways became increasingly apparent to me as I grew to know her better. In any event, my attempts to dissuade her failed, and off we drove together to the Roosevelt estate. Conducting me around the Library, she took trouble to be sure that I would not miss those exhibits she considered particularly interesting—for example, the correspondence to President Roosevelt regarding the development of the atom bomb—commenting upon them as we progressed through the galleries and into the Library stacks. In her tour of Springwood (the Big House), no room was omitted, including those generally off-limits to the public, such as children's playrooms and bedrooms on the attic floor. Spying what I thought was an oddly placed mirror at the very top of a tall chest in an upper-story dressing room, I remarked upon it. "Who could possibly see anything in a mirror so high?" I asked. "Franklin tied his ties in that mirror," Mrs. Roosevelt replied, making her husband's height vividly clear to me for the first time. I realized that until then I had had in mind only the image of a seated president.

Sunrise at Campobello

Starring Ralph Bellamy as FDR, *Sunrise at Campobello*, the play describing the dramatic events that took place at the Roosevelt family's island retreat off the coast of Maine during the summer of 1921, opened on January 30 (Roosevelt's birthday), 1958. It was a Broadway hit. Dore Schary's drama dealt with the traumatic time when thirty-nine-year-old Franklin Roosevelt was stricken with a life-threatening case of poliomyelitis and how he, his wife, mother, and children valiantly coped with his paralysis. The idea of the production strangely seemed to satisfy Mrs. Roosevelt and she willingly shared with Mr. Schary some of her memories of the heartbreaking events of that summer that had so changed their lives. David and I met the playwright-producer more than once in Hyde Park and with Mrs. Roosevelt in New York when he came to interview her in preparation for the play. Her motivation for cooperating with the project became clear when she explained to David that her five children, seemingly always in need of money, were to share in the royalities. A dutiful mother, she did her best to ensure the play's success.

It was unusual that so many of the Roosevelt offspring were present on any one occasion, but the four handsome brothers—only Anna was absent—were front and center in the audience on the night of the opening. Their mother and her escort for the evening, her old friend Harry Hooker, along with David and I, were seated together on a side aisle. There was a buzz of anticipation as the theater filled with famous figures from the worlds of entertainment, government, and politics. Whenever I stole a glance at Mrs. Roosevelt as her life was enacted onstage, her expression was impassive. She simply did not react to the performance. The mass of admirers crowding her during intermissions made moving through them impossible. She did manage to pass the word to us that at the final curtain we four were to make haste for the exit. We did. Gladly leaving the limelight of the occasion to her children to enjoy without her as the final applause began, we dashed up the aisle of the still-darkened theater, Mrs. Roosevelt resisting all attempts to help her into her dangling ermine jacket. She could not get out to the waiting limousine fast enough. Poor Harry Hooker was breathless as Mrs. Roosevelt instructed the chauffeur, "Just drive around." We were too early for the after-theater party given by a member of President Roosevelt's cabinet, Secretary of Commerce Oscar L. Chapman. As we'd left the theater at such a clip, we continued on our aimless drive so as not to arrive at the Savoy Plaza before we were expected. Mrs. Roosevelt seemed relieved that the performance was over. No sooner had we settled into the car than Harry Hooker promptly asked, "Eleanor, how did it feel to see yourself on the stage tonight?"* "The play had nothing to do with me," she emphatically replied, looking straight ahead. "Nothing?" he repeated incredulously. "Nothing at all," she answered coolly. "I did not recognize myself at all."

It was the best party I can remember. It even began memorably, although I didn't know that at the time. We entered the elevator with an attractive young couple. The man deferred respectfully to Mrs. Roosevelt. His elegant wife was close to my age. Mrs. Roosevelt introduced us: "Senator and Mrs. John Kennedy," she said. The Chapmans had arranged a splendid supper for more than two hundred, a who's who of old New Dealers. I can't recall actually seeing Mrs. Roosevelt during the party. She was always surrounded, as were James, Elliott, Franklin, and John. The air was filled with hearty greetings as the jovial men of the Roosevelt administration remembered heady shared experiences of past triumphs and great events. I noticed the Kennedy couple only once or twice as they remained seated by themselves a bit self-consciously on an upholstered bench against a wall. A different generation, they evidently did not have a sense of belonging. It was well after midnight when we prepared to leave. Mrs. Roosevelt looked tired. Had she enjoyed the party? She didn't say. As a rule, looking back at the past did not interest her and she didn't waste time or emotions on it. She had fulfilled her obligation. The play had been successfully launched.

Two Plus One

David moved into a larger apartment and we began to furnish it, but still no wedding date had been set. I would have given up on him by then had he not been so different from everyone else, so beguiling, tender, comforting, and close. I had never known a person like him and have

---

*Harry Hooker was one of the few people who called Mrs. Roosevelt by her first name, having shared a part of her distant past. Actually, one could always distinguish those who knew Mrs. Roosevelt well from acquaintances and strangers by how they addressed her. Those who knew her referred to her as "Mrs. Roosevelt." Those who did not spoke of her—and still do—as "Eleanor."

never known one since. Nothing escaped David's notice. His observations and often-original viewpoints were fascinating. An independent thinker, he approached subjects inquisitively and with fresh vision, wanting to learn. What luxury it was to see through his eyes aspects of life I would otherwise have missed. The time we spent together either stood still for me or flew.

One day, he asked me to marry him in Paris, where he was flying to attend a patient's wedding, but the anxious request had more of an undertone of wanting the deed done than of romance. I refused. He had evidently voiced his qualms to Mrs. Roosevelt, who wrote him plainly:

New Year's Day [1958]
David dear,

Just after midnight and as the New Year begins, first of all I want to wish you happiness and success in the year to come. May you know what you want and then I know you will achieve it and may those who love you be helpful and give you what you want.

My first wish is for you and I pray you may be your best for that is really very wonderful.

My love and a blessed New Year be yours.

On his return from the Paris weekend she, not I, met David at the airport, having left the following letter at his apartment in case they missed connections. Thoughts of his marrying were definitely on her mind:

Darling,

Just in case I miss you at the airport, for you should be gone before I arrive, these flowers will brighten up the apartment and tell you how happy I am to have you home. It is good to have you near. A thousand welcomes and I can hardly wait to see you tonight.

Your mother and 2 friends went with me Sunday pm to the French lecture on the "Mime." Too long, but she loved the demonstration and admired his body control and wanted you to see him!

The Pendars [friends they had met in Morocco] were here to-night to go to Washington Thursday and return in February. They leave the 8th so could you dine here with them the 6th for a farewell?

That would mean being here two nights in succession but please come the 9th and let me go to hear you speak for I go the 8th and won't be home til the 18th and that to me seems a long time!

How I hope you have had good weather and a wonderful time and come back with no more trouble with your shoulder and feel-ing really rested.

I have kept free time the days I am here in case you have any important news for which you want quick arrangements made!

I miss you and love you dearly and may you always be happy and healthy and blessed.

E. R.

To this David replied:

1/31/58

Dearest Mrs. R.,

Just a word to thank you for the wonderful welcome home from Paris—You sitting there—having come all the way out [to the air-port] so early! And then your letter and the flowers—I so often receive without acknowledging my joy. Thank you again and again. Last night [I had] a deep impression [of living] these days and years with you being there—it was strange and moving. Just my love. And my thoughts and thanks.

As 1958 began, Maureen, privy to many of her boss's private affairs, was puzzled by Mrs. Roosevelt's unaccountable behavior.* She was with-drawn, a sure sign that something was wrong. Maureen knew of no un-usual ongoing family problems, no impending upheavals that would have produced that kind of strained silence. On Mrs. Roosevelt's various fronts

---

*Author's interviews with Maureen Corr, 1988 and 1989.

of activity, private and public, things seemed to be going smoothly. Yet, thought Maureen, something had to be troubling her. Mrs. Roosevelt was not herself. They had left New York on a speaking tour. In a postcard to David stamped "Phoenix, February 9, 1958," Mrs. Roosevelt wrote:

IN AIR NEAR TUCSON
Feb., 8 pm
A thousand thanks for the telephone call. It was good to hear your voice again. Take care of yourself. Your speech yesterday was excellent and will help me in those I make. My thoughts are with you and my love.

E. R.

She sent him another card the following day:

Sunday eve [February 9, 1958]
First speech over and successful. Here it is lovely and you might enjoy it as a rest. This is a place of memories for me tied to Isabella Greenway.* Between a tea and the lecture I dined with 2 of her children in her old house. A good time with Elliott and Minnewa. I hope all is well with you.

E. R.

After his return from Paris, David firmly and happily asked me to marry him on my birthday, February 23.

Just as she and Maureen were about to leave the Arizona Inn for Los Angeles, Mrs. Roosevelt was handed a telegram from David announcing our wedding date. By then, I knew that David had told Mrs. Roosevelt about his interest in me soon after we'd met, and that discussions about us had been ongoing between them behind the scenes. Besides, it was

---

*Isabella Greenway and Mrs. Roosevelt had been debutantes together and their friendship lasted into adulthood.

obvious that David and I had become a couple, and Mrs. Roosevelt could easily draw her own conclusions. Nevertheless, the news that David was getting married, when it came, was a shock to her. I did not imagine that would be the case. As far as I was concerned, in terms of our courtship, Mrs. Roosevelt had been in the background all along. She was not the subject of our conversations when David and I were alone. She knew that marriage was in the air, but it was not yet a fait accompli, and she had been in and around the maze of David's indecisions before. She had accepted the idea of his marrying once before, and, in my case, she had even encouraged it, understanding that he was a man who needed love and companionship and was not happy living alone. But the actual announcement of our wedding date was so final. When she read the telegram, her face turned ashen, Maureen said, and the cause of her brooding in the two preceding weeks became clear. She had been expecting this news, but now, confronted by its reality, her feelings were mixed and turbulent. Miserable memories of abandonment returned. She struggled between the anxiety of losing David and heartfelt hopes for his happiness. More than any other, theirs was the close companionship she had treasured ever since their friendship began on their fateful flight to Switzerland eleven years earlier, when they first recognized in each other common longings, loneliness, and compassion. Would it now end? David wisely followed his telegram to Mrs. Roosevelt with a telephone call on the same day. Heavy heart or no, she rallied as usual, prepared to support him.

At day's end, she was able to write:

Wed. night [February 12, 1958]
David dearest:

It was so good to hear your voice today and you sounded happy and I hope it is because you are fully satisfied with your decision.

I am free till 3 P.M. on Sunday the 23rd if you need me later than that, wire me St. Francis Hotel, San Francisco and I'll get out of the afternoon and evening dates.

God bless and keep you and give you love and happiness.

E. R.

Once the date was fixed, David became so elated and hopeful at the thought of it that I could not possibly object to its closeness, a mere two weeks away, or to the fact that he preferred that we have a small wedding arranged by Mrs. Roosevelt in her apartment. He explained that she wished to give the wedding. (In hindsight, I think he needed it to take place in familiar surroundings.) I was not in the mood to dwell on the curiousness of the arrangement as long as we could be surrounded by people we loved. Preparations for the event were almost insignificant to me. Never having cared for ceremony, I agreed to this wedding plan, hoping that my parents would not be too disappointed. Actually, they were less than enthusiastic about my marrying David altogether, although they liked him well enough. I was considerably younger than he, had not been married before, and the fact that he was divorced, with a teenaged child, made him not exactly ideal for their only daughter. But events were happening too fast and they, good parents that they were, had no choice but to be open to persuasion.

Relieved and happy that her son was at last settling down, David's mother responded to our news with a rush of joy. Her excitement when she telephoned me compelled her to lapse into German in expressing her delight over the coming event. David, who was with her, took the receiver from her hand and gently reminded her that I did not understand German. Whereupon, she repeated her exuberant message in Russian. After a further reminder about my language limitations, my future mother-in-law showered blessings upon us in English.

Mrs. Roosevelt rallied.

ST. FRANCIS HOTEL
SAN FRANCISCO
Sat. Feb. 15th, 1958
David dearest,

I hope this will await you Monday and I think of you with Grania and hope the pictures and lecture were a great success. I'm sure they were. Perhaps Edna went with you which would give you a pleasanter trip. Give her my love.

Life was hectic in Los Angeles but it is worse here! However, all went well at Stanford yesterday and will pray all goes well here and my plane is on time going back.

I'll call you Tuesday P.M. and I'm all prepared to do anything you wish the 23rd. Wouldn't you like a buffet lunch? I hope for you the deepest and most satisfying happiness. My thoughts and love go to you.

E. R.

We dined with Mrs. Roosevelt on an evening before our wedding. She had lovingly arranged at my place at the table a little ceramic bird with a verse she'd composed:

Edna:
At your wedding you should wear
Something old and something new,
Something borrowed and something blue,
So I give you a little blue bird who brings happiness;
May you be happy and you will then make the man you love happy.

There was a small object at David's place also: two standing wood figures, one male, the other female, paddling in a canoe. She'd written these lines:

David:
These little figures may be a symbol
May they take you on smooth seas
Where the storms are few
May you have the understanding
*   which gives kindness*
And may you both give and
*   receive the warmth of love*
Which will bring you both happiness.

Old-fashioned, even quaint as these expressions may be, they show the freshness of Mrs. Roosevelt's appreciation of love. She had entered into our prenuptial celebrations with all the warmth of which she was capable. Here was a woman determined to keep David close as well as to ensure his happiness. I cannot judge exactly how she thought she would fit into our picture, but I imagine she hoped for the best, and without artifice, she made it clear to me that we could be friends. I responded in kind. In ever-increasing contact with her, I was discovering day by day the extraordinary grace she brought into the lives she touched. Here are excerpts from a letter I wrote her:

February 22, 1958
Dear Mrs. Roosevelt:
  ...I am most grateful to you for the wedding tomorrow which I know will be beautiful....I know how much you mean to David and what your feelings and opinions mean to him. [How easily I thought I knew things in those days.] I can repay you in part by doing all I can to make David happy. I shall try very hard.
  I have admired you so much all my life and to this I add my love....

Edna

Our wedding day was cold, overcast, an eerily quiet New York winter Sunday. Vestiges of sooty frozen snow ran in irregular patterns along the street curbs. David's was the first car to pull up at Mrs. Roosevelt's apartment. (He told me later that when he stopped for a red light on the way, something inside him clicked, and for the first time he felt he had entered the mainstream of life. I couldn't resist a mischievous thought: What if the light had been green?) Immediately upon our crossing the threshold—my parents, brother, and I—Mrs. Roosevelt held out a gift to me—a necklace: a long gold chain of smoky crystals in a narrow black leather box. "This is not valuable," she said, "but I wanted you to have something which has been close to me." I saw at once that she was pale. Her manner was cordial but restrained, different from before—kind, not warm. We were married in Mrs. Roosevelt's large flower-filled living room in the presence of our families and a few close friends. A friend of David's from his Berlin days, Rabbi Joachim Prinz, performed the ceremony. It was a lovely wedding, joyous for us and everyone present, except for Mrs. Roosevelt, whose apparent weariness I attributed to the fact that she had just returned from California. David knew the occasion would take its toll on her. But for him to have rejected her offer to arrange our wedding would have heightened her sense of exclusion. I am sure he also needed the security of her closeness on this occasion. It still had not occurred to me that David's marriage would be a trial to Mrs. Roosevelt, that she believed it could wrench from her the person who meant the most to her. To all of this, I was blissfully oblivious. As the afternoon party progressed, I noticed her gradually warming to her accustomed role of hostess, and now and then, among the convivial sounds around the several luncheon tables, I even heard her laugh. How could I have guessed her apprehension when the following evening she wrote me this note?

Monday night, Feb. 24th, 1958
Edna dear,

Your lovely roses are giving everyone who comes in a joyful welcome and as I go in and out I think of you. Many thanks but above all my thanks for your sweet note.

I loved having the wedding here, as I have always loved doing anything I could for David and now I shall love doing anything I can for you and for you both. I never want to be a burden, but it is a great joy to me to feel close to the few people I really love and to be able to do anything for them. I need you both very much, but don't let me be a nuisance for David and you both need time alone in your own home.

Will you let me know if you are going to the concert on the

26th? I can't get there till 9:30 so I won't go unless I'll find you there!

My thanks and love to you.

E. R.

My mother received a similar letter, written two days later, to which a touching and unexpected postscript was added:

Dear Mrs. Perkel,

How kind you are to send me the lovely red roses! They are a joy and will give me pleasure for some time.

It was very nice to meet you and your family and I was more than happy to arrange the reception for David and Edna.

With many thanks and my warm good wishes,

Very sincerely yours,
Eleanor Roosevelt

P.S. I hope we will meet often in the future and that you will feel I belong a little in your family circle.

She wrote to David on our wedding day:

David dearest,

I have no wedding present for you and Edna but I think what will bring you the greatest pleasure is the gift of your next real trip whether it is to Russia, China or Timbucktu, so I hereby promise you 2 tickets for the next real trip you want to take! Sometime when I find something you could use and enjoy in your home I will get it as a *post* wedding gift.

You know you have all my love and may this day bring you the perfect relationship you have dreamed of and I hope you can fully enjoy.

God bless you always.

E. R.

Not long after, Mrs. Roosevelt invited me to have lunch alone with her. I started out in a driving rain from our apartment on West Fifty-fifth Street. Unable to find an empty cab, I walked to East Sixty-second Street, arriving at Mrs. Roosevelt's door soaked to the skin. Most unusual for her, she hardly noticed that I was dripping rivulets, other than making the offer, which I refused, of a pair of slippers to replace my wet shoes. Her behavior was strained, almost unfriendly. We were both self-conscious, our conversation was forced, and I hoped for the grim lunch to end. When I was at the door, ready to leave, she suddenly turned and made a surprisingly hostile remark, which had no bearing whatsoever on our previous conversation. Bitterly, vehemently, she said, "Don't worry. David will give you *everything* you want!" Taken aback and offended, I made no response other than a strangled "Good-bye."

Mrs. Roosevelt was never bad-tempered with me again. It was beginning to dawn on me that I had stepped into a deep and established friendship with possible pitfalls. But I was still too full of my own happiness to realize the threat I posed to Eleanor Roosevelt, or the emotional adjustments she had to work through.

The Three of Us

Although I now knew that David and Mrs. Roosevelt were accustomed to sharing their innermost thoughts and feelings, he had at no time discussed with me the many sides of their attachment, nor had he revealed how central they were to each other's lives, how one depended upon the other. In recounting so much of his past to me, he had deliberately excluded Mrs. Roosevelt. He had had too much respect for her even to hint about her romantic feelings for him, which both of them had dealt with maturely and honorably. David simply never alluded to the subject. It was like him not to stir the waters and to assume that I somehow knew what he knew. He gave me more credit than I deserved. Mrs. Roosevelt had not counted with me in my love for David. Whatever I realized or did not realize about the complexity of their relationship, I correctly sensed that he and Mrs. Roosevelt had done nothing that needed to be hidden or disguised, so neither had had to alter his or her behavior when I came on the scene.

Occasionally, early in our marriage, someone would cautiously bring up the subject of David and Mrs. Roosevelt's friendship, hoping to satisfy a long-standing curiosity. But there was nothing racy to tell. I had never seen any sign of romantic love between them. Her admiration for him was, in many respects, much like that of other grateful patients, men and women, or so I thought, except that she was such a larger-than-life person, one assumed her responses would be fuller, more generous than those of others. If further evidence is needed to explain how freely I could accept her closeness to us as a couple, it is that David had established his considerable reputation as a physician independently, and his career did not require patronage. It was plain that Mrs. Roosevelt preferred David's company to that of anyone else. Who could understand that better than I? Why should I think that she loved him in any way other than as a doting and affectionate friend? I had not yet read her letters to him. Had I done so at the time, their relationship would have been clearer, but nothing would have changed. I am sure I would have thought then, as I do now, that her feelings for David were a tribute to him. She was a very intelligent woman. And, confident of David's love, I could freely admire Mrs. Roosevelt and enjoy close contact with her.

I found it odd when I would occasionally be asked how I could not have been "jealous" of Mrs. Roosevelt. But I had no reason to be. When I met Eleanor Roosevelt, she was more than four decades older than I, older than my mother. I never considered her to be a threat to me. Her loving David, however she loved him, took nothing away from me. Quite the contrary. She was an inspiring person and utterly disarming in her modesty and in the kindness that came so naturally to her. She was wise and experienced, someone from whom one could learn a great deal. When I was with her, I was always aware of what a fascinating woman she was, and that she lived the life she preached—of loving one's fellow-man. David used to say that Mrs. Roosevelt was the same person in public and in private—indeed, even more wonderful privately. It was true.

Mrs. Roosevelt never "held court." Members of her intimate circle were not required to flatter, attend, or accompany her. She fled from superficial behavior and unessential formalities. Any "homage" paid to her was totally uninvited and unwelcome. Often when applauded for her own accomplishments, she would attribute these to her husband. We considered ourselves privileged to enjoy the company of such a rare human being, whether it was traveling, at home, or anywhere else just *because* we were free to be ourselves with her, free to say what we thought and to behave as we felt. She wouldn't have had it any other way. She was one of the few people in this world in which greatness and modesty coexisted. I was enriched by her intelligence and by the unique experiences that closeness to her offered, and by the very caring friendship that she and I came to share. This speaks for her enormous tact, her empathy for me, and, of course, for her resolve to keep David near. Mrs. Roosevelt was able to transcend her fear of losing David by befriending me. I didn't know it then, but I know it now. This could not have been easy for her at first, but she made it work. Her ability to love unselfishly and unpossessively enabled her to be with David more, and for us to have peace at home. (Later, I suspect, I even freed her of feeling responsible for looking after him, which must have been a relief.)

I never sensed that Mrs. Roosevelt acted toward me in any way contrary to her feelings. If she had, being together as often as we were and sensitive as I imagine I would have been to being merely tolerated, I would have been aware of it. Besides, falseness was alien to her nature. It was her strength of character and her pragmatism that triumphed over her neediness to love deeply and be deeply loved by a few. Promoting David's happiness was her primary incentive. Rising above her own feelings of lost love to draw me in made him even more available to her than before. Her devotion to me was based on her love for David, although I cherish the memory of her warmly telling me otherwise.

By the following May, only three months after David and I were married, she could already be sure that her forebodings of losing him were groundless, that he would continue to be the strong presence in her life — which was her first priority — and that real friendship with me was possible. She made it happen. So did I, but it was easy for me; I had everything I wanted.

Mrs. Roosevelt was sufficiently reassured to write David buoyantly:

May 27th

. . . I want you to know how happy I am to see and feel your happiness with Edna and hers with you. I fully expected that our relationship would have to change but I think Edna is so lovely that I can mean something to you both and not hurt the happiness and closeness between you. It is good, so good, to see you well cared for and happy and to feel that I can keep [you] and share and perhaps contribute a little to both of you. . . .

David's mother, Maria Gurewitsch, died suddenly one Sunday afternoon in April when, after visiting a patient, she stepped off the curb to cross the street and a bus abruptly backed up, nearly hitting her. She died instantly of heart failure. She was eighty-four years old. David and I raced to the police station where she'd been taken. Married only several months before, I had not yet had a chance to know her well.

The first time my mother-in-law stepped across our threshold with her many boxes of candy for me, this tiny, delicate woman, barely five feet high, a luxurious mass of snow-white hair crowning her head, eyes shining, murmured, "Wonderful." "What is wonderful?" I gently asked. "Everything here," she replied, reaching up to me.

Seated on a wooden bench in the faded green litter-strewn hallway of the police station, I waited, shaken, for David to emerge from the room in which his mother's body lay. The longer I waited, the more anxious I grew about him. He finally appeared. With glistening eyes that were the same bright blue as his mother's, and looking so wounded and vulnerable, he smiled at me. "The bus never touched her" were his first words. "I examined her. How wonderful to die with your boots on," he added. This thought seemed to console him. The renowned psychologist Dr. Eric Fromm, Maria Gurewitsch's patient and friend, spoke at her funeral. He reminded the hundreds of people who were gathered in her memory of the Talmudic tradition that each generation must produce thirty-six righteous people in order for the world to continue, the thirty-six unaware of their significance. "Maria Gurewitsch was one of those who unknowingly upheld the world," said Dr. Fromm. I remember her radiance and serenity, her small, strong, healing young hands. Inspiring by example, loved by her two sons, she was "Omama" to her grandchildren, who still revere her.

Although hospitable and gracious to David's mother because she was David's mother, and respecting her for her accomplishments and independence, Mrs. Roosevelt had not much cared for her. I learned this from stray remarks. She would say resentfully, "David's mother doesn't really appreciate his achievements. She did not instill self-confidence in him." I disagreed, saying: "But she adores him. Her face lights with joy when she sees him. He knows she is proud of him. It is enough." I remember one of my own earliest impressions of David, when as a stranger I thought to myself that it must be wonderful to have such a son. Mrs. Roosevelt probably felt the same, maybe even more ardently.

Val-Kill Vignettes

During the first summer of our marriage, David and I alternated our weekends more or less between the town of Watermill on Long Island, and Hyde Park. We were given a room of our own at Val-Kill, large and airy, with a mixture of ponderous, dark, old-fashioned furniture and lovely pine bookcases and tables. Except for the spacious porch extending from Mrs. Roosevelt's upstairs bedroom (on which she often slept summer and winter), ours was the only room with a terrace, and from it one could easily see Stone Cottage through the trees, the residence of the John Roosevelt family. The land on which the two cottages had been built belonged to Franklin Roosevelt. By the time he and his wife had grown apart, he had understood her need for a place of her own and generously gave her a life-interest in the Val-Kill land. He offered to supervise the building of a cottage for her use, as well as to house her friends Marion Dickerman and Nancy Cook. These women were both active in state Democratic politics with Mrs. Roosevelt and were her colleagues and co-owners of the Todhunter School in New York City.

Built in 1925, Stone Cottage was a retreat for Mrs. Roosevelt, where she could be happy with friends of her choice, professional people, talented and socially aware, from whom she could learn. When her husband and children were in residence in the Big House, which belonged to her mother-in-law, Mrs. Roosevelt stayed with them. Otherwise, when in Hyde Park, she lived at Val-Kill. The property turned out to be something of a retreat for FDR, as well. There he relaxed in the company of his wife and the interesting people who gathered at Val-Kill. The important addition of a swimming pool to the grounds of Stone Cottage, where FDR could freely exercise, gave him added purpose for visits, and he drove the short distance to Val-Kill from the Big House in his hand-controlled Ford whenever he could get away. He was an affable, informative member of his wife's picnic parties, where he passed many pleasant summer afternoons. In 1926 Mrs. Roosevelt and her friends, the Misses Dickerman and Cook, decided to add a furniture factory to the property to provide employment to the many fine craftsmen living in the Rhinebeck–Hyde Park area. Proceeds from the sale of well-made examples of American-style furniture were intended to help support local workmen through the winters, when times were hard and farmwork minimal. Under the artistic supervision of Nancy Cook, the project, largely financed by Mrs. Roosevelt, never prospered, and ten years later, when she felt she could no longer afford to make up the business deficits, Mrs. Roosevelt closed the factory. Following difficulties with her partners, Mrs. Roosevelt left Stone Cottage and converted the furniture factory into a house for herself, which included an apartment for her secretary and best friend, Malvina ("Tommy") Thompson.

With its pond, stream, and woods, Val-Kill Cottage was home to Mrs. Roosevelt until she died. She envisaged retiring there. David said: "From whatever distance, for however short a time, she would try to get back there." Val-Kill was where Mrs. Roosevelt counted bed linen and towels before distribution to rooms, where she picked flowers from her garden, walked in the woods with Fala, the president's dog, then Tamas and Duffy, the last of her Scotties. At Val-Kill, she wrote out the day's menus, stopped at local produce stands in summer for fresh corn and strawberries, called the gas station attendant by his first name, slept outside on cold winter nights on the glassed-in porch beyond her bedroom, and retired there in summer when the screens were in. Val-Kill was home to the family, the place where they swapped political stories, argued, carried their troubles home to mother, took meals together, brought their children. From there, her identity as an independent and powerful woman was underscored, enabling her to fulfill her life's mission of service.

Mrs. Roosevelt was often her husband's stand-in after he was crippled by polio. In the seventeen years she lived after he died, in addition to being recognized for her own accomplishments, she was the symbol of FDR in the eyes of the world. She took this responsibility very seriously because she had believed in her husband and was proud of his achievements. She appreciated that visits by prominent world leaders continued to be made to his grave, to the presidential library (he was the first president to establish such a library), and to his family home. Mrs. Roosevelt's efforts to keep Franklin Roosevelt's policies alive went far beyond wifely loyalty. It was constant hard work. In her inimitable style, she personally welcomed dignitaries and special groups who made the trip to Hyde Park, often rearranging her schedule to accommodate them. She would drive the two hours up to Hyde Park and later made the two-hour trip back to New York City in order to receive these prominent guests, if even for a very short time, knowing they had come from a distance or had a special purpose for their visit. She was their hostess and guide, and she realized that her presence would add to their memory of the visit. She hoped that her children, grandchildren, and great-grandchildren would continue to gather in Val-Kill, so close to the Hyde Park estate, long after she was gone.*

---

*No members of the Roosevelt family now live there. Val-Kill is a National Historic Site.

As one drove up the narrow, winding dirt road and rumbled across a short plank bridge over a stream to the modest house, lovely wide fields opened on either side. Behind the cottage were the woods Mrs. Roosevelt loved. The gray stucco building was never a pretty place from the outside. Having once been a factory, it still had an industrial look to it. Of no particular exterior design, the house had simply changed and expanded with need. Mrs. Roosevelt received first-time callers, and some of the most important world leaders, including royalty, at the building's small, awkward side entrance, where there was barely room for two people to stand on the top stucco step. Once across the threshold, however, you were welcomed by cheerful knotty pine–paneled rooms designed for peace and comfort. The only jarring note was the skin of a tiger Mrs. Roosevelt's father had shot in India, spread on the floor before the living room fireplace, jaws ajar and teeth bared.

In addition to Mrs. Roosevelt's Val-Kill Cottage and Stone Cottage, there was Top Cottage on the Val-Kill property, the president's Hyde Park retreat. The other buildings included a stable-garage and the playhouse.* The latter had been turned into living quarters for Archibald (Tubby) Curnan, Mrs. Roosevelt's chauffeur. These buildings, the tennis courts (poorly maintained), the pool, and a large stone outdoor fireplace for cooking picnic hot dogs and hamburgers for visits by organizations, were the essential elements around which Val-Kill life turned.

David and I had lovely holidays in Hyde Park. Mrs. Roosevelt personally arranged the flowers in our bedroom and left books to interest us. All guests were free to do entirely as they pleased. We were expected only to be prompt for meals—and even that was not a hard-and-fast rule. It was, in fact, easy to comply, as mealtime gatherings could be such fascinating social occasions. On July and August weekends, it was rare to find a spare

---

*The playhouse is currently used as a small auditorium. Hung with photographs, including those taken by David on his trips with Mrs. Roosevelt, its main function is to show a short film on the life of Eleanor Roosevelt to visitors to Val-Kill.

seat around the table outside on the screened-in porch. When we left on a Sunday night, bundles of vegetables and flowers from the garden were placed in the trunk of our car.

Mrs. Roosevelt had an "open-door" policy wherever she lived. The extent and style of Val-Kill hospitality was awe-inspiring. Friends, neighbors, and some members of the family were there often and I was becoming acquainted with them. Mrs. Roosevelt's ninety-four-year-old uncle, David Gray (formerly U.S. ambassador to Ireland), came up from Sarasota for the summer. In and out were sons and their wives— most often Franklin and Sue, who had a farm in nearby Poughquag, occasionally, Jimmy visited from his home in California, alone or with his wife, Irene. John, living a stone's throw away, was always in evidence on weekends. Having her grandchildren about the place meant a good deal to Mrs. Roosevelt.

On one of my first summer weekends in Hyde Park, I met Anna Roosevelt Halsted, who was as handsome as her brothers. She had come to spend a few days with her mother, as well as to see her daughter, Ellie ("Sisty") Seagraves and her grandchildren, who were vacationing there. (Mrs. Roosevelt was particularly fond of Ellie, Van, and their children.) The eldest grandson, Curtis ("Buzz"), was an occasional summer visitor, but he was more often than not in Hyde Park for Thanksgiving and Christmas. He was always attentive to "Grandmère," as Mrs. Roosevelt was known to her grandchildren. We saw a good deal of Curtis's half brother, John Boettiger, Jr., during the summer, as well as Mrs. Roosevelt's niece Ellie Elliott Roach, who lived in Rhinebeck with her four children and husband, George. Another visitor was Laura Delano, the president's cousin, who had been with him in Warm Springs when he died. "Cousin Polly," as she was known in the family, was an interesting, odd-looking little woman with the beautiful, chiseled Delano profile. The Reverend Gordon Kidd, rector of St. James Church, was one of the regulars, as were Lorena Hickok, Father George Ford, a sprinkling of Hudson River neighbors, and staff members of the Franklin D. Roosevelt Library. Occasionally, Maureen Corr would come up, as well as my brother, Bertram Perkel. My parents, too, were among the visitors, often driving Mrs. Roosevelt's literary agent, Nanine Joseph,* to Hyde Park. Into this revolving mix around Mrs. Roosevelt's table were included many beguiling, well-known people. They arrived in Hyde Park at different times, singly or in pairs, with children or entourages, and their names read like a who's who of world figures. To presidents of countries, royalty, prime ministers, Nobel laureates, maharajas, politicians, scientists, labor leaders, teachers, Mrs. Roosevelt was always herself. When protocol required, the occasion became more formal, but, generally speaking, important guests, whoever they were, were delighted and honored to be in Mrs. Roosevelt's company, relieved to be placed at their ease and treated like everyone else. Table conversation was stimulating and informative.

David's and my Hyde Park weekends began in early spring. Mrs. Roosevelt would sometimes drive back to town with us on Sunday night. Occasionally, the three of us made a brief stop at the Fishkill summer house of Henry Morgenthau, Jr. (President Roosevelt's secretary of the treasury), and were sent home with baskets of apples from his orchard. At other times on the way to New York, we stopped off at Blythedale Children's Hospital in Valhalla so that David could look in on some worrisome young patients as well as to see how things had calmed down in the hospital after crowded family weekend visits. Mrs. Roosevelt was always warmly welcomed there. While he looked things over, she and I would visit with some of the children and staff members. From Mrs. Roosevelt's own experience in dealing with infantile paralysis, she was familiar with the trials of the physically disabled and the struggles of the

---

*Nanine Joseph once told David and me the following story: When Franklin Roosevelt was governor of New York, she received a call from a friend in Albany. It was late at night and she'd been awakened by the ring. The friend asked whether she would be willing to be Governor Roosevelt's literary agent. Annoyed at the lateness of the call, she replied, "Only if he can write!" The hearty laugh of another man could be heard on the line. "Judge for yourself," Governor Roosevelt interrupted good-naturedly. "I will send you some samples of my writing and look forward to hearing from you after you have read them." Nannine said she was embarrassed to have been so brusque, but she was impressed by the fairness of Roosevelt's answer. He sent her his material for consideration and she did become his literary agent.

professionals who worked with them. Listening to a physical therapist recount her frustration when a child she was treating reached a plateau, Mrs. Roosevelt replied that one should not minimize the value of any stage reached in treatment, saying that even the smallest gains should be appreciated. She added that "President Roosevelt would have loved to have been able just to stand at his desk and take two steps to the window."* The work at Blythedale is inspirational. I remember Sundays on the hospital lawns, on which were spread a lively mixture of young patients in wheelchairs, some on self-wheeling stretchers (giving them independence to move about despite their inability to sit up), enjoying themselves with parents, siblings, friends, even pets brought from home, all kinds of reunions encouraged to keep patients' ties to family and home as normal as possible. Notwithstanding his medical directorship of Blythedale, David's main professional home remained the Neurological Institute of Columbia-Presbyterian Medical Center.**

The observance of Memorial Day was taken particularly seriously by Mrs. Roosevelt, a great patriot, as were other national holidays. In my Hyde Park Memorial Day experiences, the day inevitably dawned hot and sunny, and the Hudson River Valley can be broiling. I do not recall David or Mrs. Roosevelt ever mentioning the weather. She took it for granted that sizzling summers were simply to be borne, and David seemed to like both heat and cold. But the knowing, dressy New York–Washington crowd, who often came up to Hyde Park for Memorial Day lunch with Roosevelts, neighbors, and houseguests and for the services that followed, arrived wilted, though prepared with fans and parasols. A buffet lunch was set shortly after breakfast dishes had been cleared. Although there

---

*This anecdote was repeated to me by executive director Robert Stone, who was told it by the physical therapist in question.
**He was attending physician in the Department of Physical Medicine, as well as being clinical professor of Rehabilitation Medicine, Columbia University, College of Physicians and Surgeons.

would be anywhere from sixty to ninety or more luncheon guests on Memorial Day, no extra household help was ever hired and all food and desserts were prepared at home. Mrs. Roosevelt's system of offering meals to large groups of people was simple and efficient. Usually, there was a basic serving crew around the large dining room table: Anne Roosevelt and her daughter, Nina; Marie Morgan; Trude Lash and I, and sometimes Grania, too. Armed with utensils, each of us manned two dishes, from which we served the steady flow of guests circling the table. There were salads of all kinds, cold meats, and rolls and biscuits spread out on one side of the long, broad table. On the other side, in double rows, were banana and cranberry breads, marvelous fruit pies, and rich cakes. Tea and coffee were poured from the sideboard by Becky, the housemaid, while Marge Entrup, Mrs. Roosevelt's cook, oversaw the table. Those with filled plates distributed themselves throughout the downstairs of the house, many settling on the front and back porches, others comfortably seated in the study and large living room.

When word was passed that it was time to leave for the Memorial Day celebration, we paid attention. Mrs. Roosevelt could be counted upon to see that none of her guests trailed behind and that the event began on time. She supervised an efficient exodus to the ceremony, which took place at the Rose Garden, the grave site of President Roosevelt, on the estate of the Big House. Local residents were usually already seated by the time our large Val-Kill party arrived on the scene. Waiting also were local Boy Scouts and West Point cadets, who annually came to participate in the Memorial Day services, for which members of the Roosevelt Home Club were official hosts. Usually, Franklin or Jimmy would invite the speaker for the occasion, generally a person well-known in public life. A raised platform ringed in bunting faced the audience; on it were seated Mrs. Roosevelt and as many family members as were present, the speaker, the president of the Roosevelt Home Club, a United States Service ranger, and the director of the FDR Library. The unrelenting sun beat down upon us all as the band played, cadets marched, the speaker delivered his resounding message, wreaths were laid on the president's grave, and taps were sounded. It was very important to Mrs. Roosevelt that President Roosevelt be remembered on the occasion when those who had died on the battlefields of our wars were being memorialized. Added to her compassion for the significance of the holiday was her determination that her husband's memory be honored as one who had given his life for his country.

Before my second Memorial Day at Hyde Park, Mrs. Roosevelt wrote me on April 28, 1959:

Dearest Edna,

I am asking Buddy [my brother] and your father and mother and Mr. Silberman [my boss] if they would care to drive up for lunch at 12:00 noon on Memorial Day as Mr. Truman is going to give the address this year and I thought they might like to come. Of course it may not be of any interest to them so this is just to let you know about it and to tell you if they don't want to come they must not make an effort to do so, but I would love to have them.

I would be happy to have Buddy stay over Sunday and if you and David care to come I would love to have you. As you know, your room is always ready but I am not going to burden you because I know you both have so many things to do particularly with the excitement that comes towards the end of the school year in getting Grania into a job. You will want to be around here [New York City] as much as you can then, so I don't want to urge you to do anything you really don't feel would be pleasant.

Much love,

E. R.

Of course Grania is always invited too.

I recall that Mrs. Roosevelt particularly appreciated Senate Majority Leader Lyndon Johnson's appearance one Memorial Day. Exuberant extrovert that he was, he obviously relished having his picture taken with his arm around as many Boy Scouts as possible, in groups and singly (some with their mothers, as well); he also enthusiastically participated in a tree-planting ceremony on the property. Some uncharitable remarks were made about Mr. Johnson's eagerness to pose for cameras, but Mrs. Roosevelt heatedly defended him. He was her guest, after all.

The day that Adlai Stevenson came to speak, he was late to lunch. He was staying with his good friend Mary Lasker at her summer house in Amenia, about a half-hour drive away. By the time Governor Stevenson, Mrs. Lasker, and their party finally arrived, making a total of ninety for lunch, Mrs. Roosevelt was very tense, concerned that the gathering at the grave site would be kept waiting. She received the Stevenson party graciously, of course, but she didn't like the fact that they were late. The governor was no longer a needy candidate, and his tardiness seemed a slight. At the ceremony, he spoke well, as he always did, and Mrs. Roosevelt, fond of him, was grateful. When the ceremony concluded, we returned to Val-Kill for Mrs. Roosevelt's open-house tea for members of the Roosevelt Home Club and other Hyde Park residents. That evening, just as dinner ended for the few of us remaining overnight and Mrs. Roosevelt prepared to go upstairs to her bedroom, Marge, the cook, appeared and, with a triumphant gleam in her eye, gaily asked, "Well, Mrs. Roosevelt, how'd I do?" Mrs. Roosevelt laughed, told her she'd done splendidly, and kissed her good night. It had been a long and tiring day. As Marge turned to go, Mrs. Roosevelt reminded her cheerily, "Only seventeen for breakfast, Marge." That number is somehow forever etched in my mind.

One summer afternoon, Mrs. Roosevelt asked me if I would mind making a short stop with her on our way to visit her niece Ellie Roach* in Rhinebeck. A middle-aged member of an old-guard Hudson River family was having an engagement party, and she felt obliged to make an appearance. On arrival, we could see that the wide porch encircling the house was already filled with people. Some simply stared at Mrs. Roosevelt,

---

*After the death of her husband, George Roach, and a subsequent divorce, Ellie retook her father's name and is now known as Eleanor Roosevelt.

while others acknowledged her with curt nods. Those who spoke to her called her by her first name, a sure sign they had known her since youth. She kept a firm grip upon my wrist as we entered. I assured her that she wouldn't need to look after me and suggested she could release me. "Don't be foolish, dear," she said. "I want to leave in five minutes and don't want to waste time searching for you." She and I moved in lockstep until we left. Mrs. Roosevelt was estranged from this society of her past, and they from her.

Relationships: The Lively Brood

At weekend gatherings at Hyde Park, the famous Roosevelt faces were becoming familiar to me. As I've mentioned, we saw John and his family regularly in Hyde Park, and Franklin and Sue were frequent summer callers. We used to meet Jimmy when he visited his mother during the course of the year on solitary business trips to New York. Anna came to see her mother when she could. While they were family and were friends, one somehow sensed when in their company that the two lacked intimacy: There was perhaps too much *effort* being made to speak affectionately. I had the impression that they were almost too polite with each other. Mother and daughter tried to be close, yet Mrs. Roosevelt's correspondence with Anna over the years suggests that they never quite succeeded.* I remember the evening Mrs. Roosevelt told me that she would never have a secretary who might hinder people's direct access to her, adding there was a time during the war years when she had to go through Anna, then acting as her father's secretary, to reach the president. She said no more about it, but one knew it had hurt her. Nor did she forget Anna's role in facilitating FDR's later meetings with his old flame, Lucy Mercer Rutherford. Mrs. Roosevelt used to tell David, "I can forgive, but I can't forget," to which he always answered, "If you can't forget, you don't forgive."

---

*Bernard Asbell ed., *Mother and Daughter. The Letters of Eleanor and Anna Roosevelt* (New York: Coward, McCann & Geoghegan, 1982).

Mrs. Roosevelt felt an especial affinity with Anna's three children, however, and in the summertime she enjoyed watching John's son and daughters growing up next door to her in Stone Cottage. Elliott's children, especially Chandler, David, and Tony, were dear to her and she traveled to see them whenever she could. Then there were the grandchildren she hardly knew. In some cases, they were very young when Mrs. Roosevelt died. In other instances, certain ex-wives in the family did not encourage their children's contact with their grandmother — for example, Betsy Whitney. Sometimes Mrs. Roosevelt felt too estranged from certain ex-wives to have much hope for any real relationship with their offspring, as in the case of Jimmy's children with Romelle Schneider. I remember being surprised to learn that Mrs. Roosevelt did not consider the youngsters adopted by her sons James and Elliott as "Roosevelts." This resistance was due partly, I think, to her pride in the family bloodline, and partly because she was justifiably uncertain that her sons' marriages to those particular wives would last.

David told me more than once that he thought Elliott had been Mrs. Roosevelt's favorite. In 1945, when Elliott had gone home with his mother after FDR's funeral and had made plans to stay with her, she was grateful to him, loved the idea of having family again settling in Hyde Park, and entered into his plans for the place with uncritical enthusiasm. While all the Roosevelt offspring were rightly famous for their charm, Elliott was especially disarming. David told me that Elliott had been the most worrisome child. He was the next infant born after the first Franklin Junior died, and because he had been a sickly boy, his mother had been preoccupied by him. David wrote in his notes, "Mrs. Roosevelt loved all her children, but I have the suspicion that she loved Elliott most. . . . Certainly she was more vulnerable where he was concerned; she could be more hurt by him than by any of the others, I think. . . . She was overwrought when Elliott and his brother John (both living in Val-Kill at the same time) had terrible quarrels, especially those in her presence. Quick to blame herself whenever the family did not get along, friction among them gave her moods of sadness and tension, though she cried very infrequently." Perhaps she responded to him so caringly because Elliott had been named for her father and he reminded her of that beloved parent in his tender nature and broken promises. David had prepared me for meeting him by saying, "He is the sweetest of them all." As David was forgiving to a fault, I tended to be a bit skeptical of his susceptibility to Elliott. The tales I'd heard about the many times he had disappointed his mother caused me to feel somewhat restrained when I first met him, on the occasion when he brought his new (fifth) wife, Patricia, to our house. However, the more I saw of him, especially during the last period of his mother's illness, when he seemed so defenseless, the more I liked him. At his best, Elliott was a hard man to resist.

On the surface, the Roosevelts and David got on reasonably well, as, for example, do most family members who "inherit" one another. They were cordial to him and looked to him to solve some of their own medical problems, and occasionally a marital one, as well. Indeed, Elliott and John's wife, Anne, were both patients of David's. (I still remember Anne's kindness to my mother on her first visit to Hyde Park.) The family treated David's beautiful daughter, Grania, as one of them. Consequently, it took a while before I saw that they had very mixed feelings about David. They were relieved that he looked after their mother, but underneath, they harbored deep hostility toward him, which they disguised by charm and good manners. The competitive Roosevelts were jealous of the approval and attention that their mother lavished on David, especially in light of her often-critical attitude toward them. They were mindful of their mother's permissiveness toward him and the few others of her "adopted family." They might have accepted what they viewed as their mother's inability to be freer and more intimate with them had they not seen her show so effortlessly to her small, chosen circle, especially to David, the kind of tenderness denied to them.

Mrs. Roosevelt evaluated situations affecting her children quite matter-of-factly. When, for example, Franklin lost his election for New York State attorney general in 1954, her postscript in a letter to David read: "I've just written to F. Jr. I'm afraid it will be hard but losing, if you take it well does no harm." She would not have been so objective had David suffered some defeat. She did not want *him* to learn from disappointment.

This sensitive family had to feel the disparity. Vying with one another for the advantages their famous name produced, each brother jealously guarding what he had, how could they be expected to feel expansive and generous toward this "chosen son" so admired by their mother?

Mrs. Roosevelt was as critical of her children (with the possible exception of Anna) as she was uncritical of David. He had to prove nothing. He could do no wrong. She looked to him, not to them, for advice and recommendations. She never regarded David reprovingly, the way she did her sons at times. What should they think of an outsider on whom their mother doted and who was unhappy if he were not present? Having David, then me, as well as Joe and Trude Lash, in their midst on holidays and other family occasions throughout the years added, I am sure, to the general irritation of Anna, James, Elliott, Franklin, and John. They were indignant among themselves, but it is doubtful that they dared raise objections to David with their mother.

They had an enviable natural charm, were charismatic public speakers, and attracted attention wherever they went. Yet, despite all their advantages, the daughter and sons of Franklin and Eleanor Roosevelt, tall athletic figures bursting with energy and good looks, somehow never realized their full potential. The sons gave the impression that they felt entitled to a luxurious style of living. Good times called and they followed.

It was the brothers' lack of discipline, wavering principles, and faulty judgment that were such a trial to Mrs. Roosevelt. Family tensions were deeply distressing to her, and there were times when it made her nervous to have more than one of her grown children under her roof, when tempers were apt to fly. They knew how to arouse her guilt, always close to the surface. When their plans and/or marriages did not succeed, she had a tendency to blame herself. She felt that she had let them down in their childhood, when her own feelings of inadequacy, unhappiness, and ignorance of child rearing made her dependent upon governesses and her overbearing mother-in-law. She had never experienced a mother's love, and having missed it, she was not warmly demonstrative with her own youngsters. Anna told me that her mother had never played with them as children, saying that she did not know how. Their father had played with them. "Mother was forced into the position of disciplinarian," Anna commented dryly. "Mother did her duty."*

Now as adults, her children counted on her for political support, advice, and help in emergencies, both financial and marital. Mrs. Roosevelt was vulnerable to them and could be hurt as only they could hurt her. She felt responsible for them and tried to compensate for whatever lack of closeness they had experienced in childhood, although this dearth of affection seemed to loom larger to them with age. In fact, Mrs. Roosevelt loved her children and was proud of their achievements. Considerate of their friends, she stood by them resolutely, even when she disapproved of their ventures. David said that Mrs. Roosevelt had long outgrown being bothered by criticism of herself, by cartoons and jibes at her expense. She trained herself to ignore these things, he said, repeating her explanation: "If she stopped and worried every time anybody said or wrote something disagreeable about her, it would be a waste of time." But she reacted strongly to any criticism of, or threat to, her children. Their enemies were her enemies. David wrote:

> No child could count more on a mother than her children could count on her. . . . [Mrs. Roosevelt] has a reputation of not being a good mother when they were young. Her mother-in-law had such a big part in bringing up her children. She [ER] didn't pay enough attention . . . she went on speaking tours, traveled. . . . I hadn't seen her at that time, but when I knew her, she could not have been a more remarkable mother, loyal and standing by her children in an admirable way. She knew her children from all their sides, she knew all their short-comings and all their failings and what they did well and did not do well, where they could be trusted and where they couldn't be trusted. She knew them better than anybody. But nothing interfered with her loving them and standing by them.

*Conversations with Anna Roosevelt Halsted when she visited us during the period of her mother's last illness, October–November 1962.

She wrote David:

May 12 [1948]
... The children have often thought that I did not do the right things for them but when things go wrong they usually bring them [their problems] to me. I would feel I had really failed if they didn't. ...

They changed wives (and husbands), lifestyles, and ambitions, and pursued a variety of careers and professions. Elections and fortunes were won and lost, and, with the possible exception of Anna, they felt they didn't have to *do* anything to prove who they were. To them, politics was the family business and they yearned to be in high places. Although their petty quarrels and domestic problems irritated their mother, and their seeming lack of commitment disappointed her, Mrs. Roosevelt enjoyed the company of her sons and daughter, especially when they got along well with one another.

Still, regardless of the rancor her children harbored, wherever their mother was was home to them, and she was their tie to one another. They made the best of her determination to lead her own life—they had no choice—and their natural geniality often overrode their grievances.

With regard to David and me, nothing changed very much after Mrs. Roosevelt died. The family kept in touch with us, continued to consult David from time to time, and invited us to family weddings and other social occasions. Fundamentally, the children appreciated that David had been good to their mother—they knew he had truly cared about her and had not exploited his friendship with her—and they respected him in spite of themselves.

Nevertheless, in Mrs. Roosevelt's lifetime, there were two separate and distinct social circles in Hyde Park. One revolved around John and Anne's Stone Cottage; the other centered around Mrs. Roosevelt's Val-Kill house. While family occasions and important visitors brought John and Anne over to Mrs. Roosevelt's cottage—for propriety sake, Mrs. Roosevelt liked a son beside her to help represent the family when the Queen Mother and other notables came to call—it was clear that John and his mother preferred different sets of people. The John Roosevelts certainly did not care for their mother's parade of Democrats, "do-gooders" or intellectuals with social programs needing airing or funding, or both, whose cars came rattling across the Val-Kill bridge. The polarization between the two cottages stemmed only in small part from the fact that John, Anne, and their circle were Republicans* and the people close to Mrs. Roosevelt were Democrats. That John and Anne singled out their friends mainly for the gaiety they provided was not particularly tempting to those of us gathered in Val-Kill Cottage, and this was another reason the two camps had little in common. It was easy to ignore the sounds of late-night high hilarity and occasional boisterous quarrels that floated across to us in the soft summer air from John's house, and it goes without saying that nothing could have had less appeal for Mrs. Roosevelt than frivolity for its own sake. The two camps got along, albeit self-consciously. Differences could, however, be forgotten at the picnics and swimming parties together and meals shared; underlying tensions between the two houses could be suspended on those sunny summer afternoons. Still, the family's fundamental antipathy to their mother's small group of special friends remained. It was a point on which *all* of Mrs. Roosevelt's children were united and one they had to accept.

As a latecomer to this situation, I didn't realize the truly complicated relationships that existed between David and the Roosevelt siblings, and David, true to form, gave me no hint of them. Again, he saw no need to confuse my relationships with them by uncovering their resentments, and he himself preferred not to think about the subject. I wanted to like these people. Their unfailing friendliness to me made it easy to do so, and I did not look too deeply into the whys and wherefores of the pleasant

---

*One of the rare occasions on which Mrs. Roosevelt turned on her television set was the evening of the Republican National Convention, when John Roosevelt was scheduled to deliver a nominating speech for Richard Nixon for president. Mrs. Roosevelt watched the screen intently as John appeared at the podium, greeted by tumultuous applause. She was irked indeed. "Look at them. How they love to have a Roosevelt introduce a Republican candidate" was her scathing comment.

times I had with them. And looking back, I recall the times when they responded to David as a friend—a curious ambivalence. On a certain level, Mrs. Roosevelt's children were pleased to have their mother well looked after, and, interestingly, I believe they *were* grateful to him. David communicated with them easily about their mother's health, which proved to me that professionally he had their trust. Just how deeply their jealousy cut, I learned much later.

· 5 ·

SETTLING DOWN

Travel with Eleanor Roosevelt

GRANIA GRADUATED FROM THE Putney School in May 1958, then went to England for a round of debutante parties sponsored by her mother's family. She was to join us in September in Brussels to visit the World's Fair. Mrs. Roosevelt and David were delegates to the World Federation of United Nations Associations, meeting first in Brussels, followed by conferences in Moscow and Leningrad. I had very much looked forward to the trip, especially our visit to the Soviet Union, eager to see for myself something of the country about which I'd recently learned so much from Mrs. Roosevelt and David. The three of us decided to stay on there for several weeks after the WFUNA meetings had ended. I was excited about the prospect of seeing the fabulous collections of paintings housed in the Hermitage Museum as well as Russian icons and Byzantine mosaics, still largely off-limits to Westerners. In addition, I was formulating a project of my own. The Bolshoi and Moiseyev dance companies had been most enthusiastically received in New York and everywhere else they had toured in the United States, a fact pleasing to both countries. Though not a specialist in theater art, for some time I had admired the original drawings and watercolors I had seen in Paris and New York of ballet costumes by Léon Bakst, Nathalie Gontcharova, Michel Larionov, and other gifted Russian artists, as well as the original stage designs for ballet and opera. As our own theater art was so highly developed and appreciated, my plan was to have an exchange of this noncontroversial material, theirs and ours, which would tour both countries. The art would be of equal quality, an important factor for Soviet approval. At the height of the Cold War, even cultural contacts between the United States and the Soviet Union were fraught with suspicion. I began to make inquiries. On Mrs. Roosevelt's suggestion, I first contacted the people responsible for cultural affairs in the State Department in Washington. They could not have been more cooperative. Our artists were thrilled at the prospect. All that was needed was the green light from the Soviets. For that, I needed to be there.

Mrs. Roosevelt invited the Soviet cultural attaché to the United Nations to a Saturday lunch in her apartment. Not needing an English interpreter, the lady came alone. Mrs. Roosevelt, David, and I had already submitted separate lists of our special interests. I received the good news that in Moscow, appointments had been made for me to meet with the director of the Bakhrushin Museum, a splendid institution devoted to theater arts, as well as with government officials in a position to aid me with my project. Privately, Mrs. Roosevelt had told us that she suspected her critical speeches and newspaper columns about the Soviet Union in the past year had jeopardized her chances of being granted a visa to reenter the country. "I will not be welcome there again," she had said. But the attaché gave no indication that Mrs. Roosevelt's visa was a problem, and she entered willingly into a discussion of what we hoped to see and do.

That David would be our stumbling block to admission did not occur to us. Only later, when the Soviet official accepted David's offer to drive her back to her office and she saw that in our convertible she could speak freely—into the air, as it were—did she tell David confidentially in Russian, and in no uncertain terms, that a visa for him this second time would not be a simple matter. Despite the fact that it was a risk for the attaché to be candid with a foreigner, she took trouble to explain that during his previous visit to her country, he, gentle, civilized David, had been known as a madman. He had dismissed his Intourist guide when she insisted that a hospital he had asked to visit simply did not exist, when he knew perfectly well that it did. (It materialized, complete with staff and patients, on Mrs. Roosevelt's request.) In addition, each morning in Moscow, upon entering Intourist guide headquarters in the National Hotel, where they were staying, he had repeatedly asked for a telephone book. When solemnly told each time that he would be given one "later" and it never appeared, he became visibly annoyed. "One such answer should have sufficed," said the attaché reproachfully. There was other unacceptable behavior. He had photographed old and dilapidated housing sites, in addition to the new buildings pointed out to be photographed. In fact, he had taken pictures of crumbling ruins, which the Soviets were not proud to have foreigners record. They were intent upon showing off their modern improvements and they expected examples of the remains of the war's devastation and signs of their poverty to be politely ignored. They had other problems with David's attitude. He especially empathized with colleagues whose accomplishments in medicine and science were achieved in the face of the poorest, most difficult circumstances. He was sensitive to the limits imposed on their travel, sympathizing with their being cut off from the international medical community. Pity for them and anger against the system did not mix well in him.

On the other hand, there had been positive aspects to his 1957 visit, which were not lost on officials. David's honest appreciation of the scientific progress that they had made and the welcome medical lectures he'd given were remembered, too. In any case, David interpreted the cultural attaché's threat of withholding a visa to be a warning to control his frustration on a second trip and to stay within the established rules for foreigners. We were relieved when his visa came through. The summer drew to a close and our departure for a month in the Soviet Union was imminent. It was to be my first trip with Mrs. Roosevelt.

Our first stop was Brussels. Fortunately, Maureen was on hand to deal with the countless messages and letters awaiting Mrs. Roosevelt on our arrival at the Hotel Metropole. Grania was already there. Also waiting for Mrs. Roosevelt were her cousin Marie Morgan and her two children. Mrs. Roosevelt didn't touch the many superb dinners at different national restaurants, which we flocked to at the fair. She was impatient and ill-humored. Perversely, she had chosen this particular time, in a city famous for its excellent food, to diet. My guess is that she felt beset by too many people and demands, so she gave herself added reason for her bad mood by being chronically hungry. When David finally succeeded in coaxing her off her grim rations, she noticeably relaxed.*

It was gratifying to see the warm reception given Mrs. Roosevelt by people abroad. Everywhere, they smiled and waved and stopped to chat with her as we toured the fairgrounds, especially around the U.S. pavilion. She often joined David and me on visits to art exhibitions, enjoying the newness of this exposure. The week at the fair passed quickly, as did the World Federation of United Nations Associations meetings, to which Johnny Boettiger, a junior member of the organization, accompanied his grandmother. After a formal dinner party one evening at the United States ambassador's residence, excursions in and around Brussels, and a final banquet, Maureen flew to Ireland for a holiday with her family, Johnny went back to school, and Grania returned to England. Just David, Mrs. Roosevelt, and I boarded an Aeroflot jet for the Soviet Union.

Dusk was just beginning to fall when we landed in Moscow. A Russian limousine and driver—at our disposal throughout our stay—met us at the airport and took us to our hotel. Like other official cars, ours had little white ruffled curtains at its windows; these were drawn to obscure the

---

*David's notes explain more fully Mrs. Roosevelt's approach to dieting: "She was five-foot-ten and weighed between 150 and 180 pounds. We both tried to keep her weight down and her efforts came in spurts. When Mrs. Roosevelt went on a diet, it was the most rigid and disciplined affair imaginable. She would practically stop eating. . . . It was remarkable how she could be as active as she was . . . with the small amount she would eat on a diet and then she would lose some thirty pounds. Her old clothes didn't fit anymore and occasionally she would go to a French couturier and fit herself out with a becoming suit. But even when her clothes were simple, she paid attention to them. Mrs. Roosevelt was very neat. She was a woman, all right, with all womanly qualities. . . . She generally chose her clothes in the stores in which she started to buy—she was faithful to whoever gave her service. In my time, she would get her clothes at Arnold Constable [extinct Fifth Avenue department store]. . . . She went to the same hairdresser in New York where she started, in Washington Square, from the time she lived down there. The same was true with her florist."

occupants. To a New Yorker, the emptiness of the broad Moscow thoroughfares was almost eerie. There was simply no traffic to speak of, anywhere. We were staying at the National Hotel, where the WFUNA meetings were to be held. Situated on Red Square, with a view of the vast Kremlin beyond, it was extremely impressive and had doubtlessly been more so when Lenin stayed in the hotel in 1918, enjoying its amenities. But now, the remnants of its former grandeur were dismal. Signs of splendor from bygone days—frayed carpets on its intricately designed ironwork staircase, spacious but clanking old elevators, dim lights in majestic halls—were all sad to see.* Lenin had once lived in the suite we were given. It had a tremendous double-bedded room with bath, and a smaller second bedroom and bath, each room having a door opening onto an imposing sitting room, which the three of us shared. (Who could forget the painted pink cupids cavorting on the sitting room's ceiling?) The master bedroom was obviously meant for Mrs. Roosevelt, but she would not hear of occupying it. Over David's and my protests, she insisted that we two would not feel as lost in it as she would. Later, as we prepared to leave the Soviet Union, we learned that, out of respect for Mrs. Roosevelt, the government had had the bedroom furniture used by President Roosevelt during the Yalta Conference with Stalin and Churchill flown to the National Hotel in Moscow for her use. It was a truly grand gesture, and subtle, too, the information coming as it did at the end of our stay. The thought pleased Mrs. Roosevelt, though David and I cringed at the news, having used the furniture ourselves.

On most of our mornings in Moscow, we took our breakfast downstairs in the hotel's immense dining room, where a small frayed-edged American flag on a little metal stand was placed in the center of our table at every meal in honor of the wife of the Soviets' wartime ally. Food at the time, generally speaking, was simply awful. Caviar, inexpensive and abundant, and ice cream, which Russians love, were compensation.

---

*In recent years, the National Hotel has been restored. I understand that Maxim's, the famous Parisian restaurant, has opened in the hotel. What a contrast it must be to the shabby old dining room we knew, not to mention the tasteless old food.

Eager that I see the Lenin-Stalin Mausoleum in Red Square, the three of us set out early. Fronting the Kremlin wall, it was probably the prime sight-seeing monument in the whole of the Soviet Union. It was odd to be with Mrs. Roosevelt in a place where she was hardly recognized. Later, thanks to her special request, we were granted permission to visit Lenin's private apartment in the Kremlin, something that David did not want me to miss.*

They both accompanied me to my first meeting with the Soviet minister of culture, who was keen on an art exchange with the United States. That important step settled, I called on the director of the Bakhrushin Museum. He, too, was amenable to the plan. We made preliminary general selections and our conference went well. Every so often, and without dampening my enthusiasm, Mrs. Roosevelt suggested that I not pin my hopes too much on the realization of the project. She reminded me that I was dealing not with a museum but with a Communist bureaucracy. I paid attention to this, as I usually took heed of her advice. Her warnings were correct, for though plans for the art exchange actively continued on my return to New York—the news even made the front page of the *New York Times*—it finally turned out that the Soviets were too mistrustful about the fate of their treasures abroad to allow them to leave the country. The eventual failure of the project was a great disappointment all around. But at that time, my own work in Moscow accomplished for the time being, I was enjoying making the rounds with Mrs. Roosevelt and David.

We met with heads of Soviet ministries, agencies, and departments; we toured scientific institutions, many different kinds of schools—universities and specialized training institutions—physical therapy units,

---

*In her September 10, 1957, newspaper column "My Day," Mrs. Roosevelt referred to her visit to Lenin's apartment: "He [Lenin] wished to live as nearly as possible the way the workers lived and, to some extent, seems to have succeeded. One thing Lenin could always completely control was his food, and we were told that his meals always were frugal. . . . Despite this frugality, his study and an adjacent room where meetings of his government took place showed he had the reins of power with a concept of the potential strength of the great nation he was beginning to build, [and that he] was widely read and [was] a highly intelligent and cultural man."

clinics, hospitals, children's day-care centers, and orphanages. I experienced for myself how David and Mrs. Roosevelt made their educated appraisals following these visits, how they constantly shared with each other the facts and observations they had accumulated, sifting through their impressions in an attempt to get to the truth of a thing. They had their daily routine down to a science. They focused on a few particular subjects and studied them in as much depth as possible within a limited time period. We moved at a swift pace, following a prearranged schedule, not a moment wasted. Afternoons were filled with trips to other designated places, sightseeing, and so on. When we were alone, Mrs. Roosevelt and David exchanged views on what we had seen and been told, and on how services in a Communist country were or were not actually delivered to a huge and far-flung population. They usually came to similar conclusions, sometimes reached by different routes. It was fascinating to me to be introduced to subjects entirely new to me and to hear them being analyzed by such keen observers. I learned many things that might otherwise have gone unnoticed. Though they spoke together comfortably, as intimate friends do, I always felt included and enjoyed myself tremendously.

Our traveling as a threesome had gotten off to a good start, as I knew it would. We each felt it. There was no tension among us, no secrets, much goodwill. Never did Mrs. Roosevelt impose her own desires upon David or me. It was she who accommodated us whenever she could. We discussed everything openly, the three of us easily agreeing on things to do and when to do them. I am sure Mrs. Roosevelt remembered resenting her mother-in-law's intrusion into her own married life, and she went to all lengths to ensure David's and my privacy.

Although lunches and dinners often included others—members of the U.S. press corps, the few Western officials in the Soviet Union on special missions, the handful of American businessmen there—David, Mrs. Roosevelt, and I dined alone whenever we could, especially before a concert or ballet. After our hotel dinner—we were told there were no acceptable restaurants—we would be whisked off in the Russian limousine with the little curtains at the passenger windows to protect our identity—from whom, nobody knew. It was rare that we socialized with any Soviet citizen we had met in the course of our daily activities. Such contacts were not encouraged.

At the Brussels's World's Fair we had seen a performance of the Moiseyev Dance Company and afterward had attended a gala backstage reception. We again met this triumphant group at a party celebrating their return to Moscow, an affair held in the only private residence we visited during our stay there. One of the few remaining beautiful log houses, it was the home of *Time* magazine's Moscow correspondent and his attractive red-haired Soviet wife.

We lunched at Ambassador Llewellyn E. Thompson's residence. Both David and Mrs. Roosevelt found many of the comments about Communist life made by the dozen or so American embassy staff seated around the table to be provocative, as their own opinions differed from these. David entered into rather brisk discussions, while Mrs. Roosevelt said almost nothing, quietly eating her meal. As we drove off the grounds, I asked her why she had not responded to certain positions with which I knew she strongly disagreed. "Anything I said would have been reported back [to the U.S. State Department]," she answered quite simply.

One evening, we were to attend the Bolshoi Ballet's *Swan Lake*. David was coming down with a head cold, and, happy to have an excuse not to go, he decided to turn his illness to advantage. "Let's see what happens when an ordinary hotel guest in Moscow needs a doctor," he said, and called down to the desk clerk for a physician. Most internists in the Soviet Union were women, and David's female doctor soon arrived, carrying not only the usual medical bag but one containing medicines, as well. (It was not a bad idea that the doctor making house calls came complete with her own pharmacy, instead of just a prescription pad.) As she pulled up a chair to the bedside, Mrs. Roosevelt and I left for *Swan Lake*.

The magnificent theater was filled to capacity. We were without our Intourist guides. At the first intermission, we were invited to the office of the English-speaking director, who had had prepared a refreshment table for us with fruit, soft drinks, cakes, wine, and vodka. He explained that it was the custom of the Ministry of Culture to assign active roles in the management of cultural institutions to retired performing artists. "What was your specialty?" I asked him. When he told me he'd been an opera singer, I asked if he still sang, and he assured me that he did. We could not refuse a return visit to his office during the second intermission. Where there had previously been a dining table, there was now a grand piano, a seated accompanist, and our director, who was standing smiling, ready with a song. His voice was still strong. Mrs. Roosevelt and I finally had to hasten back to the swans and the real lake that magically rippled onstage, eliciting gasps of awe from the audience, including me.

We returned to our hotel to find David still in animated conversation with the Russian doctor, who was listening intently as he described what he had learned about the organization and state of medicine in the Soviet Union, a subject about which she knew very little. While this was going on, an amused Mrs. Roosevelt remained standing on the threshold of our bedroom. The scene of the two doctors, one of them a patient, in such earnest discourse in Russian struck her funny. Our return had signaled that it was time for the physician to leave. Glancing at the medication she had left for him on the night table, David commented, "Here, even the pills are gray."

David had succeeded in tracking down an uncle, the son of his maternal grandfather, with whom David and his brother, Vladimir, had lived for five years as children. The uncle was the only member of the family who had escaped being murdered by the Nazis. He and his wife had agreed to come to the National Hotel, but he made it clear we must not visit them. One day, they came to see us. It was a deeply emotional meeting. On his harrowing flight from the Germans, David's uncle had saved only one thing from home: family photographs. He carefully withdrew these from his pocket to show us. When asked how things were going with them, the aunt and uncle told us that now everything was "wonderful." They spoke self-consciously, as though they were being overheard. They would not or could not give us their telephone number. After Mrs. Roosevelt joined us for tea, David took photographs of them and then, setting the camera, asked Mrs. Roosevelt to photograph the four of us together.

On the day following the photograph session in our hotel room, David's uncle wanted to walk alone with him in the street, and only there did he feel free to ask David not to give them any pictures that included Mrs. Roosevelt. After this, they telephoned us several mornings, always with excuses for being unable to join us for any meal upstairs in our sitting room or in the hotel dining room. Nor would they accept an invitation to socialize with us in public. It seems that just having tea was the safe decision. In 1958, it was still a miracle that they braved seeing us at all. Everywhere in every way, one felt the oppression of the Communist regime.

After arriving in Leningrad,* we visited a children's hospital in an airy suburb. A large staff of doctors, nurses, and teachers showed us around their sprawling modern facility. That Mrs. Roosevelt was deeply moved by the plight of the children we saw in this hospital was clear by her intense concentration as she made the rounds of the various wards, bed by bed, and looked into the schoolroom and lockers. Her wise eyes everywhere, she was entirely focused, listening to all that was told to her, carefully asking penetrating questions. As we left, she quietly inquired if I had noticed the beautiful embroidery done by the children. When I replied that I had, she murmured, "What a pity they work on such poor fabric. It won't take many launderings." Mrs. Roosevelt didn't miss much.

Although my eyes had been opened to countless new experiences, I still could not wait to reach the Hermitage in Leningrad. The five-building addition to the Winter Palace begun by Elizabeth, daughter of Peter the Great, was the place where the 1917 Revolution began. Under Catherine the Great, the original building had been expanded into a magnificent eighteenth-century Russian baroque palace and now contained glorious masterpieces of European art, which Catherine had vigorously collected during her thirty-four-year reign, from 1762 to 1796. There were so few visitors to the Hermitage Museum in those days that the guards (only women were employed in this capacity) remembered

---

*Its original name, Saint Petersburg, was later restored.

David (or his well-cut English suit) from the year before, and they exchanged friendly greetings in Russian with him.

In Leningrad, we took many walks along the banks of the Neva River. One time, we were taken to a small island to see the log cabin in which Czar Peter the Great had lived while supervising the building of the great new city of Saint Petersburg. The humble word *cabin* betrayed its most palatial interior, awash in sable coverings, mysterious icons, and golden chalices, all a privilege to have seen. Our next stop was quite a contrast — the ancient fortress Peter and Paul. Used as a prison for revolutionaries under the czars, it was a forbidding prison museum when we were guided through it.

One night, I surrendered to fatigue. Finding the schedule grueling and needing time off, I skipped the formalities when the Soviet delegation arranged its sumptuous banquet for the departing WFUNA participants. David understood, of course. I went to bed and he and Mrs. Roosevelt went down to the hotel dining room together. About ten o'clock, I was awakened by the sound of a key in the lock of our bedroom door. In the darkness, I could see it slowly being pushed open and the outline of a tall, slightly stooped figure stealthily approaching the bed. Rising from my pillow, I called out with an authority I certainly did not feel, "Who is there?" "It is I, dear," replied Mrs. Roosevelt, to my great relief. "I thought you were ill and came up to find out how you are." She had not believed David's explanation that I was tired. As far as Mrs. Roosevelt was concerned, if I went to bed, I had to be sick. It was difficult for her to understand that a woman so much younger than herself did not have her physical stamina. She could generally count on her unusually strong constitution, not to mention her discipline, to keep her going.

But one morning, Mrs. Roosevelt came down to breakfast looking exhausted. She'd been ill during the night and had not slept. Of course she would not disturb David, her doctor, in the room next door. She didn't say a word when we met, so determined was she not to change (or miss) the plans for the day. David pulled her upstairs at once, declaring, "You look awful." He examined her and, giving her the necessary antibiotic from his pharmaceutical bag, prescribed a day of bedrest. Mrs.

Roosevelt would not hear of it, and when I went upstairs, I heard them quarrel. She thought that her staying behind would cause too many complications for the people who had arranged the schedule. When the car came to take us to the famous Pavlov Institute, Mrs. Roosevelt was there. I remember how attentively she listened to the translators as she watched demonstrations performed on small animals to retrain behavior, all the while looking gray-faced and weak. I felt squeamish in those surroundings, and when I soon indicated I was ready to leave, David gave excuses for shortening the visit. This time, Mrs. Roosevelt did not protest, even though this was her habit when she suspected David of changing pace or activities to accommodate her.

How ordinary people lived was always Mrs. Roosevelt's chief concern, and wherever she went, she focused on it. Having visited collective farms the year before, she had asked to see an urban family this time. It had been arranged that we have tea with a couple and their children who, after years of waiting, had recently been awarded a much coveted apartment in a newly erected apartment house. The tall concrete building was unadorned and ugly. We proceeded up the eight flights of stairs, as the elevator was not working. But it didn't matter to the family. To a couple with four children who had lived in a hovel with a dirt floor, an airy three-room apartment with its own kitchen and bathroom was pure luxury. In the dining-living room, there were daybeds for two of the children; a narrow folding bed against a wall in the small entrance hall was for the third child. The youngest shared the parents' bedroom. Our hosts seemed pleased to have been chosen by the authorities to have Mrs. Roosevelt as their guest. Proud of how they were living, they freely answered Mrs. Roosevelt's queries about their work, the children's school, the cost of food, how they managed. Side by side on a daybed, the three children who were present sat quietly throughout our visit. To Mrs. Roosevelt's question as to the whereabouts of the eldest child, a boy of twelve, the reply was translated, "He is at his after-school sports class." Later, David told her that the mother had really replied that the boy was at his Communist indoctrination class.

Today, it is hard to imagine the degree of poverty we saw in the Soviet

Union in 1958. Memories are still fresh of the shadowy figures standing
on long lines in the evening darkness to buy food after the day's work was
done; men in the general population with rags wrapped around their legs
to ward off the cold; a large department store with no goods to sell; a
sparkling new subway system with few stops. It takes courage to live only
for the future.

The one thing David and I had wanted to take back to the United
States was an authentic Russian icon. But by the time we prepared to
leave the Soviet Union, we had about given up on the idea. Several
inquiries had confirmed that it was impossible to buy a genuine icon
legally for export. Shortly after we reached home, Mrs. Roosevelt, remembering our disappointment, gave us a Russian icon that had been presented to her by the former U.S. ambassador to the Soviet Union, Joseph
E. Davies.

The members of the international press corps, especially Americans,
were sorry to see Mrs. Roosevelt go. Most had known her for years, although in different circumstances and places, and had a warm and
friendly relationship with her. The press conferences she gave were
marked by respect even when, in the end, she explained she could not
give them too much news because she would be using the material for
her own newspaper and magazine articles. Nevertheless, as she stood before them for the last time in Moscow prior to our departure, she answered many questions in detail, giving a final satisfactory interview. It
was clear that wherever Mrs. Roosevelt went, she represented the United
States, officially or not. To Americans in distant lands, she brought memories of home, even to those who disagreed with her politics. Her directness and natural simplicity were appreciated by everyone.

Mrs. Roosevelt had invited both our Intourist guides and their spouses
to join us for the ballet on the evening before our departure, but this was
not allowed. After we'd had final tea together in our sitting room and
they had left, Mrs. Roosevelt asked me if I would mind going over with
her the tips we should leave for the hotel staff. I was surprised. I thought
the subject of tipping would be second nature to her. But I guessed that,
like everyone else, even such a worldly traveler was pleased to have some-

one at hand with whom to talk over little things. With scissors from her sewing kit, Mrs. Roosevelt cut the few envelopes we had in half to double their number, and we slipped in the amounts we thought fair, labeling them for distribution. We did this together on other trips, too. I remember how I prized these unremarkable moments we shared.

As the rich brown farmland skirting the city of Prague came into closer focus from our plane window, we felt an enormous sense of relief to be out of the Soviet Union. The United States ambassador to Czechoslovakia had driven out to the airport in the early morning to have an informal private meeting with Mrs. Roosevelt and to give her certain unofficial messages to take back to Washington. "This is the place we can talk," he said, indicating the empty airport cafeteria. David and I left them alone for a while. Even after we rejoined them, the ambassador continued to speak, was reluctant to leave, and waited with us until our Paris flight was ready to depart. I thought he was a bit homesick.

At the Hotel Crillon in Paris, we again shared a suite. Mrs. Roosevelt and I left David to his telephoning and went to the hairdresser around the corner. He and I were going to meet later at the apartment of the widow of one of his oldest friends, Mme. Andrée Vienot, in rue Cognac-Jay. When our hairdressing had been completed, I set out for the Louvre and Mrs. Roosevelt went back to the hotel. When I returned, she was still in our sitting room, dealing with her accumulated mail. "Where are you having lunch?" I casually inquired, certain that her day's plans had been made. "No place," she snapped. I ignored her irritation. "I am on my way to Mme. Vienot, and from there we are going to a restaurant," I said. "Why don't you come with us?" "I was not invited," she replied. "But I am inviting you," I said. As she hesitated, I quickly added, "David and Mme. Vienot will have so much to talk over, I will be glad if you are there." By now, I had learned one or two things from David about dealing with Mrs. Roosevelt's sensibilities. She accepted, saying, "When you arrive, say that I'll be along in a half hour. It will give you time to get acquainted. I will not go upstairs, but will wait in the car." From past conversations with David, I understood that the two ladies did not care for each other. As I was preparing to leave, she came to the threshold of our room. Standing close, her hands on my shoulders, she looked down into my eyes. "I love you," she said. "I love you not only because of David. I love you for yourself." We embraced. She could have given me no higher compliment.

David was delighted when I arrived at Mme Vienot's with the news that Mrs. Roosevelt was joining us. He rushed to the balcony of the apartment every ten minutes or so to look down for her car so as not to keep her waiting. ("Why do you jump up and down so much?" Andrée complained.) It was hard for me to believe that Andrée Vienot's circumstances were modest, which she so often claimed, especially when I learned she had purchased both apartments on her floor of the building, although the duplex she occupied was quite spacious. "I like to choose my neighbor," she explained. She invited David and me to dinner in her apartment that evening. David was disappointed when I later told him I did not want to go. I did not like the overbearing Mme. Vienot, either. When I confided this to Mrs. Roosevelt, she said we should accept. "David rarely sees her. Her husband was his close friend. It is contact with his past. And," she advised me, "Mme. Vienot must get accustomed to seeing David as a 'couple' now." I always took Mrs. Roosevelt's advice.

Our visit in Paris was all too short. David and I were usually out seeing art exhibitions, lunching with friends, walking, shopping, buying pastries. It was a momentous time to be in Paris. De Gaulle's name was on the ballot for the presidency of the republic, and excitement about the coming election reverberated in the air. All over the city were huge signs with one dramatic word: OUI—for De Gaulle. Our hotel sitting room was steadily occupied by callers, government people as well as Mrs. Roosevelt's personal friends. One afternoon, we three briefly settled ourselves on those uncomfortable small metal chairs near the Jeu de Paume in the Tuileries, overlooking the Place de la Concorde. David paid the few francs for the use of the chairs, only to have the woman who collected the fee try to return the money after she recognized Mrs. Roosevelt. On the night before we left, we dined at the Relais de Porquerolles, the restaurant David had discovered ten years earlier and which Mrs. Roosevelt had since made famous by her patronage. Our plane landed in New York on an early October morning, and John Roosevelt and my parents were at the airport to greet us. Shortly after, Mrs. Roosevelt wrote me on stationery with the Hotel Crillon letterhead, enclosing a gift (a beaded evening bag).*

Edna dear,

A little remembrance from Paris. It has been a lovely time for me. It would be if we sat at home together a lovely time for me but we added interesting things!

The gloves being the only thing David wanted will be my remembrance to him.

To you both a world of thanks and deep and enduring love.

E. R.

Everyday Life

I returned to work at the gallery. Mrs. Roosevelt wrote her columns, coped with her wide range of social services, was active in Democratic party politics, traveled around the country giving paid and unpaid lectures for various organizations, raised money for the causes she championed, attended to the affairs of the Franklin D. Roosevelt Library in Hyde Park, dealt with her family, and gave innumerable dinner parties. Most of her evenings were programmed. Late at night, when no one interrupted her, from about eleven o'clock till the early-morning hours, Mrs. Roosevelt signed the mail she had dealt with in the morning and wrote personal letters. Especially when on the road, after returning at night to an impersonal hotel room, it was imperative for someone as lonely as she to

---

*It is sometimes difficult to fix the time and place of Eleanor Roosevelt's personal letters. She often used available hotel writing paper wherever she happened to be traveling, or stationery of former residences, and rarely did she add the year to the date of the letter. The content of a letter allows one to place it in time.

feel connected to people she loved. Long handwritten letters were her "visits home." She stopped when she was tired enough to sleep well. She was apt to succumb to forty winks in public occasionally, more from lack of sleep the night before than from boredom, as was rumored. She never fell asleep on the job, however.

Fees from lectures, her daily newspaper columns, regular articles for *McCall's* magazine, some broadcasting, and the sale of her books provided Mrs. Roosevelt with most of the income with which she supported her large and bountiful households and contributed to her lengthy list of charities. Indeed, she lived on earned income until the day she died. While she had private means, the Roosevelt fortune had not notably increased with the passing years. In addition to allowing her to live in the style she chose, earning her living made it possible for Mrs. Roosevelt to move about freely yet keep more or less intact her own inheritance to pass on to her children. Her lecture agent, Mr. Colston Leigh, kept her busy. The sight of her tall figure, stooped as she grew older, weighed down by the large black leather handbag she held firmly in one hand and her heavy briefcase gripped in the other, was familiar in railroad stations and air and bus terminals throughout the land. She was a strong woman, but there were times her step slowed with fatigue. Strongly focused on her goals, she had taught herself to disregard the inconveniences and discomforts of life on the road. She was a very effective fund-raiser for many organizations, the American Association for the United Nations, the Citizens' Committee for Children, and the NAACP, among the others. For Israel Bonds, which she so ardently supported, she solved the problem to her conscience of accepting fees for addressing their audiences by giving an unpaid talk for each paid one.

David used to tell Mrs. Roosevelt that he marveled at how much she could accomplish in a day without ever being *late*, to which she would reply that she could function as she did only because she strictly adhered to her schedule. Rejecting this approach for himself, David answered that if he were to follow a timetable closely, he would feel too pressured to enjoy his work. These exchanges usually ended with mutual sympathy, but nothing changed. David was grudging about integrating clock watching with seeing patients. Too-tight schedules crowded him, interfered with his freedom to concentrate on a patient for as long as he felt was necessary. Despite long working hours, which included teaching medical students and physical therapists, he loved evenings out, though we tried not to make them consecutive or late. He found them refreshing, and he happily donned black tie at a moment's notice. We had guests at home frequently; for me, the party began only when David arrived.

He telephoned his mother early every morning. This was shortly followed by Mrs. Roosevelt's call to him. He was the first person she called each day she was in town and whenever possible when she traveled. In the beginning, she had asked me whether I would mind it, suggesting that it had become something of a habit with her. She asked rather hesitantly, in an especially low voice, the way a hard-of-hearing person sometimes speaks when she is cautious and cannot judge the tone of her words. I did not mind, and she continued the practice. Her calls were always brief; each minute counted with her.

Lorena Hickok was visiting one winter afternoon when I stopped by Mrs. Roosevelt's apartment. I had had previous brief contacts with her in Hyde Park. All I knew about her at the time was that she was a friend of Mrs. Roosevelt. I later learned of the significant role "Hick" had played in Mrs. Roosevelt's struggle for an independent life, and what good friends they had been. Lorena Hickok was a respected female reporter in the days when that was a rare achievement. As a self-made professional woman, she had been a welcome adviser in Mrs. Roosevelt's search for an identity apart from that of wife of a governor and First Lady. Miss Hickok, without family, and hungry for affection and stability, provided the loyal friendship and guidance important to Mrs. Roosevelt in a period when she was trying to turn her life around. These two women, from such diverse backgrounds—one born into privilege, the other into cruel poverty—had found they could sustain each other in different ways. Other nontraditional workingwomen had played roles similar to that of Lorena Hickok in Mrs. Roosevelt's drive to develop her own resources, but Hick had been needier, more constantly attentive, and perhaps more possessive. The two friends had shared their loneliness, were vacation traveling companions and confidantes, and, in the style of the period in which they were close, wrote endearingly to each other when apart.

When Miss Hickok no longer worked for the Associated Press, Mrs. Roosevelt arranged other employment for her, took her in to stay at the White House for a time, and finally, when she became ill with diabetes and was partially blind, established her in a house of her own in Hyde Park, where she could be looked after when necessary. Always faithful, Mrs. Roosevelt took care of Hick for the rest of her (Mrs. Roosevelt's) life.*

In some quarters in recent years, especially in connection with Miss Hickok, Eleanor Roosevelt has come to be regarded as having been a lesbian. It is to keep the record straight that I say I believe this is a false assumption and that it is based on wishful thinking by those who claim it. Mrs. Roosevelt and my husband confided in each other. She was not a secretive person. Quite the contrary—she had an entirely open nature. Yet nowhere in David Gurewitsch's journals, diaries, notes, private medical chart of Mrs. Roosevelt, or in his intimate discussions with me— indeed, I had the opportunity to form my own perceptions of her in so many different circumstances—was there any indication that Eleanor Roosevelt was ever attracted to same-sex love.

Seeing Miss Hickok more frequently, I came to dislike her. I was not alone in this. Hick considered most of the people close to Mrs. Roosevelt intruders in her best friend's life, with the possible exception of Anna's daughter, Eleanor Seagraves, whom she made a concentrated effort to befriend. To the rest of us, Hick was impersonal, even condescending. Nevertheless, she wanted to impress us with what she considered her dominant position in Mrs. Roosevelt's circle and showed this in such ways as addressing Mrs. Roosevelt as "Darling." (Mrs. Roosevelt paid no attention.) Through a haze of cigarette smoke from her seat in the Val-Kill study, Hick would ask, "By the way, darling, do you have a hat I can borrow?" Mrs. Roosevelt would go upstairs to her bedroom and return

*Lorena Hickok outlived Eleanor Roosevelt.

with a hat. No, that would not do. Miss Hickok asked for another. Silently, Mrs. Roosevelt climbed the stairs again and came back with two hats in hand. Hick pondered her choice. This playlet was to demonstrate her power to send Mrs. Roosevelt on errands. Now old and frail, Miss Hickok firmly clung to the one person on whose loyalty she knew she could always depend. She was adept at exploiting Mrs. Roosevelt's sense of duty, and she knew that once Mrs. Roosevelt's friendship was given, it was never withdrawn. An older, wiser friend of Mrs. Roosevelt, Esther Everett Lape,* once said, "Eleanor felt that people did the best they could with the genes they inherited and the experiences life had given them, and she viewed the results with compassion."

On October 13, 1958, two days after her seventy-fourth birthday, Mrs. Roosevelt wrote:

David dearest,

I want to write and thank you for your birthday letter, it did make me happy on my birthday and I will keep it by me and read and reread it for it is hard for me to believe my presence is at all necessary to you or to any-one else and if just my being here does add a little to your happiness, I shall be happier.

You should not thank me however since it is you who make life interesting and worthwhile to me. I love to be with you and Edna and am so happy to see you happy and appreciated and loved, and using your great capacity for love to make Edna happy for she is a lovely person.

---

*Of Mrs. Roosevelt's dearest friends, David, and later I, knew Esther Everett Lape best. A social scientist and activist, she led the unsuccessful battle for United States participation in the World Court in the 1920s and 1930s. She had been sent by President Calvin Coolidge as his envoy to Europe in connection with the World Court. The independent Miss Lape had also influenced Mrs. Roosevelt in her early years, and they remained in steady lifelong contact with each other.

Thank you for saying you love me, you know I love you and admire you and trust you.

E. R.

Thanksgiving was approaching, as well as Grania's New York coming-out party in December, a social event that meant a good deal to Grania and her English mother. David had decided to follow Grania's London debut of the previous summer with a dance for her and the friends with whom she had grown up in New York; it was to be held at the private women's club of which Mrs. Roosevelt was a member. One morning, Mrs. Roosevelt and I went together to settle which rooms were to be reserved. As we were leaving, a woman standing at the downstairs reception desk delightedly greeted Mrs. Roosevelt, clearly ready for a good chat. Grasping my hand, Mrs. Roosevelt unsmilingly nodded in greeting, then, after hurriedly introducing us, led me to the door. The lady was Edna Gellhorn, mother of Martha, from whose clutches, in Mrs. Roosevelt's eyes, David had narrowly escaped. Mrs. Roosevelt didn't say a word as we walked to the street corner.

In addition to the majority of young people, guests at the dinner dance included several of Mrs. Roosevelt's and our friends, and those invited by Grania's mother. Governor Stevenson was going to be in town around this time, staying with Mary Lasker, and they, as well as Franklin and Sue Roosevelt, were among those invited.

I danced with Adlai Stevenson that evening. He was a good dancer. Enjoying ourselves, we were abruptly interrupted by the clap of a young man's hand on Mr. Stevenson's shoulder and I was transferred into the arms of a grinning youth. "Why did you do that?" I asked him, plainly disappointed. "Because when I go back to school," he jauntily replied, "I want to tell everyone that I cut in on Adlai Stevenson."

Every tenth of December, the United Nations celebrated the anniversary of the adoption of the Universal Declaration of Human Rights with a special concert in the General Assembly Hall. The celebration in 1958

Val-Kill in winter. I am standing below Mrs. Roosevelt's windowed sleeping porch on the second floor of the cottage.

Cotton balls affixed to windowpanes substitute for Christmas snowfall. Clockwise from far left: Eleanor Roach and her daughter, Lorena Hickok, Jonathan Lash, Margaret Cutter, Mrs. Roosevelt, Becky, the housemaid, Curtis Roosevelt, Anne and Joan Roosevelt, me, Eleanor Roach's son, and Joe Lash, standing.

Mrs. Roosevelt
and my brother,
Bertram
("Buddy")
Perkel, Christmas,
Val-Kill Cottage,
1958.

Mrs. Roosevelt
celebrating a
birthday.

Top: Eleanor Roosevelt and her friend Lorena Hickok, who lived nearby in Hyde Park, 1960.

Right: Mrs. Roosevelt picking flowers from her garden for her cottage guest rooms.

Top: David called this photograph "Four Generations of Anna Eleanor": Mrs. Roosevelt's daughter, Anna Halsted; Mrs. Roosevelt; Anna's daughter, Eleanor Seagraves, holding her little daughter, Anna (now Mrs. David Fierst).

Right: Mrs. Roosevelt celebrating Memorial Day near the grave site of President Roosevelt in the Rose Garden of the Hyde Park estate. Seated beside her is Franklin D. Roosevelt, Jr. Her son John is seen behind them.

Top: Mrs. Roosevelt reading Kipling's *Just So Stories* at her annual picnic for the Wiltwyck School of Boys.

Right: David's daughter, Grania, with Marcelle (Mrs. Henry Morgenthau, Jr.), Val-Kill Cottage.

Adlai Stevenson receiving some editing advice before his speech at a Memorial Day service in Hyde Park. Mrs. Roosevelt is wearing her usual flowered hat, reserved for summer ceremonial occasions. It was also worn at Fourth of July Hyde Park parades.

Nina Roosevelt presents her sister, Joan, to the Queen Mother and her lady-in-waiting, Val-Kill Cottage.

Top: Princess Beatrix, now queen of the Netherlands, being warmly received during a Hyde Park weekend visit.

Right: Our house on East Seventy-fourth Street.

Eleanor Roosevelt arrives at the 1960 Democratic National Convention in Los Angeles to support the candidacy of Governor Adlai E. Stevenson for president.

Portrait of David.

Top: A corner of Mrs. Roosevelt's bedroom at East Seventy-fourth Street.

Left: Mrs. Roosevelt receiving Senator Kennedy on the front steps of Val-Kill Cottage, August 10, 1960.

Top: Eleanor Roosevelt and candidate John Kennedy lunching at Val-Kill, August 10, 1960.

Left: Satisfied with their private luncheon meeting, Senator Kennedy and his hostess happily rejoin us.

Left: Mrs. Roosevelt and I with our friends Rolf and Kyra Gerard at Saint Moritz. Maureen Corr is at far right with a camera.

Bottom: Mrs. Roosevelt's first vacation. She's reading Arthur M. Schlesinger, Jr.'s book *The Coming of the New Deal.*

Maria Gurewitsch, five weeks old, Val-Kill Cottage, July 1961. Mrs. Roosevelt later signed this photograph: "To Maria Anna, from one of her most ardent admirers. Eleanor Roosevelt."

David at Maria's first birthday party.

Front view of the Roosevelt house on Campobello Island.

Maria exploring Campobello Island, August 1962, the summer before Mrs. Roosevelt died.

Mrs. Roosevelt and I
on the boat from
Campobello to Saint
Andrews Island. She
is carrying a book
written by her friend
Fannie Hurst.

Maureen Corr
and I on
Campobello.

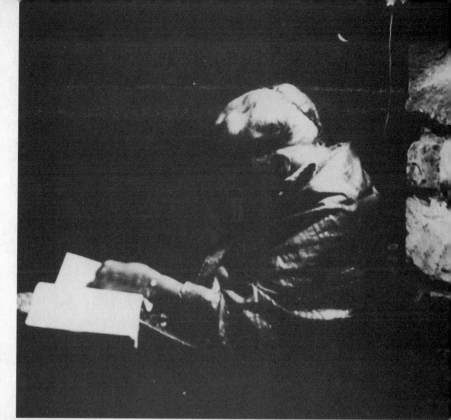

Mrs. Roosevelt reading on the porch of her Hyde Park cottage. This is the last photograph taken of her.

The Roosevelt sons walking in their mother's funeral procession. Left to right: John, Franklin, Dr. James Halsted (Anna's husband), James, and Elliott (barely visible).

Top: President and Mrs. John F. Kennedy arriving at St. James's Church, Hyde Park, to attend the funeral service for Eleanor Roosevelt.

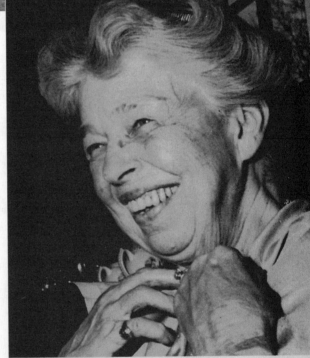

Left: This photograph, which David took at a Thanksgiving dinner, was selected by the U.S. Postal Service for the stamp to honor the one-hundredth anniversary of the birth of Anna Eleanor Roosevelt, October 11, 1984.

Eleanor Roosevelt

USA 20

DE PARK, NY
OCT 11 1984
12538

FIRST DAY OF ISSUE

was particularly noteworthy, as it marked the tenth anniversary of that Paris morning when, at three o'clock, the vote to adopt was unanimous, due in large measure to the commitment and diplomatic skill of Eleanor Roosevelt. David, Mrs. Roosevelt, and I usually went to this event together. That night, David was late for dinner, she was nervous, and the three of us rushed through the meal. "Eat! Don't talk!" Mrs. Roosevelt bid him. Breathlessly, we arrived in the United Nations Assembly Hall, which was already filled to capacity, and quickly walked in single file through a side aisle to our seats, Mrs. Roosevelt in the lead. The audience rose to its feet, applauding. She turned to us, face flushed as she rushed ahead, and over her shoulder announced in an angry stage whisper to David, "I *told* you we were late. The conductor is already at the podium." I looked at the orchestra. The podium was empty. It was Mrs. Roosevelt whom the audience had greeted with such thunderous acclaim.

That year, the renowned cellist Pablo Casals came to play at the United Nations to honor international human rights. It was his first appearance in the United States after having left his native Spain years before. For a frail man in his eighties, the trip from Puerto Rico, where he had settled, to New York was long and tiring. His performance would be a great musical event, attended by every important musician, the diplomatic community in New York, and those who could manage to get a seat in the United Nations Assembly Hall that evening. We in the audience held our collective breath as the aged Mr. Casals was slowly helped onstage. When he began to play, he became transformed, and his brilliant interpretation of Bach more than fulfilled expectations. After the concert, we accompanied Mrs. Roosevelt, whom Mr. Casals had expressly asked to meet, to the apartment of his business manager for a late supper. The party had deliberately been kept small. We learned that immediately after the concert, Mr. Casals had been whisked away from the UN and was now napping in the bedroom of the apartment. A half hour or so later, he entered the living room rosy and eager. Looking tenderly up into Mrs. Roosevelt's eyes as she leaned down to hear him, Mr. Casals greeted her with reverence, delicately kissing her hand and telling her in heavily accented English of his admiration for her.

Around this time, a friend of mine telephoned me at the gallery to ask if I could make an appointment for his friend, Supreme Court Justice William O. Douglas, to see Mrs. Roosevelt. Will wonders never cease? I thought when I arranged the appointment. David and I were present at the meeting. Justice Douglas was thinking of running for president and he wanted Mrs. Roosevelt's opinion of his chances. She gave him no encouragement. After he'd gone and David asked her reason for her cool response, she replied simply, "I do not think he would make a good president." Sometime after our return from the Soviet Union, I met Mr. Douglas again at a reception at the Soviet embassy in Washington. I had gone alone to sign the guest book for the three of us. I made my way up to the reception room, where endless trays of champagne and caviar were being passed, to find not one familiar face among the Washingtonians. Just as I decided that this would be a short spectator event for me, Justice Douglas approached. I was no longer solitary. The good judge remained by my side, which meant that every young Washington lawyer present came to say hello, others to shake his hand and stand with us. He was a popular man. I refused his repeated kind offer to drive me back to the airport and soon left for home. To this day, I regret that I never had the chance of casting my ballot for William O. Douglas.

1958 Draws to a Close

Mrs. Roosevelt's Christmases were major productions. Again aglow and filled with people, Val-Kill Cottage was beautifully decorated, right down to the white cottonball snowflakes Marge pasted to windowpanes. A fire crackled on the hearth. The tree was heavy with ornaments. A few of the hundreds of cards Mrs. Roosevelt received were on the mantels, among them those from the British royal family.

Tables for grown-ups and children overflowed with gifts at each place. John and Franklin carved the roasts, as usual. Plates were filled with traditional Christmas dinner and vigorously passed. Grandson Curtis served the wine. As on all other such occasions, Mrs. Roosevelt spent the predinner cocktail hour working, while we all chattered around her, the accelerating hubbub of our voices in the room not seeming to bother her at all. The same system prevailed at Christmas as at all other large dinners. From her seat at the head of the table, she concentrated on filling plates, aware of everyone's preferences. It was only when the doors of the living room were thrown open when the meal was done that she became animated. Mrs. Roosevelt did not put her gifts for us under the tree in the far corner because there were too many of them. Instead, each of us was allocated a chair on which the individual's selection was piled. Guests added their own presents to the heaps on Christmas morning. Large empty containers were set up in the room for discarded wrappings. During the gift-opening procedure, Mrs. Roosevelt circulated, watching our faces as we undid parcels. What an assortment she had provided. I spent a few Christmases in Hyde Park, and we received numerous gifts, including Siamese silk scarves, Japanese hair ornaments, brass ashtrays from India, silk underwear, Brooks Brothers shirts, English wool socks, hors d'oeuvre forks, fruit plates, ceramic platters made by Hyde Park craftsmen, books, records, Maine maple syrup, finger bowls, cuff links, and sweaters from England and from the New York Exchange for Woman's Work. As she passed among us, she watched our reactions. Were we really pleased with her choices or just being polite? Were the sizes and the colors right? I remembered the time in the summer that Mrs. Roosevelt, David, and I went to visit the new apartment of a friend. She and I walked out onto his balcony to see the view. The city was stifling, as humid July evenings so often are. As she looked around the small empty terrace, mopping her brow with a handkerchief rolled into a damp ball, she said, "I know, I shall give him an outdoor chair for Christmas."

After our gifts had been sorted and packages bundled for taking home, Mrs. Roosevelt turned dutifully to her own collection. The long window seat of the living room, near the now-deserted outdoor porch, was reserved for the mountain of Mrs. Roosevelt's gifts. Material things did not matter to her. She cared only about their donors. She liked best practical items, presents of food—cheeses, jams, cakes, boxes of candy—delicacies she could offer to her stream of visitors in Hyde Park and New York. She also appreciated a large new handbag now and then. One Christmas, David gave her a set of antique ivory-handled comb and brushes for her dressing table and handsome frames for the many photographs she liked to have around her. She kept the garnet roses we sent her by her bed; she liked the cases of champagne for her parties. It took quite awhile for her stack of packages to diminish. Some guests went upstairs to read or nap as twilight fell; most had gone home. As was her custom, Mrs. Roosevelt settled down to read aloud favorite passages from her worn copy of Dickens's *A Christmas Carol* to those of us remaining in the room.

· 6 ·

UNDER THE SAME ROOF

Moving In

IT WAS MY IDEA that we buy a house together. I knew instinctively, as well as from experience, that Mrs. Roosevelt would not intrude upon David's and my privacy. Before we had left for the Soviet Union some months earlier, Mrs. Roosevelt had mentioned that she'd been notified of a rent increase that would take effect upon expiration of the lease on her Sixty-second Street apartment. She was planning to look for a larger one, since she needed more space. At about the same time, David needed to move his private office. "Do you think Mrs. Roosevelt might be interested in buying a house together with us?" I asked him. "We could arrange to have your office there and Mrs. Roosevelt and we could divide the house so that we could each have a comfortable apartment. It would give her the additional room she requires." David mentioned that years earlier, in his bachelor days, she herself had proposed this to him, but he had not agreed to it. But now, Mrs. Roosevelt was happy to be our partner. She first discussed the matter with her children for their approval, and I imagine they could not refuse her wishes. (Franklin, in fact, liked the idea.) She might have reminded them that, at seventy-five, living in the same house as her physician would be a comfort to her as well as a relief to them. I was soon given the task of finding a house that would accommodate our various needs. When her apartment lease expired and the house had not yet been found, Mrs. Roosevelt moved back temporarily to the Park Sheraton Hotel.

Accompanied by a real estate broker, I began looking at town houses in the part of Manhattan where we wanted to live. There were two houses on East Seventy-fourth Street that I found interesting. Mrs. Roosevelt had seen one of them, but before making any final decision, I naturally wanted her to see the one she had not yet visited. The owner assured me she would be delighted to have me bring a friend for a second viewing. Early the following morning, she cheerfully swung open the door, but her smile froze and her eyes narrowed when she saw that my companion was Eleanor Roosevelt. She waved us inside without a word and rudely sat down at her desk, turning her back and ignoring us completely. Roosevelt-haters die hard. I was ready to leave at once, but Mrs. Roosevelt was not a bit perturbed and calmly proceeded to inspect the house with me, calling out a polite "Thank you" to the still-stiff back of the owner as we left. Seeing that I was upset, Mrs. Roosevelt suggested we stop to have a cup of coffee at the corner drugstore. (This was certainly not one of her customs.) We sat at the counter and talked things over. It didn't take us long to agree on the other house on Seventy-fourth Street.

A five-story limestone-fronted town house, it was built in 1898 in a neo-Renaissance style, with five steps leading up to a central entrance door framed by Greek-style columns. Once the home of a prosperous middle-class family, it was converted in the mid-1950s by its architect-owner to a multiple dwelling with four floor-through apartments and a doctor's office on the ground floor. A good modern elevator had been installed next to the interior stairway. The roof of the four-story brick extension at the back of the building formed a floor for the terrace of the fifth-floor apartment.

We divided the house as follows: Mrs. Roosevelt was to occupy the larger parlor floor, and the third-floor apartment; David and I were to have the fourth- and fifth-floor apartments. The first-floor office did not work out for David after all, for he decided that the stairs leading to its separate entrance, even if capped by a ramp, would present too many difficulties for his more physically handicapped patients. He took offices in a nearby medical building. I was glad of this. David's inability to say no was well known to his patients, and with his office in the house, I could imagine streams of postmidnight callers in distress. Our doctor tenants, therefore, remained.

Mrs. Roosevelt and we were co-owners. Our agreement included the clause that in the event of the death of one partner, the remaining one had first option to buy the other's half.* President Roosevelt's old law firm, Hooker, Alley and Duncan, represented us in the purchase of the building and established the partnership of Roosevelt and Gurewitsch. I was house manager, but fortunately, the administration took little time from my work at the gallery, four short blocks away.** Running expenses were met by rent paid by the doctor tenants and monthly maintenance payments by Mrs. Roosevelt and ourselves, supplemented when needed. The three of us excitedly looked forward to our new home, together yet separate, and to the prospect of being neighbors.

Meanwhile, still in her close quarters at the Park Sheraton Hotel, Mrs. Roosevelt gave us a party to celebrate our first wedding anniversary. She sent me a gift, accompanied by a note:

VAL-KILL COTTAGE
February 23d, 1959
Edna dearest,

May you use these [dessert plates] often and enjoy them. My love goes to you on this doubly happy occasion. You are very dear to me, and I love you even more because you make David so happy and have given Grania so much that she does not yet realize is deeply important and valuable.

Bless you for being you and may every year bring you and David increasing happiness.

Devotedly,
E. R.

---

*When she died, we purchased Mrs. Roosevelt's half of the building.
**E. and A. Silberman Galleries, 1014 Madison Avenue, New York.

Our half of the house was available first, allowing us to move into it quickly while the space below was being renovated. Mrs. Roosevelt impatiently remained in her hotel suite on West Fifty-sixth Street while one of her floors, consisting of living and dining rooms, kitchen, and housekeeper's bedroom, was remodeled.

The director of a charitable foundation was once heard to say, "Eleanor Roosevelt could accomplish more in a day with one secretary and a box of sharpened pencils than an entire office staff." Mrs. Roosevelt made her plans for the apartment and moved into the one floor she had at her disposal without altering her schedule or sacrificing any of her obligations. In the early morning of the appointed day, together with burly moving men and furnishings taken from storage, she arrived promptly at Seventy-fourth Street. Her flushed face reflected her excitement. It was almost as though it were her first apartment. In a certain sense, it was, for she told me this was the first time she had ever arranged an entire living space for herself exactly as she wanted it.

Every preplanned detail was efficiently executed on moving day. Two Hyde Park carpenters arrived to check the cabinets, closets, and bookcases they had previously made and installed, and to hang pictures and photographs. The watercolors of Venice bought on her honeymoon were among the first pictures to go up on a living room wall. In the modern new kitchen, the housekeeper put away quantities of dishes, glassware, vases, trays—the stuff of large households. A wall of dining room closets with rows of newly constructed shelves took the overflow. Maureen arranged the office and filled in elsewhere as needed. Mrs. Roosevelt's actor friend Charles Pursell, who often worked on special projects for her between theater roles, indexed books as he unpacked and shelved them, so that by nightfall the library was cataloged and in place. Mrs. Roosevelt, wearing a stylish velvet hat by Sally Victor, a well-known milliner of the day, supervised everything, directing the moving men as to the placement of each chair, table, and lamp. My offers of help had been refused when I went downstairs early that morning. But I persevered. "I can send down some lunch, sandwiches and coffee." I should have known better. It was a conditioned reflex of Mrs. Roosevelt to arrange to feed people working for her. Ample provisions had been ordered from the hotel before she'd left that morning. When I stopped in again after work, the crew had gone. Every carpet had been laid and every curtain hung; even the plants had been watered. Mrs. Roosevelt's elegant hat, still on her head, was the only visible sign that the day had been unusual for her. She'd forgotten to take it off. Later that same week, she gave a cocktail party for sixty people in her new apartment to celebrate Joe Lash's birthday.

Like all her dwellings, her new home reflected her natural simplicity and style. There was nothing in it for show, nothing forbidding; everything was inviting. Each picture, photograph, and object either meant something special to her or was of practical use. The large high-ceilinged living room looked like the room of a statesman. A magnificent Persian rug covered the hardwood floor. Her many-paneled Japanese screen now hung on the long wall above dark red couches that ran practically the entire length of the room. Together with deep easy chairs on either side of the fireplace opposite, and those by the three bay windows, the line of couches provided abundant seating for Mrs. Roosevelt's large parties. Always practical, she noted that one of them could be converted for use as a guest bed if needed in an emergency. The glow of old-fashioned lamps, askew as before (bumped by the usual room traffic), added coziness to the room. There were floor-to-ceiling bookcases and mementos and photographs on the mantel and on assorted tables, affirming a rich personal history. In the far corner of the living room was the cumbersome cabinet that housed the oversized television set of the day. I saw it in use only twice: when Mrs. Roosevelt and her guests gathered after dinner to watch the first of the Nixon-Kennedy debates in 1960, and on election night of that same year. Set out on living room tables were boxes of chocolates and other good things, always available to those who stopped by.

In addition to two small round tables in each corner, capable of seating a total of eight people, the dining room had a central rectangular table. When extended, this seated twelve. Additional mealtime guests sometimes spilled over into the living room, where a table or two could be set for them. Anna Polenz, who had been David and Nemone's housekeeper when they had first settled in New York, often came to help Mrs.

Roosevelt's New York City cook. By themselves, these two efficient women dealt with the countless luncheon and dinner parties for guests from everywhere. When she was in town, Mrs. Roosevelt wrote out the daily menus, but otherwise she steered clear of all culinary matters.

Against the east wall of the dining room was a couch, which for the time being was transformed nightly into a bed. We tried to persuade the occupant of Mrs. Roosevelt's other apartment to move out earlier than the near expiration date of his lease. Despite financial incentives and David's entreaties to accommodate a woman in her seventies, he balked, saying, "I love living in the same house with Mrs. Roosevelt." Until she could take possession of the second floor sometime later, she lived only on the third, which she did without complaint—indeed, almost triumphantly, I thought. The arrangement was inconvenient but too unimportant to her to fuss about. Beyond the dining room were the kitchen and small temporary office.

We were all relieved when she could finally move into her second-floor apartment. There, she had a splendid bedroom; spacious and sun-filled, it was crammed with all the things she was accustomed to having around her. The dressing table beside the double bed was closest to the built-in closets. A night table on the opposite side, heavy with manuscripts and books waiting to be read, had leftover space only for David's photograph. This, Mrs. Roosevelt had placed in a polished brass frame with her initials, A. E. R., incised in its top. Beside the bedroom fireplace was a clear blue silk damask settee with a needlepoint footstool before it and a chair opposite. Her desk was placed, like the one in her Val-Kill Cottage bedroom, near the blue-curtained windows. A gateleg table with a small floral-patterned club chair stood at the south end of the room in the center of an arc formed by three curved eleven-foot-high windows and a circular balcony that faced Seventy-fourth Street. There, Mrs. Roosevelt had her breakfast as she scanned the morning paper before her busy day began. In spring and summer, a leafy sycamore tree in front of our house masked the large apartment building across the street. A narrow corridor led from this room to another well-proportioned though smaller one, which became her office. Two desks were in its center. (Almost every day, a secretary, Gabrielle Gutkind, came to pick up mail that had been separated for standard replies. (When Maureen traveled with Mrs. Roosevelt, Gabriel remained in the office and forwarded correspondence.) An often-used guest room completed the apartment. Fresh flowers filled the rooms. Promptly at 9:00 A.M., still reading the paper at her breakfast table, Mrs. Roosevelt would call out to Maureen Corr, who'd just arrived. "In a minute, dear," she'd say.* Entering the office, she dictated her daily newspaper column to Maureen, who typed it out directly on the typewriter.

One evening when David and I went downstairs for dinner, Mrs. Roosevelt pointed out a new light fixture she had had installed on the ceiling of the living room. David gave his standard response when he saw something he didn't like. "I guess I'll get used to it," he conceded. "You don't have to like it," Mrs. Roosevelt snapped. "I like it." That was all that was said. But the fixture was soon quietly removed to the ceiling in her bedroom.

If I did not understand the private loneliness against which Mrs. Roosevelt struggled, I would find it hard to reconcile the description of the shy young woman full of self-doubt one reads about with the strong, wise woman I knew. By the time David came into her life, and certainly by the time I did, she was clearly aware of her capacity to assume burdens and to follow her commitments through to the end. Everyone felt this, and she attracted the world to her door. Our house bustled with the comings and goings of the great, the near-great, and everyone else. This was utterly apparent from the doorbell and telephone ringing, the food, flower, telegram, mailbag, and parcel deliveries, and the greetings and farewells of Mrs. Roosevelt's children and friends, politicians — local, national, and international — an assortment of diplomats, philanthropists, lawyers, educators, actors, folksingers, writers, trade unionists, classes of school children, and anyone else seeking advice, counsel, and support. Mrs. Roosevelt was comfortable in a home constantly humming with activity.

---

*Author's interview with Maureen Corr, October 1992.

Shortly after we all moved in, she produced a mezuzah, a small object, a little vessel—it can be made of silver, wood, ceramic, anything simple— containing a parchment on which there is a prayer from the Talmud. Observant Jews often attach this small object to their front doorpost. Someone had sent it to her, she said, and if we agreed, she thought she would like to have it on our house. To fix it to the door required a short ceremony. A traditional prayer was to be made just before the mezuzah was nailed to the door; I asked my boss, Abris Silberman, to do the honors. David and I used the occasion of a dinner party we were giving to have the mezuzah attached. In addition to Mrs. Roosevelt, our dinner guests on this ceremonial evening included Nachman Karni, a colonel in the Israeli army, who was then the military attaché of the Israeli delegation to the United Nations. Immediately after dinner, I asked Mrs. Roosevelt for the mezuzah. She said she had already given it to me, but I didn't have it, and neither did she. Colonel Karni rose to the occasion. Following his instructions, we gathered down at the front door, having taken the hammer, nails, and prayer with us. He left us there, then reappeared in ten minutes with a mezuzah, which was proudly fixed to our door. Nachman then confessed he had taken the mezuzah from the door of the Israeli consulate, which was only four blocks away and closed for the night. He would replace it with another the next morning. The blessing stayed on our front door for two years, until someone stole it.

First Real Vacation

The September following Mrs. Roosevelt's move into Seventy-fourth Street, we took a short holiday. The three of us went to Puerto Rico for nine days and stayed at the newly opened Rockefeller resort, the Dorado Beach Hotel. It was her first real vacation, Mrs. Roosevelt confided, the first time she would not be responsible for driving, camping, meeting trains or studying road maps, organizing supplies, or feeding people; it would be the first time she wouldn't have to *do* anything. She was seventy-six. But at the last minute, she almost changed her mind. Maureen telephoned to warn me that Mrs. Roosevelt was going to cancel her visit to Puerto Rico, her excuse being that she had too much to do. "Her real reason is that she thinks she will be intruding on David and you if she comes." After a moment's hesitation, Maureen added, "She is very tired, Edna."

It was just because she was badly in need of a rest that David and I had urged her to join us. That evening, I saw Mrs. Roosevelt. Before she could speak, I told her what a comfort it was to me that she was coming along. I reminded her that David was not good at doing nothing and that she could help entertain him if he became restless. No other coaxing was necessary.

Actually, David took to the lazy days quite easily, happy to swim, try the new golf course, and read in a hammock. It was Mrs. Roosevelt who couldn't resist taking trips around the island. During the Depression, President Roosevelt had sent bright young men to Puerto Rico to start up local industries that would provide jobs for the local population and products for export. The economy of the island was still poor, but conditions had improved since Mrs. Roosevelt had been there years before. Adrian Dornbush, a former New Dealer and now permanent resident of San Juan, had gotten in touch with her, and she accepted his invitation to show her around. When David told Adrian that we might like to buy some property there, Mrs. Roosevelt recalled, "Franklin was also interested in different kinds of business investments. He took the advice Henry Morgenthau gave him occasionally, but he never succeeded in any of his ventures. Franklin didn't understand money."

We spent our days mostly reading and swimming. Mrs. Roosevelt had brought with her Arthur M. Schlesinger, Jr.'s thick volume *The Coming of the New Deal.** "I've wanted to read this for a long time," she said, "and now at last I can." The array of detailed information it contained about Father Coughlin's group (Native Union for Social Justice) as well

---

*Arthur M. Schlesinger, Jr., *The Coming of the New Deal* (Boston: Houghton Mifflin, 1959).

as other extreme right-wing organizations in pre–World War II America disturbed her. "If I knew then how effective some of our homegrown fascist movements were, I would never have let Franklin talk me out of worrying about them." When I sat beside her to read, she would stamp her foot on the grass to scatter away the little tropical lizards if they came close to me. I was grateful for such attention—and amused by the fact that, secretly, she was just as wary of them as I.

While in Puerto Rico, Mrs. Roosevelt and I would have a frozen daiquiri together before dinner. With no pressing schedule, she had time to take more trouble with her appearance. When David complimented her on the pink chiffon dress she wore one evening and asked if it was new, she replied dryly that he had seen it for years. Walking to the hacienda where we generally lunched, David took a shortcut by balancing himself precariously, one foot before the other, on a wobbly wooden plank laid across a little rushing stream. Noting this, Mrs. Roosevelt commented, "Remember, Edna, the nicest men in the world always keep something of the boy in them." She paused, adding, "Franklin was like that."

Heady Days

Our evenings together were often rushed, owing to David's unavoidably late office hours. Typically, we three would hurriedly gulp our dinner in Mrs. Roosevelt's apartment downstairs, then dash out, David in the lead, to hail a taxi. Anxiety was high and breath was short as we reached the theater or concert hall in the nick of time. On such evenings, I would generally have arrived in her living room before David got home. Mrs. Roosevelt would fix us both an aperitif and we would settle down to talk and wait. One night, I said to her, "Mrs. Roosevelt, do we always have to rush out somewhere after dinner? Couldn't we just stay at home once in a while?" She was handing me my drink, her face close to mine, her expression serious. "Do you mean, dear, that you think you would not be bored?" I was stunned by her reply, the reason for her having gotten tickets to various entertainments on our evenings together becoming sadly clear.

I stammered as I facetiously replied, "Let's try it and see." To my added embarrassment, she accepted this answer as reasonable. From then on, unless there was something special, Mrs. Roosevelt, David, and I really wanted to see, hear, or do, or social obligations one of us felt we had to meet as a couple or a threesome, we would stay at home after dinner, either upstairs in our apartment or down in hers. For me, it was then that the really wonderful evenings began.

One night while we were waiting for David in her apartment, Mrs. Roosevelt told me that there were a number of events to which she would like to invite us. She had to plan well in advance, she explained, but she also knew that David did not like to be pinned down to social appointments far ahead. "He feels 'claustrophobic,' " she added. I replied, "Every morning before he leaves, we stand for a few moments at the elevator. David asks me, 'What do we do tonight?' and I tell him. If you give me the dates you have in mind, Mrs. Roosevelt, I'll simply answer his usual question." Without further hesitation, she brought her engagement book from her office and gave me a number of dates, which I wrote down. From that time on, Mrs. Roosevelt would go over her calendar with me at the beginning of the month and we would make our appointments.

She often knit or did needlework as we talked things over together on the evenings we waited for David's arrival from his office. Sometimes I wish I had had the foresight or incentive during our many peaceful tête-à-têtes to ask her questions about FDR's presidency and other topics of historical importance or to discuss her own past activities. I do not think she would have minded. There we were, just the two of us, with time on our hands. But quizzing Mrs. Roosevelt on these subjects was not characteristic of our relationship. While we did discuss our activities from time to time, I was more interested in learning how she approached problems and solved them, how she persevered, how she garnered courage. Being close to her in the present was enough, without thought of past or future. I was fascinated by the stories she volunteered to tell. It was a self-indulgent time of my life. Through our conversations, I wanted to understand how she had evolved into the exceptional person she was, how she had overcome early disappointments. I listened to how she had handled being alone in the world at an early age, how she had tran-scended fears and become brave. She would mention, for example, that obstacles were given us to grow strong on. "That works for you, Mrs. Roosevelt," I replied, "but not everyone grows strong on obstacles. Some stumble and fall down." But she insisted, "You are not allowed to fall down. You must stay on your feet and keep going." She also told me more than once, "If you've done something which you think is wrong, it doesn't matter so long as those who love you understand." I still have one of her quotations pinned above my desk: "You must do the thing you think you cannot do." She lived by her beliefs.

She told me about her visit to the South Pacific during World War II, recalling how she had sat, frozen, wrapped in a blanket in the bomb bay of an American plane, typing her column with two fingers. She spoke of the awkwardness she felt when she arrived at military bases. News would have gone out that a woman was coming, but naturally the fact that it was the wife of the president was withheld for security reasons. Mrs. Roosevelt was always sure, she said, that they were expecting a Hol-lywood star and felt that she would be a disappointment to the men. She remembered her visits to hospitals behind the front lines, how moved she'd been by the heroism of wounded servicemen, and how she'd had to steel herself before her tours of hospital burn units. She never forgot the smell of burned flesh in those wards, she said.

Mrs. Roosevelt described how horrified she was to find the floor of her cabin in Guadalcanal covered with crawling insects. "I soon discov-ered why the floor was slatted," she explained. "If you stamped hard on it, the insects scurried out of sight down between the slats." She stamped often, and spent a good part of the nights sitting up in bed with the lights on to keep them away. She was afraid of mice as well as bugs, but "I could not show I was squeamish," she said. Traveling in dangerous war zones, however, never fazed her. She told me how happy she was to have seen Joe Lash, who was stationed on Guadalcanal in the Signal Corps' weather service. On that trip, she had carried letters to him and parcels from his mother all the way from San Francisco to Hawaii then to Christmas Island, New Zealand, and Australia, until she reached him. It was an important reunion for Mrs. Roosevelt and Joe.

Once when we were walking together on the street, a taxi pulled up alongside us. "Mrs. Roosevelt," the driver called out. "Remember me? I was one of the wounded soldiers you visited in the hospital in Australia." She waved and smiled at him, whispering to me that he could have no idea of the thousands of wounded men she had seen on her Pacific tour.*

How I've regretted not having taken advantage of Mrs. Roosevelt's often-repeated invitation to show me a sculpture she loved in Rock Creek Cemetery in Washington. It is an over-life-size bronze by the American artist Augustus Saint-Gaudens, commissioned by Henry Adams as a memorial to his wife, Marian ("Clover") Hooper Adams, who had committed suicide. Entitled *The Peace of God* (better known as *Grief*), it had been reproduced in photographs I'd seen. I didn't want to impose on one of Mrs. Roosevelt's heavily scheduled trips to Washington to see a work that had little appeal for me. I did not understand its real significance to her when she told me she had spent many hours contemplating the sculpture. In its secluded place, it had offered her tranquility when her official life became too hectic, I assumed. Had I been aware that it was there that she had restored herself after Franklin Roosevelt's romance with Lucy Mercer, I would have treasured the experience of seeing the sculpture together with her. I did not know at the time that the solitary, mournful figure had given her the solace and inspiration she needed to work out her problems. *She* was not going to give up. She was going to *live*, and be useful. Her enthusiasm about showing the sculpture to me was proof, if indeed any was needed, that Mrs. Roosevelt had long ago freed herself from the despair that had originally brought her to that spot. Typically, she dwelled on the positives. *That* is what I learned from her.

Chatting together one night, she told me that she had not been happy

---

*New York taxi drivers had a great fondness for Mrs. Roosevelt and sometimes asked her to sit beside them in the front of the cab as they drove to her destination. She always obliged.

when Mr. Churchill came to stay at the White House and that she was glad when he went home. She thought he was inconsiderate of the president. "He should have known better than to keep Franklin up till all hours of the night. He knew Franklin rose early and did not take two-hours naps in the afternoon as he did, and his visits wore Franklin out."

She recounted her early days as a member of the women's division of the New York State Democratic Committee and expanded on how hard women had had to work to prove to the men in the party that they were worthy of support. One time, she drove her old car to an upstate farm to track down a committeeman who was dodging her. She stopped at the farmhouse. "And when his wife came to the door, I asked if I might see him. 'My husband isn't in,' she replied. I then politely asked her, 'Do you mind if I wait?' Without stopping for an answer, I sat down on the porch rocker and took out my knitting. I knit for two hours before her husband came out of the house." Mrs. Roosevelt smiled as she told me this story to the tune of her clicking knitting needles.

She liked to recall her friendship with Mary McLeod Bethune. A talented and resourceful educator from the rural South, Mrs. Bethune had founded Bethune-Cookman College, an institution devoted to the education of black youngsters. Mrs. Roosevelt had supported Mrs. Bethune's many projects over the years in the struggle for civil rights. She had invited her to be an overnight guest at the White House, the first black person so honored. Reminiscing about her trip to Birmingham, Alabama, to attend the founding meeting of the Southern Conference on Human Welfare, Mrs. Roosevelt said, "The hall was already quite filled when I arrived with Mrs. Bethune, and I took my seat beside her on the Negro side of the segregated auditorium. A young city law-inforcement officer was immediately sent over to me. He was red-faced with embarrassment and apologetically asked me to change my seat, explaining that I was breaking a city ordinance by sitting in the section reserved for Negroes. Well, I certainly didn't want to break any laws," said Mrs. Roosevelt gently, "so I asked him to put my chair down in the center aisle. I listened to the conference from there."

One time, Mrs. Roosevelt described the wooden stocks she'd seen displayed that day in a small country town, primitive devices once used for punishing lawbreakers. The victim's head and arms would be locked into position, causing great strain on the body. She looked so pained as she detailed the discomfort that I was prompted to ask how she knew it was so bad. "I tried it," she replied.

She reminisced in the most casual way and most informatively. She spoke of her childhood, her family, of her distant cousin who had danced with Lafayette, of her paternal great-grandfather, Cornelius Van Schaack Roosevelt (1794–1871), who had made his money in the construction business. Her snobbish family preferred to forget the humble source of his money, "although," she added, "they never minded spending it." She suddenly jumped up from her chair to show me his photograph, taking it from the mantel and holding it an extra minute to smile into the face in the small picture. Her only references to her mother-in-law were to the instances in which she "spoiled the children." She rarely talked to me about President Roosevelt, although I know that she had revealed a good deal about him to David, especially in the early years of their friendship, when she talked about the president's infantile paralysis and its effect upon her and the family. David once told me that Mrs. Roosevelt had said the president was an expert at denial. "Unpleasant things just did not 'happen,'" David quoted her as saying. If she came across an incident not meant for her eyes, the president would wheel himself over to her and say, "You *did not see* anything." (She recounted what would happen if she ever had to fire a member of their household staff: "Franklin had me tell him in advance so he would be sure to be out of the house at the time.")

Sometimes when we were alone, she would ask me about events in the art world, about which she knew very little. She listened attentively, either to learn or to help. If she had gone somewhere that she thought would have some significance for either David or me, she had notes about it or printed material to discuss with us. She told me about letters she'd received from people we knew. She would show me a book on children's art that had come in the mail, tell me about a special school she had visited. Letters sent to her requesting medical and other advice were set aside in a pile for David, with her penciled reminder at the top: "Show David," or "Ask David," or "D. to keep," or "D—see and return." We talked over the day's events. David would explore politics and international affairs with her—shop talk. I learned a good deal. These were wonderful times, and we were happy. It was only after Mrs. Roosevelt had died, when I deliberately applied myself to it, that I learned about the specifics of her incredible record of accomplishments.

On the rare occasion when Mrs. Roosevelt complained about a physical problem, she did so openly in my presence. It saved her the time of going to David's office. While she had every right to a patient's privacy, her naturalness made it clear to me that she and David kept few, if any, secrets from me. I moved out of view when he would examine her, but I felt she would not have minded if I hadn't. Sometimes as we were seated together, talking, David would lean forward and casually poke her around her ankle to check something about her circulation. If all was well, nothing would be said. If not, he would schedule an office visit. David would pull her over to the window in daylight, or bring her to a bright light at night to have a good look at her. She would be quite amiable about it. He used to say she was a good patient and followed instructions well, generally speaking.

David noted:

One day, sometime in the mid 1950s, Mrs. Roosevelt came to me with a medical question. She asked if there was some kind of medication she could take that would improve her memory, which she felt was failing. I asked whether I could give her a story for an answer. When I was taking my M.D. examination in Switzerland, I was questioned about a patient with arteriosclerosis, whose supply of blood to the brain was being affected by the disease. The examiner then asked me the same question Mrs. Roosevelt had just asked. In an examination one has to give answers; therefore I replied, "I did not really know of a remedy for the problem, but there was an old remedy used for a long time, especially in Italy and France. The remedy was garlic. These people believed that garlic had a beneficial influence on circulation in general and on the circulation of the brain in particular." Mrs. Roosevelt said, "But I like garlic. I will gladly take it." I told her about garlic pills made in Switzerland that supposedly eliminated the odor that usually goes with eating garlic. I prescribed them for her, and unfortunately for me, she wrote about this prescription for improving her memory in her newspaper column. This resulted in my receiving many inquiries from unknown people asking me to prescribe for them whatever I had given Mrs. Roosevelt. It went on for years. I was involved in another medication I gave her, which was a cold capsule. I combined into one prescription the many remedies claiming to be helpful in preventing or treating the common cold. As science does not have an exact explanation of its causes, and since there are probably multiple causes involved, I felt that combining the various components which at times have been helpful would decrease the chances of catching a cold, *especially if taken quickly at the first suspicion of a cold.* Mrs. Roosevelt kept these capsules with her and had found them to be quite helpful.

David explains her in part:

The blend of her strengths and weaknesses, her efforts to surmount the weaknesses, to continually improve herself, made her the rich personality that she was. She never wanted to be younger than she was, or younger-looking than her age. When she'd had her motor accident years ago, she was delighted that she needed a cap for an obtruding tooth which had broken. The accident forced her to do the capping. I don't think she would have deliberately changed the position of the objectionable tooth without the necessity for it. . . . There were times she had urges to be more elegant, and she liked to wear a new dress and she did. . . . She was a woman all right. But all within reason—the level of its importance was way down. . . .

She drank tea and coffee in moderation and wine in great moderation; she would drink it not on her own but for company's sake. Her alcohol consumption was not minimal, but negligible. It just didn't mean anything. And she didn't smoke. . . . That Mrs. Roosevelt was as effective as she was was partly due to her very extraordinary constitution. Her reserve energy went far beyond that of an average human being. But this was true of other members of her family. . . .

She was never, but really never, controlled by her self-importance. She regarded herself humbly, though she was quite aware of her position, her dignity, her power . . . and still she looked at herself critically. . . . I imagine she couldn't have been the person she was had she, for instance, been born beautiful. In spite of her miserable childhood, she was always conscious that she was born privileged, quite aware that she was a patrician. With all the deprivations, she was a realist and conscious of the positives in her life, and of her strengths. She understood the shortcomings of others, dealt with them and forgave them, was never patronizing. . . . Mrs. Roosevelt had a highly developed sense of diplomacy, of doing and saying the right thing.

David noted that Mrs. Roosevelt was not affected by gossip about the two of them. (It did, however, sometimes bother him.) He wrote:

She was a very strong personality and coped with everything. She stood by her opinions, her feelings and convictions. She was direct and outspoken. She did not care about rumors about herself. . . .

If she and her husband had had a real relationship, he would have been more sensitive to her unhappiness under the domination of her mother-in-law. . . .

Mrs. Roosevelt didn't think much of psychiatry; difficulties were there to be overcome; otherwise, you cannot develop strength. That was her simple belief, and in her case it was entirely true. But you have to have the strength for that kind of attitude. Not all personalities are able to overcome their difficulties and to be made stronger by them. Slowly, slowly, she became more tolerant as she saw the needs for help in people around her, needs for psychiatric help. I saw that change [in her] in my time. She realized her philosophy did not apply to everyone. But she herself certainly developed strength out of her difficulties, and there were plenty of them—and plenty of strength, too. . . .

[She] was a good patient, or rather, she was good once she had accepted advice, but a poor patient in other ways. She wouldn't go for [medical] tests. "I have no time." I had to somehow put it on the line. "If you don't go on your own, then I will take time off and go with you to the laboratory." "Well, when shall I go?" she would ask. There were times I had to use our friendship to exert medical influence with her.

He commented that she was alone a good deal in spite of all the crowds, and that when she could relax, she liked company, especially the company of those to whom she felt close. "To hear her talk, her laugh, to be drawn into her confidence was inspiring," he said.

David was once asked: "Who did the research for Mrs. Roosevelt's columns, magazine articles, and books?" He replied that she had no researchers, that she wrote the things she knew about. He noted: "She kept abreast of her correspondence so its quantity would not overwhelm her. The postman brought sacks of mail to her. She read each piece. On some she made short penciled comments on the top corners, from which Maureen could compose replies for Mrs. Roosevelt's later signature. Perfunctory replies, also noted on the letters, were handled by Gabrielle Gutkind. More complicated answers were dictated in their entirety by Mrs. Roosevelt. The mail was forwarded to her when she traveled." David encouraged her, as he did his other busy patients, to nap for a short time: "twenty minutes," he said, "every afternoon around three." While Mrs.

Roosevelt could not always follow his advice when traveling, she always kept it in mind and tried to take time out.

Mrs. Roosevelt was not adept in the kitchen. Once, seated beside me in a plane returning to New York, she told me proudly that she was going to prepare her own breakfast when she reached home. "Exactly what are you going to do, Mrs. Roosevelt?" I couldn't resist asking. "Marie has left bread out for the toaster and put water in the teakettle and taken the teacup out. I will do the rest," she replied. I couldn't help smiling. Mrs. Roosevelt never minded being teased. She was a good sport. The first time she came into my kitchen to help me as I was preparing dinner for the three of us, I had reason to be apprehensive. "What can I do?" she asked. I suggested that she wash lettuce for the salad. She went to work at my side at the kitchen sink. After a very few minutes, I excused myself and sought David. "Find a way to draw Mrs. Roosevelt out of the kitchen," I said. "We will soon be standing in water up to our ankles." After that, he was careful to interest her in something before we sat down to dinner in our apartment, and, I think, she was just as happy to be alone with him. But her conscience bothered her if I had no help, as is indicated by a note she wrote me:

> *Late in the evening of the 19th:*
> Edna dear,
> It was a lovely evening and a very good dinner and I loved being with you and David.
> Thank you very much dear, and remember next time I help with the dishes.
> Much love to you.
> E. R.

On an evening when we were downstairs, David suggested that she go to his office the next day for a vitamin injection. "I have no time," she said. She grew increasingly annoyed as David persisted. "If you repeat it once more," she angrily declared, "you will just have to leave." She was serious. I rose from my chair and made my way to the door, with David slowly following. I was already at the elevator when he stopped on her threshold and looked into her eyes with a smile. He did not budge as she pretended to push him out. Her laugh was false. Standing firm, David asked, "Don't you know how many people I worry about in the course of the day? Do you want to add to my worries?" She instantly replied, "I have ten minutes tomorrow morning," and shut the door hard behind us.

Taking Mrs. Roosevelt home after an evening out before the move to Seventy-fourth Street, I remember David stopped her in the lobby of the Park Sheraton to remind her, "You must cut down on your schedule." She replied insistently, "I can't, and you have to stop telling me that!" People in the lobby stared. A compelling exchange went back and forth, until a compromise was reached. "After this week, I shall work less the following two." She wanted to oblige him. Another time, she told us with fury that Franklin, Jr., could never be satisfied, that "he always wanted more." David casually said, "Don't blame yourself. It's in his genes. Your uncle Theodore was the same. Big appetites run in your family." And as Mrs. Roosevelt became more composed, he added, "Do you remember the time we had dinner together at Norris Point? Franklin had roast beef for his main course and ordered a steak for dessert. That is how he is, and he will never change."

He noted in his journal:

The outward sign that Mrs. Roosevelt was deeply troubled would be that she would withdraw and that one could not reach her. She would not say anything. She became silent and unapproachable. But on some of these occasions it was possible to break through her reserve and enable her to talk out the reasons for her misery. If she were able to speak, I would walk with her and listen. It was a help to her, an outlet. She sometimes actually expressed the wish to do away with herself, saying that she had lived too long, that she had become an obstacle to the success of her children, that people would turn more to *them* if she were not around. These times would of course pass. . . . I was not surprised that she reacted so strongly. A highly sensitive person who takes in all that is going on around her—and how much was going around—all the turmoil in her family—I was surprised that she took it as well as she did.

Returning from my office late one afternoon, I received a call from Mrs. Roosevelt. Could David and I come downstairs at eight o'clock? "Adlai Stevenson is leaving on a tour of Latin America and says he wants to ask me some questions about that part of the world. But his real reason for coming to see me is that he wants to run for president again and would like me to persuade him. Anyone who needs persuasion should not be a candidate, and I don't want the subject to come up. If you and David are here, he won't be able to discuss it."

"You know how hungry David is when he gets home," I replied. "An eight o'clock meeting will be too late for him."

"Please come," she urged. "I will have a plate of sandwiches ready."

I telephoned David and told him to stop off first at Mrs. Roosevelt's apartment. Mr. Stevenson and Mrs. Roosevelt were talking about conditions in Latin America when I walked in. Whatever he felt about the interruption, Mr. Stevenson greeted me very pleasantly, as he did David, who arrived shortly after. I passed the plate of sandwiches among us often throughout the discussion. Each time, Mr. Stevenson took one, but David did not. Finally, Mr. Stevenson rose to leave. Mrs. Roosevelt escorted him to the door, with David and me close at her heels, the better to rush upstairs for dinner. In the hallway, an uncommon sight greeted us. There, lying outstretched on the floor, was the body of our alcoholic housepainter. Startled, Mr. Stevenson turned to Mrs. Roosevelt. "Who's that?" he gasped. "Good-bye," she said, and helped him step over the prone body while I rushed ahead to push the button for the elevator. I still remember Mr. Stevenson's wide eyes as the elevator door slowly closed on him. David revived the housepainter, and as he took him downstairs to put him into a cab, Mrs. Roosevelt, leaning over the hall banister with me, knowingly remarked, "David has been trying to treat him with tranquilizers. But when I saw empty wine bottles in the basement the other day, I knew his efforts were useless."

On the first anniversary of David's mother's death, Mrs. Roosevelt wrote to him:

April 29 [1959]
David dear,

This time is sad for you but I hope also it brings you happy memories for that is as your mother would want it to be. She would want you to feel her love and her protective presence and she would rejoice in your growth. You probably do not realize it but you have grown in personal strength and power in this past year. Edna is doing much for you but you are doing much for her and through what you give you are able to give more to others.

I love you so dearly and I am so proud of what you are making of your life that on this day I want to bring you some happy thoughts. The 28th must have some feeling of loss but this note and the flowers are to bring you a message of love and remembrance of your Mother and gratitude to her for what she was, and above all, of her gift of you for you bring happiness to so many. All my love.

E. R.

You never knew whom you would meet in Val-Kill. Mrs. Roosevelt invited us to Hyde Park for the overnight stay of Princess Beatrix of the Netherlands. Partly because of their Dutch ancestry, the Roosevelts' personal acquaintance with the House of Orange was long-standing. Mrs. Roosevelt received the royal party warmly. The princess sat on a large chair on the lawn between her lady-in-waiting and Mrs. Roosevelt to receive the Hyde Park guests lined up to be presented to her. In spite of some observations of protocol, the visit was informal and a respite during the princess's short American stay. In our conversation, she told me how much she had enjoyed New York, describing her visits to the nightclub El Morocco and to the Metropolitan Museum of Art, where she had been shown around by Theodore Rousseau, the attractive curator of paintings. After dinner, her party retired early. The princess and her lady-in-waiting had been given the small suite off the upstairs "crossroom" of the cottage. Mrs. Roosevelt saw to their comfort, but she did nothing extra for the royal party that would not have been done for others.

On a sun-filled autumn day, Crown Prince Mered Azmach Asfa Wossen, the suave son of Emperor Haile Selassie of Ethiopia, came to visit Mrs. Roosevelt with his pretty wife. The luncheon party was too large for the dining room, so Mrs. Roosevelt had small tables for four arranged in the downstairs rooms of the cottage. I was seated at Mrs. Roosevelt's table with the crown prince and John Roosevelt. While the conversation did not start out promisingly — "It is a beautiful day," said His Royal Highness, motioning toward the bright windows — it proceeded in a more relaxed fashion. After lunch, a great crowd followed the royal couple to the Franklin D. Roosevelt Library, where Mrs. Roosevelt gave them a tour. Before they departed, the prince bade me a charming good-bye. Not long afterward, I was shocked to read in the newspaper that he had attempted to assassinate his father and been forced to flee his country. Looks are deceiving.

The visit of Marshal Tito of Yugoslavia and his wife to Hyde Park was much more casual than that of Nikita Khrushchev, his Soviet Union counterpart, the month before. A flamboyant man, the uniformed guest of honor dominated the luncheon table. One could see how his powerful personality had held Yugoslavia together. He spoke some English, expressed himself forcefully, and used expansive gestures to convey the beauties of his country, which was the main topic of conversation. Mrs. Tito was a quiet, affable companion. The famous Communist leader expounded on his hobby, carpentry. He also told us with pride that Yugoslav women were the most beautiful in the world, and indeed, he went on, there were wooden signs on various country roads declaring this fact. I carefully inquired whether he himself had carved those signs in his workshop, which he good-humoredly denied.

In October 1959 Henry Morgenthau III asked Mrs. Roosevelt to host an interview program for Boston public television sponsored by Brandeis University, the Ford Foundation, and Boston public TV — WGBH — entitled: *Prospects of Mankind.** It was a paid job. For the next two and a half years, until her failing health made her trips to Boston impossible, she traveled monthly to the Brandeis campus in Waltham, Massachusetts, where most of the interviews took place.** Some of the guests on her show were Henry Kissinger, Adlai Stevenson, John F. Kennedy (twice), and the Russian-born painter Marc Chagall. (It was on Mrs. Roosevelt's program that President Kennedy announced the formation of the Peace Corps.) She would arrive in Boston on Saturday for an advance conference about the guests to appear and the political topics to be discussed, which Henry Morgenthau and his associates had selected. Then she would attend a luncheon or dinner party given by the production group and, on Sunday, tape the interview in the Schlossberg Music Center on the Brandeis campus. Most of the nine shows each year took place at the university, although some were set at the United Nations and two or three in London and Paris. Mrs. Roosevelt gave a series of seminars on political science for Brandeis students on Mondays before returning home. Back in New York, she would tell us how stimulated she was by the attitudes and questions of serious young people and how much those weekends meant to her. She had known Brandeis University from its inception and felt a personal attachment to it, having frequently given its founder, her friend Abraham Sacher, advice and fund-raising assistance. It had been his dream to create a university having no "Jewish quota" admissions policy, a prevalent procedure at the time among first-rate American institutions of higher learning.

---

*June 16, 1997 interview with Paul Noble of Noble Productions, Inc., New York, coproducer of *Prospects of Mankind*. Mr. Noble and Diana Michaelis were coproducers, Henry Morgenthau was executive director of the program.
**The programs were also popular in New York, where they were rebroadcast on a local station, Channel 5. When Mrs. Roosevelt was too ill to travel, David reluctantly discouraged the producers' plan to continue the interviews in New York.

David came home one evening with the announcement that the Russians were coming. Two Soviet medical academicians were in New York and had telephoned him. He was glad to renew contact with the surgeons, pleased to reciprocate their kindness to him in Moscow. The following day, he gave them a tour of Columbia-Presbyterian Medical Center, showing them laboratories and departments of special interest to them. That night, we invited them out to dinner, picking them up in the shabby hotel on the northeast corner of Eighty-first Street and Columbus Avenue, where their government usually housed its citizens.* It was a glorious evening, cold (but not for Russians) and clear. We took them first to the top of Rockefeller Center to see the view. Spread out before us was the majestic, sparkling city with its fluid arcs of bridges connecting one dazzling lighted borough to another. Our guests were lost in wonder as David pointed out to them the United Nations, the Empire State Building, other skyscrapers, and places they'd heard about. He indicated the rivers, the location of various universities, and the theater district; he also showed them the Statue of Liberty, the George Washington Bridge, and the shore of the New Jersey Palisades. The doctors were visibly impressed. Finally, they could wait no longer with the question uppermost in their minds. Interrupting David's narration, and in Russian of course, they exclaimed, "But Professor, where do the *middle class* live?"

David was their guide the following day, too, taking them to the Academy of Medicine and arranging that they address an audience of doctors. In his journal he wrote, "We had a dinner invitation to Mrs. Roosevelt's the next night and she had told me that she was expecting two high Soviet government officials. I thought these Russian professors might like to speak with members of their government and I knew that Mrs. Roosevelt would allow me to bring two people along." But they refused when he

---

*It is no longer in existence. Now a refurbished building is in its place, called the Galaxy.

asked them. " 'Officials from your country' meant 'politics,' " David noted, "and no Russian interferes with politics."

Indira Gandhi, Nehru's daughter (and future prime minister of India), came to dinner at Seventy-fourth Street after a lecture tour of American universities. There were just the four of us around the table and Mrs. Gandhi described how she had encouraged students to feel free to ask her whatever questions came to mind about India or anything else. "Does the same principle apply to us?" asked David. "Of course," she replied, smiling. Very much in the current news were reports that Krishna Menon, former Indian ambassador to the United Nations and at that time minister of defense, was advocating that India seize the island of Goa from Portugal. David asked Mrs. Gandhi about this Indian policy, unfortunately referring to Minister Krishna Menon as the "Goa constrictor." Quivering with fury, she slammed her hand down upon the table as she vehemently repudiated the unflattering reference as well as any suggestion that India's claim to Goa was illegitimate. Mrs. Roosevelt, entirely unruffled, rescued David. She stated David's case for him firmly but diplomatically. (Anyway, one could not explode so easily with Eleanor Roosevelt.) The evening ended civilly enough and after Mrs. Gandhi left, Mrs. Roosevelt casually mentioned to David that she had heard Mr. Krishna Menon and Mrs. Gandhi were "extremely special friends."

Among some of the accomplished women I met through Mrs. Roosevelt was the commissioner of the Department of Correction in New York City, Anna Cross. Following one of her visits, Mrs. Roosevelt and I lunched with her at the Women's House of Detention. It was not the first time I'd been there. After David and Mrs. Roosevelt returned from their first trip to the Soviet Union, they had given a slide-illustrated talk there about conditions in Russia. Learning about life in such a distant place was a welcome diversion to the inmates, who appreciated Mrs. Roosevelt's interest in them and received her as a friend.

One day I was waiting with Mrs. Roosevelt for the arrival of lunch guests when she heard Maureen say from her desk, "There is a call for you from California. It's Frank Sinatra." "Find out what he wants, dear,"

Mrs. Roosevelt replied. It turned out that the famous singer was inviting her to appear on one of his television specials, and she accepted. Of course we couldn't wait to view the show, wondering what in the world she was going to do on the program. We were dumbfounded when we saw Mrs. Roosevelt as the star of the finale. Seated alone onstage in a long evening dress, with an off-camera wind machine blowing yards and yards of billowing white silk behind her, she gave an eloquent, uplifting recitation to the tune of "High Hopes." She performed beautifully, and upon her return from California, she was pleased to report that the show had gone well. Mr. Sinatra had been extremely kind to her, she said appreciatively, and the work had paid well and was easy. She added that when the television crew was dismantling the set, she had asked what they planned to do with all those yards of white silk. "We throw it out," she was told. She asked if she might have it and then brought it all home. "I shall give it to people who can use it for curtains," she said.

Open House

One late December afternoon, Mrs. Roosevelt called to inquire whether she might come upstairs to deliver her Christmas gifts to us. I thanked her and said she was not to take the trouble, that I would be down for them and would have our presents for her. I went downstairs, and to my astonishment, she heaped packages into my cradled arms as I thought, Was she thinking of carrying all this upstairs herself? Then I saw that she had filled her own arms with a similar number of wrapped objects. Silently, we walked upstairs together. (David had told her that walking upstairs at a slow, measured pace was good exercise.) Turning to me, she said, "I will be coming up again." Without a word, I accompanied her back down. Her thoughtfulness was extraordinary, matched only by the depth of the feelings expressed in her gifts. The fact that Christmas was a good excuse for giving added considerably to Mrs. Roosevelt's enjoyment of the holiday.

She wrote me a beautiful letter, and one to David, as well.

55 EAST 74 STREET

Xmas 1959

My dearest David,

Another Xmas and it seems to me so much has happened this past year. I hope you are thankful for some of the things I am thankful for! I love having our house, and living under the same roof, it is a great joy to me. You and Edna are the most wonderful family for me and the best possible neighbors.

For you I am thankful because Edna has given you a home at last which is really yours. She gives you happiness and has done much to enrich the mutual understanding between you and Grania. Take a little care of yourself for all of our sakes. You are the center of all our worlds and anything which goes wrong with you affects us all. You've grown in strength and in ability to heal but then you cannot carry all the world's burdens. The happiness of Xmas and New Year my dear, my love you have always.

E. R.

We spent the holiday in Hyde Park. On New Year's Eve, we were back in New York, and the three of us, along with my brother, Bertram ("Buddy"), had an early dinner together and went to see an Off-Broadway play. We returned home before midnight, when Mrs. Roosevelt was expecting her usual crowd for champagne to toast the New Year. About a month earlier, she had suggested to me that now we were settled at home, it might be nice to have a joint open-house party on New Year's Day. The very idea of giving a party with Mrs. Roosevelt made me apprehensive. I nervously inquired, "How many people do you want to invite, Mrs. Roosevelt?" "Not many," was her reply; "we can keep it small. Perhaps each of us can ask a hundred or so." It was the "or so" that troubled me. She saw my concern, because she quickly added, "Don't worry, dear, most people won't come. On New Year's Day, many are away, and others have celebrated late the night before and won't care to go out again." "Mrs. Roosevelt," I replied, "everyone will accept an invitation from you." She seemed so pleased with the idea of a party that I stopped objecting. On my way to my office one morning soon after, I spotted two piles of cards downstairs. Maureen answered my query: "They are the invitations to your open-house party." Just as I thought, there were a great many of them. I bundled off our share.

We made the house look especially welcoming on the day of the event. People were everywhere, in every room upstairs and down, and seated on the staircases as well, with a narrow center aisle left for the flow of traffic. And traffic there was. It was one of the rare times Mrs. Roosevelt had been wrong. Everyone who was away for the holidays came back to accept her invitation, and those who had been out late the night before roused themselves in good time to appear. Many called ahead to ask if they might bring friends and relations. Just before the party began, Mrs. Roosevelt reminded me to remove any monogrammed matchbooks, ashtrays, or other similar items we might have, explaining, "People like to take away souvenirs." "Souvenirs!" I exclaimed. "They want *your* monogram, not ours."

After New Year's Day, the atmosphere in our house changed. Eleanor Roosevelt's power to persuade was particularly sought after by various politicians in 1960 as they geared up for the combat of the presidential election, in which she would play a vigorous and influential role.

· 7 ·

THE LAST YEARS

Kennedy Versus Stevenson

THE EXCITEMENT OF ELECTING a new president dominated 1960. Although Adlai E. Stevenson had twice lost the race, Mrs. Roosevelt, after due consideration and not as wholeheartedly as before, still believed that he was the best man for the job, at least compared to the other potential candidates. She did not favor Senator John F. Kennedy, the frontrunner for the Democratic nomination, for several reasons. She was informed by a number of people that Joseph Kennedy, the senator's rich and influential father, had for some time been laying the groundwork for his son's election by putting on his payroll small-town businessmen, attorneys, and local officials across the country. This widespread network of people was therefore obligated to the senior Kennedy to produce votes for his son for president. Brazen buying of campaign support was offensive to Mrs. Roosevelt.* Though they knew she was a Stevenson supporter, the Kennedy team bombarded her for her endorsement of the senator, waging almost a campaign within a campaign. Her influence on public opinion counted. Jimmy and Franklin beseeched their mother to come out for Senator Kennedy, especially Franklin, who was a good friend of the Massachusetts

---

*Senator Kennedy complained to Mrs. Roosevelt about her "My Day" column, in which she wrote about his father's paid agents. She responded in her column of January 6, 1959, that it was the extravagance which she found most inappropriate. To be fair, she included Mr. Kennedy's own objection to her position, at the same time letting her statement stand.

senator. Franklin hoped to be appointed secretary of the navy if Mr. Kennedy won the election. (Both his great-uncle Theodore and his father had once held the post of assistant secretary of the navy, and Franklin, Jr., wouldn't have minded following in their footsteps.) Mrs. Roosevelt told us that the entire Washington office of James Landis, attorney for Joseph P. Kennedy, had been marshaled to promote the Kennedy candidacy; one member of the firm, Abba Schwartz, whom Mrs. Roosevelt knew personally, had been particularly delegated to obtain her endorsement.

She had once told me about a visit Joseph Kennedy had made in 1940 to FDR in his library at Hyde Park, when Joseph Kennedy was ambassador to Great Britain. That day, Mrs. Roosevelt received a call from her husband at Val-Kill Cottage. The president emphatically told her, "Eleanor, I am sending Joe Kennedy over to you. Give him lunch and put him on the train. I never want to set eyes on him again!" (Etiquette — the lunch — was not forgotten, no matter how deep the breach.) Joseph Kennedy had been trying to influence President Roosevelt against supporting Britain in World War II, arguing that the country could not possibly withstand Nazi German air attacks and would quickly fall. His repeatedly defeatist position infuriated the president.

Mrs. Roosevelt believed that the aggressive Joseph Kennedy, whom she did not trust, had too much influence over his son. She feared that Senator Kennedy's judgments as president might be swayed by the Roman Catholic Church, of which the family were devout members. She was also concerned by the fact that the senator had not repudiated McCarthyism. And she could not forget the letter she'd shown to David one night in 1959. A person unknown to her had written that Senator Kennedy was suffering from Addison's disease,* and that this was being kept a secret. The writer gave a detailed account of the senator's condition. David explained the illness to her and they speculated whether this letter

---

*Addison's disease is characterized by loss of strength, low blood pressure, and a brownish coloration of the skin due to disturbance of the suprarenal glands. It turned out that Mr. Kennedy did have the disease. He maintained a suntan to mask this discoloration.

was a political ploy or the truth. If accurate, the disclosure of the serious illness could ruin Kennedy as a presidential candidate. They concluded that Mrs. Roosevelt should say nothing about the letter, as she knew nothing firsthand, and that it was not her job to track the story down. Nevertheless, the allegation continued to trouble her.

Although she didn't like Mr. Stevenson's disguising his desire for the nomination by saying yes and no to it at the same time, she remained quietly faithful to him. His public uncertainty did not fool her, and she eventually supported him openly. Meanwhile, she proceeded with business as usual. She made speeches for the AAUN and other organizations, advocated that Congress prevent the disposal of radioactive waste in U.S. coastal waters, championed the freedom of the Baltic states from the Soviet Union, and denounced racial discrimination. She continued to earn her living from lecture fees, books, articles, her newspaper column, and the Brandeis University seminars.

Mrs. Roosevelt called us late one night, around eleven-thirty. She had never called at that hour before. She was very angry and asked if she could come upstairs to see us for a few minutes. When she arrived, she explained that some time before, she had given Elliott a large and beautiful silver monteith bowl, a legacy from her Livingston forebears.* Dated 1679 and made by the Boston silversmith John Coney, it had been a wedding gift to John and Alida Livingston. She treasured it as a family heirloom and had hoped Elliott felt similarly. But he had just told her he needed money and was going to sell it. His friend Victor Hammer,** the art dealer, had found a customer prepared to pay him $22,000 for it,

---

*The Livingstons were on Eleanor Roosevelt's mother's side of the family. The first of the family to arrive in this country, Robert R. Livingston, was the New York chancellor who administered the oath of office to George Washington; Philip Livingston signed the Declaration of Independence. Mrs. Roosevelt's maternal grandmother was Mary Livingston Ludlow, who married Valentine G. Hall, Jr.
**Hammer Galleries, New York. Victor was the brother of the oil magnate Armand Hammer.

a sum supposed to include Hammer's sales commission; it happened to be just the amount Elliott needed. Sympathetic as she was to Elliott's need, Mrs. Roosevelt was deeply hurt that he would sell such a rare family heirloom. She believed the bowl was not even legally his to sell, as she had not paid the gift tax on it. This gave her a way out. She would take the bowl back, she said, and find another way to help Elliott. I asked Mrs. Roosevelt to give me twenty-four hours to discover what the bowl was really worth. If Mr. Hammer said he could sell the bowl for $22,000, I suspected it was worth more. The next morning on my way to work, I stopped off at a gallery I knew that handled early American silver. When I described the bowl, the dealer blurted out, "Why, I am buying that bowl with Victor Hammer!" He was immediately sorry he had spoken so quickly. I had taken him by surprise. I, too, was surprised. Victor Hammer was buying a half interest in an object he was at the same time selling, even taking a commission for selling it partly to himself! That was quite an arrangement.

I contacted two other New York galleries that specialized in old silver. One offered $75,000 for the Livingston bowl; the other mentioned a like amount, plus a certain percentage of the retail sales price above a specified figure. Next, I telephoned my boss, Abris Silberman, in London and told him the whole story. By day's end, Abris called to say that English silver dealers would easily match the amounts I'd been offered, for early American silver was a rarity in England and much in demand, especially a piece with the provenance of Mrs. Roosevelt's. That evening, I handed her my report. She thanked me but said nothing more.

Some time later, she told David and me that she had given the Livingston bowl to the Roosevelt Library and had sent Elliott the amount she had saved in taxes by making this donation to the government. I am happy to see the Livingston bowl on exhibit in the FDR Library today. It is a beautiful object.

Mrs. Roosevelt Reclines

One rainy Sunday afternoon, Mrs. Roosevelt telephoned.

"Is David at home, dear?" she asked.

"Yes," I replied.

"Is he having a nap?"

"No."

"Do you have guests?" she inquired, her voice sounding strained.

"What is it, Mrs. Roosevelt?" I asked anxiously. "What would you like?"

"May I come up, dear? I was just hit by a car."

Her apartment was filled with a large group of girls from a Jewish day school in Baltimore, so David examined her in our quarters, after rushing down to get her. She was in much pain. David's notes read:

When she was seventy-six, a taxi backed into Mrs. Roosevelt and threw her to the pavement. She had gone down to her hairdresser's shop in Washington Square on a Sunday when the lady was giving a reception to benefit cancer care. As she was stepping off the pavement to cross the street, a taxi backed into her. Feeling that she might have been to some degree responsible for having been hit because she was hard of hearing, and because the driver was Negro and Mrs. Roosevelt did not want him to be charged with anything, when he tried to help her to her feet, she insistently waved him away "before the police come." She limped across the street to the shop unaided. From there she called Joe Lash, who lived close by, to ask him to bring her home.

After examining her, David wanted to take her to the hospital for X rays. She refused. She was scheduled to speak at a fund-raising dinner for Brandeis University that night and would not cancel her appearance. She was impatient with David for trying to detain her. He gave her medication for pain and bound her ankle, then went to his office to get her crutches,

211

which he reminded her how to use. He urged her to give her speech that evening sitting down. She spent the remainder of the afternoon with her injured leg elevated, but she was in an evening dress and ready to go when her escorts arrived. We were distressed to see how uncomfortably she hobbled off with them, leaning heavily on her crutches. David's notes continue: "I had arranged for her hospitalization the next day, to which she agreed. In doing so, she telephoned her secretary, Maureen Corr, to call her son John to ask him to fill in for her in a speech to be made the following day. When Maureen heard about a cancellation on Mrs. Roosevelt's part, she rushed over to our house, thinking something very serious must have happened."

We waited up for Mrs. Roosevelt's return before midnight. Stepping off the elevator, her face flushed with exhaustion and pain, she began speaking before David could utter a word. "Yes, I spoke seated!" she declared. And then she angrily scolded him: "*You* didn't want me to go! But when they saw what condition I was in, they were able to raise more money!" With those words, she limped into her apartment, slammed the door shut, and purposefully attached the inside chain. This demonstration was to announce to David that under no circumstances was he to use the house key to enter her apartment in order to check on her during the night. (David was later able to persuade her never to chain her door again.) In her absence, he had conspired with the doctors scheduled to see her the next day, asking them to keep her hospitalized for at least forty-eight hours. He didn't trust Mrs. Roosevelt to stay off her foot once she was free to go, and thought the accident a good opportunity to pre-scribe bedrest for her. I watched from the window as promptly at seven o'clock the following morning Mrs. Roosevelt, slowly helped down the front steps by David, left the house for the drive to Columbia-Presbyterian. She had taken the trouble to dress stylishly, wearing a becoming hat and her elegant maroon and gray plaid suit. Visible in her right hand as she clutched the crutch were white kid gloves. She looked unusually jaunty for an early-morning hospital visit, I thought, but then I realized that she wanted to appear as vigorous as possible when she arrived at Columbia's Harkness Pavilion.

David and Mrs. Roosevelt soon disappeared from sight. Hoping for the best, I waited for news, which came sooner than I expected. A little after 10:00 A.M. the telephone rang. "Hello, dear. I'm back!" Mrs. Roosevelt's cheery voice announced. I couldn't help remembering David's meticulous plan to rein her in. "David worked hard to try to keep me there," she said triumphantly, "but I gave my promise to all the doctors that I would stay in bed for the rest of the week." No one could have sounded happier. She'd escaped.

Eleanor Roosevelt's version of being an invalid was different from any-one else's. She did remain at home on the daybed in the dining room, telephone beside her, for almost a week, but her doorbell and telephones never ceased ringing when word got out that she'd had an accident. Flow-ers arrived by the shopful. Packages, baskets of fruit, and messages were delivered; friends and colleagues came to the door. Mail sacks were fuller and their delivery more frequent. She attended to everything from her post on the daybed. I tried to see Maureen during the first day. "How do you stand it?" I asked, referring to the continual piercing ring of the bell. "It's hard," she replied. I fled. But it was not hard for Mrs. Roosevelt. Totally calm and, indeed, flourishing in the center of the action, she dictated her column, dealt with the mail and everything else on her schedule. Sitting up against cushions, she looked very well when she received dinner guests that week. She wore a blue silk gown, a choker of pearls, and her usual long gold chain. A master of compromise, she had kept her promise to "stay down" and had enjoyed it. David noted the following in her medical chart:

April 18th, 1960
On April 3rd . . . she hurt her right ankle. . . . I saw her at home. By then, which was about two hours after the accident, her ankle was swollen, stepping on her foot was painful at the instep, on the dorsum and at the lateral ankle. Ethyl chloride spray did not es-sentially diminish her pain. Strapping helped enough to enable her to go to her next engagement . . . at the Waldorf. She spent a bad night. The next morning she had x-rays taken at Harkness Pavilion

and she was seen by Dr. Harrison McLaughlan. The x-rays showed no fracture. She was strapped by Dr. McLaughlan and remained at home off her right foot for five days.

On examining her sprained ankle I found that she had bilateral edema in her foreleg. Her pulse showed extra cystoles, and every 6th or 8th beat skipped. She was prevailed upon to have a checkup, and did so at the Rip Van Winkle Clinic in Hudson, New York on April 14th. Essential findings were a moderate anemia. . . . The sedimentation rate again,* as on her previous examination, was elevated. . . . She was also put on a weight reducing diet. The edema, pulse and anemia will be watched. If after building up her hemaglobin the heart still shows too quick response to fatigue, we shall have to digitalize her.

Khrushchev Comes to Seventy-fourth Street

One day, Mrs. Roosevelt called my office to ask if I could be home by three o'clock to meet Nikita Khrushchev. He was coming to tea and she thought I would find the visit interesting. (David had conferences at the hospital that could not be rescheduled.) The head of the Soviet Union was in New York to address the UN General Assembly. Mrs. Roosevelt had invited him to call on her when he came to New York, and though relations between the United States and the Soviet Union were particularly strained at the time, she encouraged his visit, believing that personal contacts kept the doors of negotiation open. I rushed out of the gallery on Seventy-eighth Street in good time, only to be stopped by a police barrier on our corner. "But I *live* on this street," I insisted, showing what ID I had. Finally convinced, the policeman waved me on, only for another officer to bar me from my front door. It was the television crewman in front of the house who came to my rescue: "She's okay; she lives there," he said. With this approval, I could pass.

---

*Sedimentation rate can indicate inflammation.

Once inside, I saw policemen standing shoulder-to-shoulder on every step of each flight of stairs from the first floor up to the roof. They were lined up at attention on the four sides of the flat roof, as well. From our windows, I saw crowds of people restrained by barricades in the street below, and heads poking out of windows from the large apartment building opposite us, cameras focused on our house. I wished I had had the time to photograph them back. Instead, I went quickly downstairs to face not only Mr. Khrushchev but also Andrei Gromyko, the Soviet foreign minister; the Soviet ambassador to the United States; and their interpreter. They had arrived moments before. No one else was there except Belle (Mrs. Kermit) Roosevelt, who did the honors at the tea table while I passed the cups. The Soviet premier had brought several gifts to Mrs. Roosevelt—a long hand-crocheted fine wool shawl, a case of Russian champagne, and perfume.

As the Russians were her guests, Mrs. Roosevelt did not bring up any of the topics currently at issue between the two countries, although they did discuss some of the differences between capitalism and communism. One question Mrs. Roosevelt asked the Soviet premier was whether he had begun to prepare his people to enjoy all the leisure time that the short workweek in the Soviet Union was soon to provide, if his arguments were correct. After an hour, the Soviets prepared to leave. Mrs. Roosevelt sent her greetings to Mrs. Khrushchev and the Soviet leader asked in turn to be remembered to Professor Gurewitsch. Then the four men squeezed into our small elevator and departed. The street was deserted when I took Belle Roosevelt to the front door. Not a policeman or spectator was in sight. Two hours later, a set of books written by Nikita Khrushchev was delivered from the Soviet consulate. Blue slips of paper had been inserted to mark statements supporting his arguments on the superiority of Communist economic doctrine, with pertinent passages highlighted for Mrs. Roosevelt's attention. The next evening, she showed the volumes with their protruding blue slips to David. As he began to translate the references, she said impatiently, clearly no longer interested in hearing Khrushchev's further explanations, "Keep them!" I have the books still, blue slips and all.

On the evening of the Khrushchev visit, David and I had a friend, Byba Coster, to dinner. For the first time, the elevator stalled, trapping her inside after the metal door slammed shut. It took the serviceman fifteen minutes to free her, and I couldn't help thinking anxiously, What if it were Messrs. Khrushchev, Gromyko, and the ambassador and their interpreter who had gotten stuck? It might have been an international incident! I could picture all those policemen with axes. Poor Byba. As she staggered out, all she needed was a bourbon.

"A Good President"

It was clear that Mrs. Roosevelt did not quite have her old energy. That and the fact that there were serious ongoing medical discussions behind the scenes between David and his colleagues about Mrs. Roosevelt's health were considerably worrying. David had always referred her to specialists whenever a situation required it, but now, as her medical needs became more complicated, he increased the number of these referrals, relying not only on the medical talent in his own hospital but on physicians from other institutions as well. Since the beginning of 1960, Mrs. Roosevelt's physical examinations had shown problems necessitating more frequent laboratory tests and consultations: In April, routine tests revealed a depressed blood count. A report of May 2 advised: "In summary, there was evidence of moderate anemia, cause undetermined." Iron replacement was advised.* A bone marrow examination in June** supported the diagnosis of a hypoplastic anemia, but no therapy was advised except to "follow the patient." I had not known these precise facts at the time, but I saw how preoccupied David seemed, and how diligently he stood watch. None of these developments, however, interfered with Mrs. Roosevelt's schedule.

---

*Dr. Girard J. Croft.
**Performed by Dr. Peter Vogel.

Although she did not have her usual vitality as she sailed into the 1960 pre-election campaign, with the approach of the Democratic National Convention in Los Angeles in July, she had a role to play in nominating a new candidate. Mrs. Roosevelt might have thought of herself as on the sidelines, but she couldn't stay there long. Mr. Stevenson had hoped his party would draft him, but when support from former Stevenson loyalists began to erode, Mrs. Roosevelt was forced to step forward to prop up his candidacy. She used every opportunity to promote his name and finally participated in the movement to draft Stevenson. Mary Lasker and Anna Rosenberg (referred to disparagingly by the Kennedy camp as "the New York fat cats"), Agnes Meyer, Ruth Field, Herbert Lehman, and Thomas Finletter also beat the drum for Stevenson. Former President Truman irritated Mrs. Roosevelt by coming out for Senator Stuart Symington, when it was clear that his first choice was really Senator Lyndon Johnson*

At the same time, Mrs. Roosevelt continued to be pressured by her sons James, Franklin, and Elliott, and others as well, to meet with Senator Kennedy, whose candidacy was gaining momentum. She refused, holding fast to her belief in Adlai Stevenson. For her, he was still the most viable in the group of contenders. Even the exhortations of Representative Richard Bolling, a strong Kennedy supporter who had come to Hyde Park to speak on Memorial Day that year, were to no avail. Yet there were signs that she began to soften toward Kennedy because of his public statements, his dignified replies to President Truman, and his thoughtful answers concerning his Catholicism. Also, she did not forget what a Kennedy victory might mean to Franklin, Jr. Senator Kennedy was particularly beholden to Franklin for his help in the West Virginia primary. There, where the Roosevelt name was still revered, Franklin had diligently campaigned by his side and turned the tide for him. She considered how successful a Stevenson-Kennedy Democratic ticket might be. Her belief

---

*In her "My Day" column of July 5, 1960, Mrs. Roosevelt wrote scathingly about former President Truman and his resentment of Mr. Stevenson's independence of mind after Mr. Truman had asked him to run for president in 1952. She stated that Truman and Stevenson "are two totally different people. Mr. Stevenson will remain a great figure in the country whether he is nominated or not."

that every American, regardless of religion, should have the chance to
run for high office was welcomed by Mr. Kennedy. When David and I
had dinner with her during this time, she would occasionally mention
some particular person who had been in that day to persuade her to switch
her allegiance. Franklin came to the house regularly to explain to his
mother the senator's positions and prod her to endorse him; Abba
Schwartz was also a regular visitor on the same mission. Torn between
the candidate of her choice for her country, and having to take a public
stand against the views of her sons, knowing their best political interests
were at stake, Mrs. Roosevelt was in a bind as the convention drew near.

Nevertheless, it was for Adlai Stevenson that she made the trip to Los
Angeles, and she invited David and me to accompany her. Because of
pressing gallery business, I very regretfully had to decline. On Monday,
July 11, Mrs. Roosevelt and David left for California. She stayed with her
old friend Mrs. Hershey Martin,* who lived an inconvenient distance
from the convention hall. David had the Beverly Hills house of a friend
who was vacationing in the south of France. He and Mrs. Roosevelt met
every morning. Watching her conduct political business fascinated David,
as usual. This time, the odds were against her, as she was backing a two-
time loser. David's notes say: "She went out to Los Angeles to fight for
Stevenson. In their important, combined press conference she spoke first,
and strongly for him, and then he got up and made a lukewarm, non-
committal speech. Not coming out [openly as a candidate], that's what
he wanted. He had probably figured out that his chances were small and
he was hoping that by not antagonizing whoever might be president—
Kennedy, for instance—he would be offered the cabinet post of secretary
of state."

David told me about Mrs. Roosevelt's first visit to the convention hall.
As they took their seats in the balcony, word quickly spread that Eleanor
Roosevelt had arrived. The entire hall rose, turned to face her, and wildly
roared their welcome. At first, Mrs. Roosevelt did not acknowledge the

---

*Mrs. Hershey Martin's given name was Myris; her nickname was "Tiny." She had
been a dancer, and Mrs. Roosevelt had known her for years.

exuberant reception, remaining seated, head down, fussing for something inside her large handbag. On watching the evening coverage on television, I saw David gently nudging her to rise, which she finally did, but reluctantly. "Why didn't you get up?" he later asked. She replied, "Didn't you see there was a speaker on the platform? To acknowledge the audience standing with their backs to him would have been rude to the speaker."

She unceasingly made the rounds of state caucuses, dinners, and meetings, but nothing could stop the surge for Kennedy. When he won victory on the first ballot, a heavyhearted Mrs. Roosevelt, with David at her heels, headed straight to the airport. She had expected to go home Friday but left a day early instead. As she waited for the announcement to board their plane, she received a message that Mr. Kennedy was on the telephone. She declined to take the call, but the senator persisted, and she relented.* Afterward, she told David, "He asked for my support. I told him, 'Mr. Kennedy, you have a son of mine on the East Coast, a son on the West Coast, and a third son, Elliott, working for you. You do not need me.'" But he did and he knew it. Her opinion carried such weight with voters nationwide that the young candidate, with a close race ahead against Vice President Richard Nixon, couldn't afford not to have her on his team. Although she had cautiously begun to like the things she was hearing about him, was warming to his speeches, and appreciated the courtesy he had always shown her, she did not succumb. It took a very unusual occurrence to bring them together.

One day, Maureen told me that she had received a telephone call from a gentleman from the Golden Ring Clubs (their members were senior citizens). He was planning a bus trip with his group to Hyde Park to visit the grave of President Roosevelt on the twenty-fifth anniversary of the Social Security Act. He needed help in making his arrangements. In the course of their conversation, he informed her that he had contacted

---

*In *Eleanor: The Years Alone* (New York: W. W. Norton, 1972), Joseph Lash writes that it was Abba Schwartz who informed the Kennedy people of Mrs. Roosevelt's hasty, moody departure (p. 296).

Senator Kennedy's office to invite him to be their speaker. Maureen asked him how many people would be coming. The proud answer was, "One busload." "*One busload!*" exclaimed Maureen. She suggested it was un-likely that a busy presidential candidate would make a special trip to address so few people. Because the man seemed so hopeful, she said no more.

Mr. Kennedy had been looking for an excuse to visit Hyde Park when this opportunity arose, but he couldn't accept the invitation unless he was certain he would be received by Mrs. Roosevelt. When she heard of the intended expedition of the Golden Ring Clubs, Mrs. Roosevelt, prag-matist that she was, invited Kennedy to lunch in Val-Kill before his talk at the grave site in the Rose Garden. It was exactly what he had been waiting for. By this time, she was on the verge of coming out for Kennedy anyway. The urgings of her own family and others whose opinion she respected—Arthur Schlesinger, Jr., Senator William Benton, Governor Herbert Lehman, all Kennedy supporters now—were compelling. Mrs. Roosevelt was not one to stay long on the fence. Two evenings earlier, she had reviewed the matter with David. As we were saying good night, David looked intently into her face and, shaking her lightly by the shoul-der, declared, "You *really* don't want Mr. Nixon, do you?" I think that was the final straw.

A few days later, Maureen stopped me. "Remember the story I told you the other day about the man who wanted John Kennedy to speak to a busload of people in Hyde Park? When members of his organization discovered that Senator Kennedy would be there, they signed up for the trip in droves. He called me recently to report how many buses they've had to add, and didn't fail to remind me that 'Mr. Kennedy *did* agree to come when there was only one bus.'"

As soon as the date of August 10 was fixed, Mrs. Roosevelt invited David and me to come to Val-Kill to meet Mr. Kennedy. Then, just the day before the scheduled meeting, she had tragic news. John and Anne's young daughter, Sara (Sally), in riding camp in Maine, had fallen from her horse and was admitted to a local hospital in a comatose state. She had suffered a fatal blow to her head and could not be saved. Her parents and grandmother immediately drove to the hospital, where Sally died that night. Mrs. Roosevelt stayed with her brokenhearted son and daughter-in-law until dawn, when she departed for Hyde Park. When he was informed of the accident, Mr. Kennedy offered to cancel their appointment. Mrs. Roosevelt told us afterward, however, that, knowing the infinite details involved in a major candidate's last-minute change of plans, she was prepared to proceed with their private meeting as agreed. But she was in no frame of mind to be seen in public. She asked David and me to meet Mr. Kennedy on her behalf at the Dutchess County Airport and accompany him to her cottage.

We set out in good time from Val-Kill in Mrs. Roosevelt's station wagon, with her driver at the wheel, and were astonished to find an overflow, flag-waving crowd from Poughkeepsie and neighboring (Republican) towns waiting at the airport when we arrived. David left the car to approach Mr. Kennedy's plane, while I stayed behind, as enthusiastic for the sight of the senator as all the others. Standing apart from the surge of people, also waiting, stood the author Gore Vidal, who had a house on the Hudson River and was running for Congress from the Twenty-ninth Congressional District. When his private plane landed, Mr. Kennedy stepped out, accompanied by his New York State campaign coordinator, William Walton, and his press secretary, Pierre Salinger. Resounding applause greeted him. He looked wonderful. Responding to the cheers of the crowd, he was helped up onto a high fuel barrel standing on the tarmac, where he gave a spontaneous, rousing short speech. Then after a quick pause to shake hands with Mr. Vidal, Messrs. Kennedy and Walton slipped into the backseat beside me. Pierre Salinger sat next to David in the front.

When Mr. Kennedy arrived on her doorstep, Mrs. Roosevelt was waiting. It was an auspicious moment. Mr. Kennedy expressed his sorrow for the death in the family and his appreciation that she was still willing to see him under the circumstances. We all went into the house. Mrs. Roosevelt introduced the houseman, Les Entrup, to Messrs. Kennedy, Walton, and Salinger as he passed drinks around. (David took a photograph of the presidential candidate with a martini in hand, possibly the first picture of its kind, he thought.) Mr. Kennedy was very nice indeed. A tall, graceful man, young, dashing, and intelligent, he was a most congenial guest. It was apparent that he was glad to be there, that he considered the occasion with Mrs. Roosevelt to be special. He smiled and laughed easily, but never with his eyes, which remained deadly serious, despite any lightness of conversation. After a while, Mrs. Roosevelt took him into a corner of the living room, where they lunched alone. David and I ate with Messrs. Walton and Salinger out on the summer porch, and while they spoke interestingly about the progress of the campaign, their main thoughts were with the two in the next room. We knew by now that Mrs. Roosevelt would endorse Mr. Kennedy, but how much she would work for his election depended on how she felt about him after this one-on-one meeting. She was interested to hear his replies to questions on topics that deeply concerned her. Both were tough negotiators who knew what they wanted. She thought that Mr. Kennedy was perhaps a bit too quick in his judgments, and that Adlai Stevenson was just the person to offer different, reflective views on matters requiring presidential consideration. She wanted some assurance that Stevenson, with his knowledge and integrity, would play a role in a new Democratic administration, though she was careful to stress that she believed a president should be free to choose his own people. Mr. Kennedy had already taken steps to work together with Stevenson in the course of the campaign. Future cooperation was promised.

Toward the end of Mrs. Roosevelt's lunch with Senator Kennedy, William Walton was called to join them to answer some questions. David was also invited, and he managed to photograph the group at the table. Soon after, the two politicians, old and young, emerged, beaming with satisfaction. We remained all together in Mrs. Roosevelt's study until it was time to leave for the Roosevelt grave site, where the Golden Ring Clubs members and others had already gathered. When we drove over from Val-Kill, I sat beside the senator in the front seat. He was intent upon his written text—which he would not read but would refer to when he spoke—making last-minute changes in it with a bright red ink marker, swiftly striking out this, adding that. Although it was a short ride, he twice combed his hair while editing the draft. Before we left the car, he turned to David in the backseat and asked, "What do you think I should tell the press about my meeting with Mrs. Roosevelt?" David took an unendurably long minute before answering. Mr. Kennedy was not at all impatient; he evidently appreciated a thoughtful reply. David said, "I would suggest that the statement about your meeting come from Mrs. Roosevelt." "Yes," Kennedy quickly agreed. David and I, along with Messrs. Walton and Salinger, stood together to listen to the speech, following which, Tubby drove the three gentlemen back to the airport. When David and I returned to Val-Kill Cottage, we gave Mrs. Roosevelt some details of Kennedy's address and how well it had been received. In the end, I mentioned to her that I found it curious that Mr. Kennedy was editing a speech he considered important and combing his hair at the same time. She thought he did it to avoid looking tousled; not wanting to present a boyish appearance before an audience, this one in particular. After a moment, she added softly, "I used to carry Franklin's comb for him."

After the meeting with Mr. Kennedy, Mrs. Roosevelt felt reassured, and she did join Governor Herbert Lehman, honorary chairman of the Democratic Citizens Committee of New York, to work to elect the top of the ticket. She wrote, "I told Senator Kennedy that I would discuss what help in the campaign I could give, for I have come to the conclusion that the people will have in John F. Kennedy, if he is elected, a good President."*

It had been an exciting day, and Mrs. Roosevelt had persevered despite her grief over her granddaughter Sally's death. Having had only about an hour or two of sleep the previous night, she was completely worn-out. She was very close to John and Anne's children. Often thereafter when she was in Val-Kill, Mrs. Roosevelt would slip away to the graveyard of St. James Church to linger at Sally's grave.

---

*"My Day," August 17, 1960.

Meanwhile, the uneasy drama concerning Mrs. Roosevelt's health quietly continued to unfold. David had increased cause for worry and had brought in Dr. George A. Hyman of Columbia-Presbyterian as the leading hematologist in Mrs. Roosevelt's case. Contrary to the different diagnoses suggested by other specialists, none certain, it was Dr. Hyman's belief that Mrs. Roosevelt's condition "could only be an aplastic anemia without developing into acute leukemia, though he felt this was a distinct possibility," as David's entry into her medical chart on August 15, 1960, reads. It continues:

> I have discussed this with Dr. James Halsted and his wife, Anna Roosevelt. It was agreed that no further consultations will take place, that she [Mrs. Roosevelt] will continue with her plans, including going to Europe in a few days. I have the names of hematologists in the major cities of Europe which she might touch upon, in case of an emergency.
>
> It was also agreed not to tell her sons any more than we are telling her, which is the Hyman version, that she is suffering from an anemia and a deficiency of the bone marrow to produce blood.

The doctors brought in to examine the patient and evaluate her laboratory tests agreed that no treatment was indicated at the time except for transfusions as necessary for the symptoms of anemia. Anna was regularly informed about her mother's condition, as was her husband, who was an internist.

David always wanted the family involved in a patient's medical treatment. In the case of Mrs. Roosevelt, it was also a form of self-protection, considering the complex, combative personalities of those in this particular family, which David knew so well. Anna, he was confident, would be a good conduit for furnishing information to her brothers, while David periodically kept Joe Lash advised about the case. As Joe was so close to Mrs. Roosevelt, David confided in him, expressing his own anxieties. With Mrs. Roosevelt's uncertain state of health, he was relieved to accept Jim Halsted, Anna's husband, as a medical spokesman for the family, and Jim seemed content with the role.

A week after Mr. Kennedy's visit, Mrs. Roosevelt wrote to Anna and Jim that David had just given her the report on her latest medical tests. She had told David to stop worrying, she said, and suggested that they both forget about her condition. She promised to take her pills and complained that the tests she was taking from time to time were "costing a fortune." Though she emphasized to Anna and Jim that she felt "quite well," she would continue the tests "just to satisfy David."*

To Poland Via Flims

David and I had planned a two-week Swiss vacation with Grania at the end of August, during which time Mrs. Roosevelt was to join us. We were going to spend most of the time at the Waldhaus in the town of Flims, a spacious hotel in a parklike setting in the Alps. Enticingly steep paths in the woods below the town lead to a beautiful cold lake. A large cagelike elevator in the forest brings walkers back and forth from the lake if the climb and descent prove too strenuous. Late afternoons at tea, David and I usually danced to the music of a good small orchestra, while Grania tried her hand at tennis. After some days of lovely idleness, a black car pulled up and deposited Mrs. Roosevelt at the Waldhaus entrance. When she checked in, it was clear from her grim expression she had not wanted to come to Flims. I was pretty sure that feeling the "odd fellow out" accounted for her reluctance. She had originally wanted to meet us later in Poland, where we were scheduled to attend conferences of the World Federation of United Nations Associations in Warsaw. But after the Democratic National Convention, the pain of Sally's death, and Mrs. Roosevelt's intensive campaigning for John Kennedy, David had insisted, "You need to stay quiet for a few days." He also wanted to keep his eye on her.

---

*Letter from Eleanor Roosevelt to Anna and Jim Halsted, August 17, 1960.

She soon warmed to our pleasure in seeing her, and, as usual, her company added to the enjoyment of our stay.

Mrs. Roosevelt declined to take the forest elevator in any direction on our daily walks. She hid it so well that I did not notice she had difficulty negotiating the paths, something I learned only later from David. Drawing on his experience from his former mountain-climbing days, he had long before shown her the technique of deep, slow, regular breathing when walking uphill (or upstairs), and the importance of keeping the rhythm of a deliberate, steady pace. One morning, we wrapped ourselves in heavy sweaters and took the funicular up the slope of a mountain. At the end of the line, David told us he'd continue to the top on foot, and Mrs. Roosevelt said she would go with him. Grania and I decided to wait for them in a café perched on a stone terrace overlooking a lovely view, which we thought far more inviting than the heap of rubble toward which the two were heading. We were soon rejoined by Mrs. Roosevelt, who confessed, "I thought I'd turn back and keep you company." Everyone noticed when she came in, and several approached our table to shake her hand. But nobody expressed surprise at seeing Eleanor Roosevelt, at seventy-six, in a little café high on an obscure Swiss mountain.

On September 5, rested and refreshed, we took a Polish plane for Warsaw. During the flight, the plane went into a sudden nosedive. I sucked in my breath and, panicked, turned to Mrs. Roosevelt, who was sitting beside me. Before I could utter a word, she calmly asked, without taking her eyes from the spread newspaper she was reading, "Anything the matter, dear?" In the face of such composure, what else could I answer but a choked "No." David looked pale and reached over to me. After a few minutes, which seemed an eternity, the plane righted itself. We made ready to land in a country new to us.

A woman Mrs. Roosevelt had known in the United Nations had been assigned as her escort by the Foreign Service Ministry of the Polish government. A Communist, of course, she had somehow survived Warsaw during the German occupation by moving through the city via its sewers and living in a complex pattern of hideouts. She took us around Warsaw on our first morning in a car provided by the government. She explained how the city had been rebuilt after being razed by the Germans. When we started out that day, David had asked that we be taken to the site of the Warsaw Jewish Ghetto, which had been destroyed after its entire Jewish population had been starved and slaughtered by the Nazis, with the cooperation of Poles. But our guide was not inclined to interrupt her tour to take us there. As we continued on the prescribed route, David lost his patience and demanded that the car be stopped so that we could go on our own. Only then did she accommodate us. There, in the Warsaw Ghetto, where a vibrant community had once lived and perished, was an immense stone monument in its memory. I can still hear the crunch of our footsteps on the gravel path leading to the towering sculpture. The sight of Mrs. Roosevelt slowly walking up that path touched me deeply — she, who represented the best a human being could be, treading the same ground as those who were most inhumane.

We were the sole visitors. Nothing separated the monument from the surrounding large housing development. Mrs. Roosevelt's first thought was that the children playing on the site trivialized it, and that there should be trees secluding the memorial to emphasize its significance. She determined to draw people's attention to this cause through her newspaper column when she returned home.

The city was impoverished at the time. There was a scarcity of food in the shops we visited, the produce available was of inferior quality, and people queued up for desirable goods. Nonetheless, evenings were gay in Warsaw, unlike those in Moscow. Somehow able to ignore their poverty, people filled the many cafés around the city, enjoying music, dancing, and drinking — they ordered bottles of beer and wine with cheerful abandon. Kraków was different, more authentic, some of its medieval quality having survived. Mrs. Roosevelt, David, Grania, and I flew there in a government jet, comfortable in its handsomely appointed salon. Much of Kraków's population worked in steel plants on the city's outskirts and lived in dreary newly built workers' housing in the city itself. Our government escorts showed us this with great pride, briskly knocking on apartment doors at random to show us how well the people lived. We stopped the intrusive procedure as soon as we could.

Before mounting the high stone staircase of an ancient castle we were to see, David quietly asked that we ascend slowly, for Mrs. Roosevelt looked weary. As our party began the climb, Mrs. Roosevelt suspiciously questioned why our pace was so slow. The guide unfortunately replied, "Your doctor requested it." Plainly annoyed, and in revolt against the attempt to regulate her, she rushed ahead while the rest of us panted up the stairs behind her. On the flight back to Warsaw, she told David never to interfere like that again.

Poland, for us, was far from an inspiring place. (Even the few good contemporary Polish artists had fled to live in Paris.) In fact, we regarded the WFUNA delegates from the Soviet Union somewhat wistfully, recalling the fascinating time we'd had in that vast and varied part of the world. We took our usual route home, via Paris.

David was constantly vigilant about Mrs. Roosevelt's health. When our trip to Poland ended, he wrote to Anna and her husband:

DR. AND MRS. JAMES HALSTED,
UNIVERSITY OF KENTUCKY MEDICAL CENTER
LEXINGTON, KY.
September 19th, 1960
Dear Anna and Jim:

I thought you would like to have a medical report.

Subjectively the trip went well. On arrival in Switzerland walking any distance proved quite difficult. She became short of breath after 50 yards of walking on the slightest incline. Gradually, however, this improved, and toward the end it had improved quite considerably. On the last day there we walked uphill slowly but steadily for close to an hour without undue shortness of breath. She, of course, registered both the disability and the improvement, and was happy about the change. There were no other symptoms except for a slight swelling of both ankles, the right more than the left, and this still persists.

On our return I persuaded her to have a blood count. . . . Her schedule for the next six weeks seems to be quite strenuous again, but then she will do no travelling after the beginning of November. Her morale is good and as far as she is concerned she is healthy and wants "nothing to do with doctors or tests." I am in continuous touch with both Dr. Vogel [Dr. Peter Vogel, hematologist, Mount Sinai Hospital, New York], and Dr. George Hyman but she has seen neither of them.

Affectionately,
David

Anna was glad to have this report. In her reply of September 26, 1960, she thanked David for it, and wrote that she was pleased to hear her mother's morale was good. Anna informed David that as her mother had not mentioned her health at all, neither had she. Instead, Mrs. Roosevelt had told her about her concern for David. "She is still worried about you," Anna's letter continued, "and didn't feel you had completely lost the 'bug' you had when you left New York. . . ." Unusual patient, indeed. David's medical notes into Mrs. Roosevelt's chart read:

October 10th, 1960
. . . In addition to Dr. and Mrs. Halsted, James Roosevelt was also told by me exactly what the medical situation is.

She has developed some ankle edema. I have discussed this with Dr. George Hyman and with Dr. Peter Vogel, and both agreed that 500 mgs. of Diuril for ten days could be given. This was done with the result that the edema diminished considerably, though it did not quite disappear. She is also on a low salt diet and sleeps with foot of bed elevated. Otherwise she lives an entirely normal life, and at present does not seem overly concerned about her health.

A Close Call

Before the first Nixon-Kennedy debate, televised on Monday, September 26, Mrs. Roosevelt had had a very busy day.

After working through lunch, she was called on at four o'clock by Prince Aly Khan; at four thirty, she received Ambassador Mates; and at five o'clock, an architect named Myller. By evening, she was ready for the debate. It was to follow her dinner party, to which she had invited Senator and Mrs. William Benton; the French statesman Jules Moch and his wife; her Arkansas friend Ray West; Anna Rosenberg; Abris Silberman; Joe and Trude Lash; and David and me to watch the much-publicized and all-important political event together. During dinner, we pretended to be calm, but we weren't. Everyone knew that a good deal was riding on the result of this first debate between the presidential nominees, no one more conscious of the fact than our knowing hostess. We finally moved into the living room, darkened it, and turned on the television set in time for the contest to start. It was soon apparent, at least to us partisans, that Mr. Kennedy was in far more control of his facts and himself than his opponent was, and that the impression he made of maturity and vigor gave him a presidential presence, a quality Mrs. Roosevelt had been worried he might lack. We were convinced the election tide had turned in favor of Mr. Kennedy. When the lights went on again in Mrs. Roosevelt's living room, I could see by her flushed face that she was quite excited. Wearing a long dress, she moved about the room with a jaunty step. Though she tried to make her voice sound casual as she asked each of us for our opinion of which candidate had been stronger, it was clear she had no doubt that Mr. Kennedy had won the debate. She perceived a Democratic victory at last and felt proud. Each of us confirmed Mrs. Roosevelt's opinion, which she was last to give. Even Monsieur Moch, the guest from France, who declared he'd not before seen Mr. Kennedy in action, was more impressed by him than by Mr. Nixon, whom he knew. The lone opposition voice was that of fellow Democrat Bill Benton, who surprised us by insisting that Vice President

Nixon had prevailed. A spirited argument ensued, in which Mrs. Roosevelt did not participate.

On October 31, David wrote James Halsted:

> Dear Jim:
>
> Our patient has had the symptoms of an infection without, however, any localizing symptoms. For over ten days she was having chills, feeling cold at night, with bouts of perspiration at night. All of this has now improved, though it has not completely disappeared. We did another blood count on October 26th. It was done by George Hyman and here are the figures: . . .
>
> He is not ready to take back his initial diagnosis, but so far so good. To me it is very encouraging that her hemoglobin has gone up. . . .
>
> She is over-doing these days by any standard, and is very tired in the evening, having at times really to drag herself. I imagine until Election day this will have to continue.

Although Mrs. Roosevelt never complained or gave any indication to me or to others that anything was amiss, David's anxiety made it clear that she was in trouble.

On November 8, election night, people started to gather early in Mrs. Roosevelt's apartment for the results. Many who came had worked hard in the Kennedy campaign; some were major contributors to it. All were loyal Democrats eager for a new administration in Washington. The buffet was frequently replenished; drinks were served and champagne passed. The front door of our house as well as Mrs. Roosevelt's apartment door had been left open, and more and more friends poured into the living room after the New York polls closed. Voices and laughter rose. Victory was in the air. All of us felt sure of it—except our hostess, the only one among the happy throng who remained somber and anxious. Serious business was at hand and she was totally focused upon it. As the first returns came in, she took her seat at the end of the long red couch closest to the television screen. She wanted to be sure she could hear everything. Early announcements showed Mr. Kennedy in the lead. Elation in the room escalated as continuing good numbers were reported from the cities and towns where polling booths had closed. Mrs. Roosevelt's manner remained remote, different from ours, and it was clear to me that she knew something we did not.

I took my place beside her on the red couch to learn something. Watching election returns with Eleanor Roosevelt was a rare experience. Each time encouraging news flashed on the screen, everyone clapped and commented, but not Mrs. Roosevelt. She sat immobile, eyes never leaving the screen. When various people approached her to share their buoyed-up spirits, her response was reserved. "It is still too early to know anything," she repeated. Noting the various voting districts in the country where numbers were high for Mr. Kennedy, she said firmly, "We *expect* good results from those districts. We must wait for news from rural areas, from the South, Midwest, et cetera." She went on to name the crucial cities and towns that were borderline for Democrats in general and indecisive about Mr. Kennedy in particular. *They* were the ones that counted in this tight election. Mrs. Roosevelt understood the significance of the vote in every area that was reported on television that night. She knew her country and its politics by heart. Here was someone who had traveled the length and breadth of the United States steadily for most of her life, attuned to the nature of its people in all walks of life, someone thoroughly familiar with their political leanings and experienced enough to be aware of the behind-the-scenes political maneuverings up to the very end.

Sitting with her that night, I was reminded of an evening on which David and I had dinner with Mrs. Roosevelt and Mr. Stevenson — just the four of us downstairs. The governor had begun the conversation by saying in a light but condescending way that he had been asked to speak in a small upstate New York community. Smiling, he named the town and asked Mrs. Roosevelt if she'd ever heard of the place. She replied at once.

Not only had she heard of it and had visited it several times, but she advised him, "If you didn't drive, the only way to get there was by bus, but now, I understand, a small airport has been built on its outskirts." Mr. Stevenson, chagrined, changed the subject.

There was no point to our lingering on election night. When David and I went upstairs at midnight, we were utterly certain, as most others were, that Senator Kennedy was a sure winner. Mrs. Roosevelt, still not convinced, remained at her post on the couch, concentrated on the television screen, wary of declaring triumph. It turned out she'd been right to have misgivings. We learned the following morning that at 1:00 A.M. the tide had turned for a while in favor of Vice President Nixon. It was near dawn when the exciting news broke that the senator had managed to squeak through to victory. It had been a close call.

Before going to sleep the night before, perhaps thinking of how effective Senator Kennedy had been on television, David said to me, "I wouldn't be a bit surprised if one day we had an *actor* for president." "What an imagination you have," I replied.

The plane bearing Mrs. Roosevelt, Maureen, Joe and Trude Lash, and David and me to Washington for the inauguration of John F. Kennedy was the last one permitted to land on the icy runway. There had never before been such a snowstorm in the District of Columbia and the city was ill-prepared to handle it. As we were waiting for our baggage inside the terminal, four sprightly uniformed naval officers, two males and two females, suddenly appeared before us, each with a dark blue blanket precisely folded across an arm. With a snappy salute to Mrs. Roosevelt, they announced they'd been assigned to be her escort for the duration of the inauguration. She stiffened. The last thing she wanted was an official escort. Our baggage had not yet rolled into sight on the carousel. Mrs. Roosevelt explained she preferred being unattended, warmly thanked them, and, saying, "Follow me," swiftly marched them to an airport exit. She returned moments later alone with the four blankets, which she distributed to us, keeping one for herself. "These will be useful when we sit in the cold for the ceremony tomorrow," she advised in her practical way. (She'd had experience with an earlier snow-covered inauguration—FDR's in January 1945.) Her car dropped us off in different places. Maureen, David, and I were guests of Abba Schwartz at his house in Georgetown. I don't remember where the Lashes were spending the three days of inaugural activities, or where Mrs. Roosevelt was lodged. She often went to Agnes Meyer. She might have stayed with Franklin, who lived in Washington. Anna, Jimmy, and Elliott were also attending the inauguration, and the convergence of all her children (except John) made her tense.

We were to gather at a reception that evening in the large house rented by United Artists executives Robert Benjamin and Arthur Krim to entertain fellow Democrats on this great occasion. The snow continued to fall heavily, and in Georgetown, at least, there was not one snowplow visible. Dressed in our finery, wearing whatever boots we could unearth in our host's closets, we entered the car we had hired to drive us to the Benjamin-Krim party. It ground its way through the drifts and stalled about a mile from the house. We were stranded, but the chauffeur showed us the direction in which to walk and reassuringly told us he would get snow tires and return for us in two hours. David was the only one who believed him. Out on the road, I clutched my coat close and bent my head against the driving wind. David supported me firmly, both of us sharply aware that I was three months pregnant. At last we saw the welcome lights of the house. Not all the invited guests made it through the storm. Mrs. Roosevelt came, brought by Joe and Trude. It was rumored that the president-elect would drop in, but that seemed unlikely.

Little by little as the party ended, those headed for the pre-inaugural gala began to gather their coats and their courage to depart. All realized that it would take skill and time, not to mention luck, to drive through the snow to the auditorium for the entertainment. Mrs. Roosevelt wanted to start out early. She didn't mention that she was scheduled to appear on the program. After unsuccessfully urging David and me to join them, she left with Joe and Trude. David would not abandon the chauffeur, who had promised to return for us, though prospects of ever seeing him again were growing bleak. When there were just an uneasy few left in the house, a voice called out, "There is a driver on the phone who says to tell Dr. Gurewitsch that he will be here in ten minutes." The estimable man appeared, proud of his snow tires. We loaded the car with people, and David, sitting beside the driver as lookout, directed him by circuitous routes to the auditorium. On the way, we passed a large number of stranded vehicles darkly silhouetted against the still heavily falling snow. Scattered here and there were a few snowplows at work, and corps of yellow-suited figures attempting to dig footpaths in preparation for the next day's event. It was almost midnight when David and I entered the auditorium. Five minutes after, to resounding applause from a standing audience, the president-elect and his attractive family appeared in a box close to us. (They'd apparently also had difficulty in getting there. The program had been scheduled for nine o'clock.) It was a great show. Frank Sinatra's songs were wonderful and Gene Kelly danced an Irish jig as only he could. We became worried about Mrs. Roosevelt when we saw her name on the program and she failed to appear. The following morning, we learned that she and her party had been stalled on the road and were not rescued until 3:00 A.M. It had been a harrowing experience.

January 20, Inauguration Day, dawned sunny and icy cold. It had stopped snowing. We set out in the arctic weather in Mrs. Roosevelt's car, with its number printed boldly on a card on the windshield—a number that took us close to the front of the long line of automobiles waiting to deposit people assigned to seats on the benches below the Capitol. It was a relief that Mrs. Roosevelt had come through the hours of being stranded in the snow perfectly well.

Thanks to her, we had a very clear view of the ceremonial platform. It was noontime when the Kennedy family, their guests, and wives of the principals—Mmes. Eisenhower, Nixon, Johnson, and, of course, Jacqueline Kennedy—appeared. Joseph Kennedy was noticeably proud that morning—so jaunty and erect. But it was young Mrs. Kennedy on whom all admiring eyes focused. "Hail to the Chief" was played by the Marine Band when outgoing President Eisenhower made his appearance with

Vice President Nixon. (I remember thinking to myself at the time that we would not be seeing Mr. Nixon again.) Following a recitation by Robert Frost of his poem "The Gift Outright," Chief Justice Earl Warren administered the oath of office to the new president, who was impressive in his cutaway coat and silk top hat. His fine, memorable inaugural address closed the ceremony.

All the while, some members of the audience, inadequately dressed for arctic Washington, were passing out from the cold and required attention from ambulances stationed nearby. We ourselves were very grateful for the U.S. Navy blankets under which we huddled. Mr. Kennedy had invited Mrs. Roosevelt to be one of his special guests on the presidential platform, but she declined, preferring to stay in the crowd below. She had been on that platform often enough in the past. While she honored the occasion, she did not care to participate in it. Instead, she sat quietly with us (her children seated elsewhere). I think she was not inclined to intrude on a Kennedy occasion, nor to be regarded as a symbol of the past. My feeling was confirmed later when she accompanied us, out of kindness, to watch the inaugural parade on its route to the White House. The jubilant crowd ignored the twenty-degree temperature to honor its new president, who was standing in the flag-draped reviewing stand. In the parade beneath him rolled the black sedans carrying U.S. governors and other dignitaries, many from past administrations, including former First Ladies. Mrs. Roosevelt remained impassive as old Mrs. Woodrow Wilson's car passed by. If ever there was a symbol of yesterday, it was the procession of the once-powerful, of which Mrs. Roosevelt would never be a willing part. No one lived in the present more vibrantly than she. We stayed only briefly. And then there was the tension at lunch.

Our large party in the National Democratic Club dining room consisted of Mrs. Roosevelt, her sons and their wives, Anna and her husband, Joe and Trude Lash, Maureen Corr, Abba Schwartz, and David and me. Some family incident must have arisen earlier, which caused Mrs. Roosevelt to take her seat at the table angrily, for she whispered audibly to David, not caring if she was overheard, "I *won't* be seated next to Jim

[Halsted, Anna's husband]!" And, shrinking as if to rid herself of any thought of him, she added, "I don't want him ever to touch me!" Jim Halsted didn't seem to react to his mother-in-law's hostility—I don't think he was listening. If she told David why she was furious, he never mentioned it to me. The atmosphere at lunch was both jocular and strained. I remember that Trude tried her best to engage Franklin's attention, but his thoughts were elsewhere.

We didn't see Mrs. Roosevelt again until evening. Abba was giving a reception in his house before the inaugural galas. Mrs. Roosevelt had promised to come, and Abba felt sure that Dean Rusk, secretary of state designate, would also attend. True to her word, Mrs. Roosevelt did drop in, but she left as soon as she could get away. Dean Rusk never did make an appearance. By nightfall, when the various balls were due to begin and to be visited by President and Mrs. Kennedy, snow-removal crews, working all day, had made roads more accessible. Red carpets had been laid toward entrance doors. David and I left for one of the formal parties by ourselves. Once inside, we saw we were among the fortunate few with tickets for chairs. It was a treat to sit down. The pressing crowd made movement, including dancing, cramped, and the din drowned out conversation. Finally, the band's "Hail to the Chief" announced the arrival of the handsome presidential couple, who circled the room, greeting people. They waved and smiled, then were off to the six or so other balls at which they were expected. We headed back to Georgetown.

We had not seen much of Mrs. Roosevelt during our stay in Washington. Before leaving New York, the three of us had made plans to fly to Tucson, Arizona, for a short winter break after the inauguration. We were going to stay at the Arizona Inn, which was owned by the son of a friend Mrs. Roosevelt had known from her debutante days, Isabella Greenway. Mrs. Roosevelt seemed especially eager to be on her way when Franklin brought her to meet David and me at the airport, where we'd been given a small private waiting room. She was visibly impatient, perhaps due to accumulated irritations from all inaugural goings-on. We were glad when our flight was called.

The Arizona Inn was calmly beautiful in its desert setting. The second day we were there, President Kennedy was to give his first presidential press conference, which was to be televised live, and we were eager to see it. Certain that the program would attract a good number of hotel patrons, we seated ourselves early in the downstairs ballroom, which housed the large TV set. But we needn't have bothered being prompt. No one else came. We were impressed by President Kennedy's deft handling of the press and his knowledgeable replies, though we were disappointed that nobody in the hotel thought the event worth watching.

One afternoon, we played croquet. I'd never played before; David had, but rarely. It took only a few minutes before we saw that Mrs. Roosevelt was an expert. Her skill and strategy were dazzling and she won straight away. Now she was in a quandary. Her natural impulse was to give winning hints to the underdog—me. On the other hand, she did not want David to come in last. It amused me to watch her struggle to remain neutral.

In Tucson, we took lovely drives in the desert, visited nature centers where Mrs. Roosevelt had friends on the staff, and David and I spent several evenings by ourselves in town. One day, Mrs. Roosevelt accepted an invitation for us to visit John Greenway in his wonderful house, within walking distance of his inn. He was a young man, probably in his late thirties, extremely nice and very glad to see his late mother's dear friend. During the visit, Mrs. Roosevelt told me that Isabella Greenway's first husband, Robert Ferguson, had once proposed marriage to her. It was during her early debutante days, before Franklin courted her and just after her return to New York from her English school. When Ferguson married our host's mother, Isabella Selmes, they moved to Arizona for reasons of his health, and after he died, Isabella married John Greenway. It took me awhile to absorb the news that Mrs. Roosevelt had had a proposal prior to that of Franklin Roosevelt. "Why, if you had married Robert Ferguson, you wouldn't be Mrs. Roosevelt!" I remarked, only half in jest.

The White House Revisited

Back in New York, our daily lives resumed. One afternoon, I received a call from Mrs. Roosevelt, which opened with one of her favorite greetings: "Hello, dear. I'm back." I knew she had gone to Washington for her first consultation with Mr. Kennedy since he'd become president. She had asked for time to discuss the Commission on the Status of Women. "The president was waiting for me at the door of the White House," she began. "He stepped aside for me to enter. 'Oh no, Mr. President,' I told him. 'Don't you know that no one precedes the president of the United States?' He then walked in ahead of me, but I could see it made him uncomfortable."

She had had a good discussion with him, she declared, and then rose to leave. " 'What's your hurry?' he asked. 'Stay awhile.' I reminded him that I had asked for ten minutes of his time and my ten minutes were up. I suggested that now that he was president, he must remember to conserve his time, and I left!" It was obvious from the lilt in her voice that the visit had pleased her.

David entered these notes in her medical chart on February 27, 1961:

> Mrs. Roosevelt was persuaded with the help of her daughter, Anna, and Dr. James Halsted, to have another bone marrow puncture and another blood count. Clinically, she looked considerably improved compared with her status during the winter. There was no ankle edema. Her heart-sounds were regular. There were no skipped beats and her shortness of breath has improved considerably. She has been working quite hard as usual, though about 3 to 4 days in the week she has taken an hour's rest.
>
> Blood count showed essentially unchanged findings against the one taken in the autumn. . . . There was however, a marked change in her bone marrow. . . . Sedimentation rate was still high. . . .

Other tests made throughout the spring did not substantially clarify Mrs. Roosevelt's medical situation.

The next occasion on which Mrs. Roosevelt saw President Kennedy was at a large party given for him at the Waldorf-Astoria Hotel in New York. We hurriedly drove back to the city on Sunday after the Memorial Day ceremony in Hyde Park, with barely enough time to change our clothes and taxi to Fiftieth Street and Park Avenue. A press corps photographic session with the president had been scheduled to precede the dinner, and David wanted to take his camera along. Mrs. Roosevelt advised against it because security would be tight in the hotel and David had not been cleared to bring in equipment. David persisted: "If I am with you, no one will stop me." But Mrs. Roosevelt took all rules very seriously—most of the time. "No," she insisted. "They won't allow you in." He replied, "If you carry my lens they will." She relented, and so we set out for the hotel with David's Nikon. Dangling from Mrs. Roosevelt's white-gloved wrist hung the strings of a buff-colored suede sack holding a camera lens; my wrist was similarly adorned.

Down on the sidewalk, Mrs. Roosevelt gasped. "I forgot my invitation!" and she started back. David stopped her. "Your *face* is your invitation," he insisted. She would not accept such an assumption. I retrieved the invitation from a cubicle in her desk and we were finally off. We easily passed the scrutiny of the security detail, not a glance given to Mrs. Roosevelt's proffered invitation, everyone greeting her by name as she entered. There was a lot of milling around while the president had his picture taken by a barrage of photographers. I heard him say to David, who was clicking away among them, "Doctor, what are you doing *there*?" It made me realize he had a remarkable memory. He then asked David, "Where is your wife?" Arthur Goldberg, secretary of labor, took me over to the president. It had been almost a year since his Hyde Park visit. My dress certainly did not conceal the bulk of my ninth month of pregnancy. The president, surprised, took a quick step backward as we shook hands. Courteously, he turned to David and said, "She looks, er, uh, nice in the, uh, face."

New Life

Six months earlier, when we had told Mrs. Roosevelt that we were expecting a baby, her first reaction was to embrace us lovingly. On December 26, 1960, Mrs. Roosevelt had written David from Val-Kill Cottage:

Monday night
David dearest,

All is quiet, and the house is empty. I'd like it even better if you and Edna were here. I love you both very dearly and I hope the new baby whom we are all going to love so much is just like you, with a few little touches of Edna to add to his or her perfection.

Thank you a thousand times for all the lovely [Christmas] presents but above all for your thought and closeness. It is good to know you are near and even a glimpse or the sound of your voice starts my day better. I don't mean to be selfish but I am afraid I am for when I have free time I always want to spend some of it with you.

Bless you for all you are and do, and God be good to you and all your loved ones is my daily prayer.

All my love,
E. R.

And to me, she'd written:

Monday night, Dec. 26th, 1960
Edna dearest,

I am waiting for your call and Lester and Marge have gone to bed. Becky and Hick were taken home about 9 and I have been reading and thinking of you and David.* You mean everything to

---

*Marge and Lester Entrup were the couple who took care of Mrs. Roosevelt's cottage. Becky was the housemaid, and "Hick" was Lorena Hickok, Mrs. Roosevelt's friend.

me, so much devotion and love and a sense of closeness. I love you so much! I love all my presents from you both because they come from you and I enjoy them and because you in yourselves are a great gift. I love Xmas because it is an excuse for giving but even more because the story of Christ is one of love. Every new baby is a little gift from God and I hope we will have many Xmas days together *with* a child to add to the joy.

My love to you and thanks.

E. R.

Maria Anna Gurewitsch, named for David's late mother and Mrs. Roosevelt, was born June 27, 1961, in Babies' Hospital, Columbia-Presbyterian Medical Center. I worked until one week before her birth and then stayed at home to raise her. Shortly before the event, Mrs. Roosevelt came upstairs to give me some of her own things to wear when the baby was born. What an idea, I thought when she offered them. Mrs. Roosevelt weighed about fifty pounds more than I, and even stooped, she was a head taller.

Handing the tissue-wrapped articles to me, she said, "These were mine when I had my first child. You will only need to hem them," and with those words, she went downstairs. I spread the items out on the bed. Included was a penciled note from Mrs. Roosevelt (which I dated "June 12, 1961"):

Edna dear,

Could you use these in bed after the baby comes? The night-gowns *wld* have to be shortened.

They were mine years ago but are now much too small and they are pretty I think. Love

E. R.

There were two beautiful pale pink silk and lace nightgowns and two bed jackets, light blue satin and pink. The short bed jackets were perfect. To my surprise, Mrs. Roosevelt had been right about the gowns. If I had hemmed them, they would also have fit me. But since the initials E. R. had been sewn onto an inner label, I did not want to alter them. It was from those nightgowns of Mrs. Roosevelt that I saw her figure as a young woman—tall, willowy, slender—and remembering that she'd once had fine, light hair, that her skin was still beautifully pale, and her blue eyes still bright, I had a clear vision of the fine-looking girl she had been.

David's colleagues made an exception in his case and allowed him to stay with me in the delivery room. (In 1961, the presence on the scene of prospective fathers was not generally welcome.) His face was as white as his doctor's coat. Worrier that he was, I knew that he'd had in mind his experience of treating babies with neurological birth defects. I watched him as he carefully examined Maria almost immediately after she was born, looking intensely into her pink face, testing her reflexes, stretching out each of her little arms and legs, and I saw his sudden relief when all was well. Filled with happiness, he kissed my hand. Moments later, he produced for me a copy of the *New York Times*. I can't think why.

My mother and father were thrilled with their first grandchild. By this time, David had won their hearts, and he, simply speaking, liked having parents-in-law and enjoyed feeling very much married. The new baby was surrounded by a good deal of love.

Mrs. Roosevelt visited the hospital almost every day of the ten days of the then-customary maternity stay. In her practical way, she sent me a large plant instead of flowers—something I could take home, she said. Each day, she asked what she could do for me, and I was hard-pressed to find answers. The only items my mother and I had forgotten were an infant comb and brush, and as Maria had arrived with a substantial quantity of hair, I was glad to have something to request. All that winter, Mrs. Roosevelt had been knitting a baby blanket for Maria—it is white, edged with pink and blue stripes. Earlier, she had given me a light sweater and cap with satin bow in which to take the baby home, as well as two carriage pillows in a gift box from Best & Company and two little smocked silk dresses from Liberty of London.

Throughout 1961, Mrs. Roosevelt was active on behalf of the Veterans of Foreign Wars, the NAACP, the March of Dimes,* the Cancer Foundation, United Jewish Appeal, Americans for Democratic Action, the AAUN, the Citizens' Committee for Children, and other organizations. She had many speaking engagements and a full social calendar, and yet she found time to visit her old friend Esther Lape. In a spring visit to Washington, Mrs. Roosevelt discussed with Secretary of Health, Education and Welfare Abraham Ribicoff her concept of a domestic Peace Corps. Altogether, she continued to be deeply involved in current affairs.

I believe it was around this time that Mrs. Roosevelt showed me a letter she had recently received from Jacqueline Kennedy, whose small handwriting covered the front and back of many pages. Mrs. Roosevelt explained that earlier the president had requested through Franklin that Mrs. Roosevelt write Jackie, who was planning a future trip to South America, to suggest that she include on her itinerary visits to public-service facilities such as hospitals or schools and not limit her appearance to social events. While the two ladies did not have any relationship to speak of, Mrs. Roosevelt told me she had agreed, feeling that her understanding of Mrs. Kennedy's demanding new position as well as the challenges she would face raising children in the glare of the White House might be of help. She had written Jacqueline accordingly and had offered some advice. She gave me sections of Mrs. Kennedy's reply to read, which confided her concerns about the care and education of her children, and her thanks for the counsel of someone so experienced. She also agreed to visit some institutions on her trip where her presence might serve to attract attention beneficial to their programs.

---

*An organization begun by FDR's former law partner, Basil O'Connor, to fund research for a vaccine to eradicate infantile paralysis.

David and I stayed close to home that summer, adjusting to our infant daughter, though we took Maria to Val-Kill for two or three long weekends, where she was pronounced a satisfactory guest. Mrs. Roosevelt spent most of July and August working for the reelection of Robert Wagner, mayor of New York City. She invited me to be present when he and his associates came to Seventy-fourth Street to ask her to support his campaign. I remember how deftly yet charmingly she challenged him about certain of his positions. (Mrs. Roosevelt used to say, "Never antagonize anyone from whom you may someday want something.") Now when she entertained in the city, she told guests whom she thought would be interested that David and I had had a baby, and several of them trotted upstairs to see the sleeping Maria. She had given us a present of an intercom system so we could dine with her and still hear the baby's sounds upstairs. But I was not comfortable with this long-distance surveillance, and on the evenings we were alone with Mrs. Roosevelt, David and I appeared with the child asleep in her cradle. Mrs. Roosevelt liked the idea of having a baby around.

At summer's end, Mrs. Roosevelt had a disturbing medical episode, which David recorded as follows:

NOTE ABOUT ILLNESS FROM SEPT. 3RD TO SEPT. 8TH, 1961
On Sunday, September 3d, while staying with Mrs. Roosevelt for the weekend, Marge Entrup called me into a corner after breakfast, apologising that it was really none of her business, but saying that I ought to know that Mrs. Roosevelt must have bled quite badly during the night. She found blood on her bed sheet and nightgown. . . .

Mrs. Roosevelt had said nothing during or after breakfast. This was not new. My information frequently came indirectly. Maureen Corr, or the people who worked in the house, or one of her children would report certain observations which I then would follow up. While Mrs. Roosevelt would not easily volunteer her complaints, once I would ask her directly, she would answer without hesitation, quickly and straightforwardly. So it was this time. It turned out that this blood was a first appearance. . . . In the afternoon she reported that there had been some slight additional bleeding. I called Dr. Stanley Bysshe [gynecologist at Presbyterian Hospital] and he had counseled that [if] no excessive additional bleeding occurred it was alright to wait until Monday morning for a gynecological examination, and we made the appointment. It was my feeling that the bleeding was due to her hematological problems. Her platelets were low and there was a bleeding tendency. But at her age a cancer could not be excluded as a possibility. Mrs. Roosevelt, I am convinced, was aware then of the implications of such a sudden hemorrhage. If, however, she was, she did not show it. She did not ask any questions in this direction and in the trip into town she behaved no differently than usual. . . .

According to David's report, while Mrs. Roosevelt was dressing following the examination, the gynecologist explained to him that there was a possibility it might be cancer of the endometrium. As he did not want to take any chances, he felt that she should be admitted for a D & C and that a biopsy be done and then a decision made according to what the biopsy revealed. When Mrs. Roosevelt left the examining room, the situation was explained to her. She was told that further steps could be determined only following examination of the tissue. David recorded:

She asked no questions, asked for her admission to be delayed until the next day. In view of the fact that the hemorrhage had virtually stopped, it seemed that waiting another day would not aggravate the situation. A good many physicians, each specializing in a separate area, were mobilized for this emergency. Dr. George Hyman, the hematologist, brought in Dr. George Perera, the internist, and

it was decided that she should be given at least 1000 cc of blood
to raise the hemoglobin in case of a major operation. Dr. James
[A.] Corscaden, the gynecologist who knew most about radium
therapy at the Medical Center,* was brought in just in case this
was the course which would be decided upon. Dr. Maurice Lenz,
the head of x-ray therapy at the Medical Center was also consulted
and volunteered to be present at the operation. Dr. [Arthur] Purdy
Stout, the chief of surgical pathology [Delafield Cancer Hospital],
would perform the examination of the frozen section in the oper-
ating room. The chief of anaesthesiology, Dr. [Emmanuel M.] Pap-
per, would perform the anaesthesia. Dr. Stanley Bysshe would
operate and I, of course, was also present. Mrs. Roosevelt had consented to this admission with the explanation to the press that she
was entering the hospital for a routine checkup. It had also been
decided to use the anaesthesia for Dr. Hyman to perform a bone
marrow aspiriation. . . . There was considerable tension in the op-
erating room at the beginning of this operation. Within a very short
time, however, the biopsy was read by Dr. Sprout as showing nothing but hyperplasia of the endometrium, no cancer present. All this
accumulation of talent, all this tension for nothing! The reaction
was strangely a mixture of relief and disappointment! . . . But of
course the main response was of relief. . . . At the suggestion of Dr.
Peter Vogel, hematologist from Mount Sinai Hospital who had
examined the very first bone marrow slides taken, Mrs. Roosevelt
had been put on small doses of Ovarian hormone, Premarin, for
the last 2-1/2 months. . . . It was concluded . . . that this hormone
therapy was the most likely cause of her endometrial hyperplasia
and subsequent hemorrhage.

She was discharged from the Harkness Pavilion on the third day
after her admission, entirely justifying the pre-admission statement

---

*In past years, Columbia-Presbyterian Medical Center was referred to as "the Medical
Center."

that she had entered the hospital only for a checkup. . . . Premarin therapy was discontinued. . . .

On the way home from the hospital Mrs. Roosevelt told me that she, of course, had known right along that our worry and our thoughts had been about cancer. Now that it was over, she did not mind discussing it.

David had been more apprehensive than she was.

At the end of 1961, Maria received her first letter from Mrs. Roosevelt.

To A Very Little Girl On Her First Christmas:

May you be well and happy and always bring your parents joy. Of what I give you only one thing is useful now but I may be near you long enough to make the others *more* useful in the next few years. You chose your parents and grandparents well and all around you love you. What more can you ask? I just add to the love that surrounds you my warmest wishes for years of happiness and much, much love from,

Your oldest friend.*

Franklin and his young daughter, Nancy, came to dinner in Val-Kill on New Year's Eve of 1961. David and I, Joe and Trude, their son Jonathan and his friend, Abba Schwartz and Maureen were also present. Franklin repeated to his mother his wish to run for governor of New York. "Mrs. R. talked him out of it at present. Much political talk," my rare diary entry noted. "It was an interesting evening, though not especially gay. . . . The other night Mrs. Roosevelt casually said at dinner that she became interested in social work at nineteen because she was a social

---

*Mrs. Roosevelt presented Maria with her first place setting of silver flatware for her trousseau and followed it, until she died, with additional sets on special occasions. She also started a strand of pearls for the baby, a gift also to be added to in the future, and gave her a necklace of seed pearls for her first birthday.

failure. . . . She went on to say that her early social work in the slums of the Lower East Side required no courage because no member of the 'Four Hundred' could do wrong, whereas today, working for progressive reform requires a good deal of courage because of the specter of Mc-Carthyism."

· 8 ·

ENDINGS

Final Long Journey

MRS. ROOSEVELT WAS GOING to Israel, and David convinced me to accompany her before he joined us in Switzerland. I hadn't wanted to leave Maria for two weeks, but he encouraged me. "You must go now," he said. "You may never again have the chance to see Israel with Mrs. Roosevelt." The urgency of these words about her failing health upset me, but it wasn't entirely unexpected. I understood there was reason for worry about her. But David's remark was his first clear indication to me of just how ill she was. Though I pressed him, he would not go into detail. I changed my plans accordingly.

In a letter from Paris, where Mrs. Roosevelt had stopped to tape programs for her educational TV series, *Prospects of Mankind*, she wrote:

February 15th [1962]
Dearest Edna and David,
    I think of you much and hope all goes well with you and that this Sat and Sunday will be fairly free so that you can enjoy each other and little Maria.
    I was tired and the first day here I worked hard so today is the first day I begin to feel normal. We worked all morning on the second show and both are, I think good. This P.M. I had several people for tea and the Mochs wanted to be remembered to you and invite us to tea on our return.

I dined with the Finletters tonight and spent an hour before with a man who will interview me for the Jewish radio tomorrow A.M.

In the afternoon we leave for London. Keep well and I look forward to your arrival [in London] next Tuesday Edna dear. My love to you David dear, I can only say the 28th seems a long way off to me. Devotedly

E. R.

I left for London on February 20, 1962. Settled in our British Overseas Airline jet scheduled for takeoff, all passengers were suddenly asked to return to the airport lounge, which we'd left just moments before. The staff had thoughtfully set up a television screen so that we could watch NASA's first launching of an American astronaut into Earth's orbit. As John Glenn successfully rocketed off into outer space, the assembled British crew turned toward the American passengers and burst into applause. It was a grand send-off to London.

There was a note waiting for me when I checked into the hotel early that evening:

CLARIDGE'S
Edna dearest,

You may be here before I get home. Just use the sitting room and I'll be here soon. You are so welcome. I can hardly wait to see you.

My love,
E. R.

We were guests of Lord Home at tea in the House of Lords.* Mrs. Roosevelt's friend lady Stella Reading gave Maureen and me a memorable tour of the Houses of Parliament while Mrs. Roosevelt and her host

---

*Alec Douglas-Home, who served as prime minister from 1963 to 1964.

met privately. (She also drove the three of us to the outskirts of London to show us a gaping hole in the ground—the beginnings of Heathrow Airport.) Mrs. Roosevelt made a brief call at the house of the Churchills, saying later how sad it was to see the ailing Sir Winston. Apart from the visit of our ambassador, David Bruce, to our sitting room the next day, she followed her own schedule and I made my usual rounds of museums and galleries. On the fourth morning, we left for Tel Aviv.

It was my first trip to Israel. Though Mrs. Roosevelt wanted me to see as much as possible, I hardly remember Tel Aviv in daylight, except for our departures. She, Maureen, and I, along with Gideon Tadmor, a companionable young Foreign Service officer, and an obliging, shy chauffeur (both assigned to Mrs. Roosevelt for her stay in Israel), drove away from the Dan Hotel each morning at daybreak, gliding silently along the streets of the quiet city to our various destinations. We returned in the dark of night. I was looking forward to seeing Degania, the kibbutz near the Lake of Tiberius. There, we were able to meet Mr. and Mrs. Joseph Baratz, who were among the small group of its original settlers. It was at Degania that David had served as a young doctor after leaving Basel Medical School. Mrs. Roosevelt had met Mr. and Mrs. Baratz with David years before. Joseph Baratz described to us how life was lived in the settlement and urged us to stay for lunch, which was served in a communal tent. We ate little, for we could see that food was a precious commodity.* Though life on the kibbutz was still a struggle in 1962, its inhabitants had an extremely fine Museum of Natural History. Another morning, we drove out to Safed, a burgeoning artists' community, staying overnight in its only hotel, newly built and situated on a raised level above a sweep of terraced land below. Construction of housing and studios had already begun, and Mrs. Roosevelt and I bought some watercolors on display.

---

*On a trip I took to Israel in the mid-1970s I revisited Degania. I was greatly impressed by its transformation into a thriving settlement with an air-conditioned communal dining room (in which I lunched), television antennas rising from substantial-looking houses, and parked automobiles where formerly there had been only bicycles.

We were also given a special tour of the Weitzmann Institute of Science in Rehovot. This sophisticated center for scientific and medical research was named for the late Dr. Chaim Weitzmann, the first president of Israel (1949–1952). I noted that Mrs. Roosevelt was strong enough to walk with me up an incline to Dr. Weitzmann's residence, transformed into an historic site. Upon entering, we were asked to sign the president's large guest book. Mrs. Roosevelt leafed through it to show me David's and her signatures from an earlier time. We lunched on the grounds before continuing on our way.

One evening, Mrs. Roosevelt and I were going to dinner in the apartment of old friends of David's from his Berlin days, Mr. and Mrs. Rudolph Kroener. Thrilled to have Mrs. Roosevelt as his passenger, the cabdriver tactfully suggested that the address David had given me could not be right. "Nobody lives there," he said. He was right. We arrived in Tel-Aviv's financial district to find the building solidly closed for the night. Our knowledgeable taxi driver located a street telephone, found our friends' number in the telephone book, and called them to say we were on our way. "You had the office address," he told me. "I will take you to their home." Mrs. Roosevelt appreciated that there were only the four of us at dinner, and she was her most charming self, relaxed and happy.

On our way to Beersheba, we had a real scare. Mrs. Roosevelt began to feel ill. She was sitting miserably in the backseat corner of the car without complaint. Suddenly she said she needed some air. Maureen went with her for a few steps, but she wanted to be alone. We anxiously watched as she walked on slowly by herself. Remembering David's words to me before I left, I was very nervous. We were all apprehensive. We were in an unpopulated area—no medical help nearby. After a few minutes, Mrs. Roosevelt returned to the car, but her face became more and more ashen as we approached Beersheba. Gideon Tadmor, our guide, knew the press would be collected at the entrance of our hotel, so to spare Mrs. Roosevelt, he quietly instructed the driver, "Drive around the block until you see me again." He then rapidly left the car and walked into the hotel while we slowly circled the neighborhood. Mrs. Roosevelt asked no questions. Retreating into herself, she didn't speak at all. When

Gideon signaled us to enter the hotel, we found the lobby empty. He had checked us all in and had gotten our keys. Mrs. Roosevelt quickly disappeared into her room, refusing all suggestions that we get a doctor. That afternoon, she was scheduled to go to a party in her honor at the house of a Beersheba family she and David had met on their visit ten years before. We couldn't believe she would be able to attend, but we dared not propose canceling the party, as that would have upset her more. Meanwhile, disguising the fact that he wanted a simple dinner available to Mrs. Roosevelt should she require it, Gideon discreetly placed an order in his name for a dinner after the reception was over: broth, boiled chicken, rice, and light tea. After an hour, I knocked on Mrs. Roosevelt's door. She had had a nap, she said, then taken a bath and changed. She insisted she was ready to go. She still looked quite pale but seemed not as shaky as before.

We found a large number of guests at the party—and a feast. It was clear that Mrs. Roosevelt's visit meant a good deal to the many inhabitants of Beersheba. Our host was honored by her return visit and eager to show her how prosperous the family had become. Mrs. Roosevelt responded so warmly to the sincerity of their welcome that one would not have believed how ill she'd felt a few hours earlier. She remained seated throughout the party, however, and did not attempt to approach the laden buffet table. When various trays of food were offered to her, she barely touched anything. I hardly took my eyes off her. She did not hurry. She stayed, listened, and discussed their affairs. She looked tired but no longer ill. Determination revived her, and contact with people had lifted her spirits. When we returned to the hotel, she was hungry, and we all went to the dining room for dinner. Mrs. Roosevelt ordered a substantial meal. The waiter brought Gideon the boiled chicken dinner. "What is this?" he asked in Mrs. Roosevelt's presence, attempting to calm any suspicions she might have. "It is your order, sir" was the reply. "My order?" asked Gideon incredulously. "You have made a mistake. It must be for someone else. We would all like to see the menu."

The following day, we toured Beersheba by car, and later, seated on a platform, Mrs. Roosevelt handled a press conference very smoothly. But the episode of her illness was not forgotten.

We went to visit Prime Minister David Ben-Gurion in his office. Mrs. Roosevelt often spoke about him, mentioning his inspirational, brilliant leadership, his courage, and his dynamic personality. She was also impressed by his ability to attract a considerable number of talented young people to work in government. I think, too, that it pleased her to see someone close to her own age still extraordinarily active in public life, with a mind as alert as ever. She mentioned at various times the fact that he had read all the books in the exceptional library at his home. We mounted the flight of stairs to the prime minister's office and were escorted to a small anteroom, where we were asked to be seated. The official who accompanied us stood to one side of Mr. Ben-Gurion's door. He had evidently been told something about Mrs. Roosevelt's health problem the day before and wanted to give her time to catch her breath after climbing the stairs. It was done so tactfully that the reason for the wait was not noticeable. When it was apparent that she was ready, we were shown into the office. The prime minister's blue eyes sparkled at once. It was a warm meeting between old friends; much was discussed in a short time, and at the end, Mrs. Roosevelt, Gideon, Maureen, and I lined up with Mr. Ben-Gurion for a group photograph.

The day before our departure for Switzerland, we finally had the opportunity to see Jerusalem. We visited Hebrew University, where we had a memorable tour of its unique library. Later, we had the great pleasure of meeting Golda Meir, the foreign minister, whom David and I had known in New York. On our last evening, the minister of education and a friend of Mrs. Roosevelt, Abba Eban, invited us to dinner at the King David Hotel, where we were staying. Mr. Eban's party was a lovely ending to our trip. Mrs. Roosevelt had felt very much at home in Israel, deeply appreciating the warm and respectful reception she'd received from everyone. Early the next morning, February 28, she, Maureen, and I left by plane for Switzerland. She appeared to be fine. But as David had predicted, I never did see Israel again with Mrs. Roosevelt.

The train trip from Zurich to Saint Moritz is one of the most beautiful journeys in the world, with spectacular views unfolding on both sides as the train climbs several thousand feet above sea level. It was evening when David, who had arrived the previous day, met us at the station. The frosty night was in stark contrast to the mild Israeli weather we had left only that morning. As soon as we were alone, I described to David the incident of Mrs. Roosevelt's illness in Beersheba.

We stayed at the Kulm Hotel in the town center, where David had stopped before. He loved Saint Moritz. He walked up and down its icy inclines as surefootedly as a mountain goat, always with a helping hand extended. Having Mrs. Roosevelt along, he was careful to choose gentle slopes on our morning strolls in the clear, thin air. The high altitude brought us so close to the strong sun that the longer we walked, the more clothes we shed. Mrs. Roosevelt was often down to a light pullover.

David noted in his journal:

One day we were invited to lunch at the luxurious Corviglia Ski Club above the town of St. Moritz, reached by cable car. The station of the cable car was a little higher than the clubhouse. The lunch went well, but on the uphill walk back to the station, about two hundred feet on the cleared path banked with high snow walls, Mrs. Roosevelt's lips turned blue, she was pale as a ghost, and she became completely breathless. I was frightened to death. We stopped. We should not have undertaken that exertion for her. She recovered somewhat. I supported her. By the time we reached the station house, her pulse was racing, her breath was very short, and she was still in some distress, but fortunately it passed once the exertion was over and we were going down to the more lower levels [of altitude] of St. Moritz. . . . Apart from that single disturbing incident, Mrs. Roosevelt took the trip well and enjoyed everything.

She was happy to see Saint Moritz in the snow, she said. She'd been there once before, but in the summer. Every night, we were seated at the same round corner table in the Kulm. "I received a message today from Mr. Badrutt of the Palace Hotel," Mrs. Roosevelt mentioned at dinner one evening. "He read in the local newspaper that I was here and wrote that he was disappointed we were not staying at his hotel. I will send him a note." She then reminisced: "Franklin and I did stay at the Palace many years ago when we were in Europe on our honeymoon. It was," she continued, naming her mother's sister, "Aunt Tissie's custom to come to the Palace Hotel after her annual shopping visit in Paris. She was a very elegant woman and arrived in Saint Moritz each year with trunks full of extravagant Worth gowns.* Toward the end of our wedding trip, she invited Franklin and me to see her before we left for home. By the time we reached Saint Moritz in August, we had been away some months and had traveled a good deal. Franklin's dinner jacket badly needed pressing and my own evening clothes were rumpled as well, and not half as stylish as Aunt Tissie's. When Franklin and I came down to dinner the first night rather untidy-looking and asked for my aunt's table, the maître d'hotel refused to seat us in the main dining room and led us to a table by ourselves outside." "Did your aunt object?" I asked. "No," Mrs. Roosevelt replied. "She thought he was right." "What a mistake he made," I said.

We left Zurich on March 11 for a few days in Paris and then flew home. The episode in the snow, when Mrs. Roosevelt experienced such acute shortness of breath, worried David exceedingly.

"Au Revoir"

"I thought I'd arrange a large family lunch," I replied when Mrs. Roosevelt asked how I planned to celebrate Maria's first birthday on June 27. "Have a real birthday party," she urged. "It may not seem important now, but looking back, you will enjoy the memory and may regret not having done it." Have I said before that I always paid attention to Mrs. Roosevelt?

---

*Charles Worth, the most famous Paris couturier of his day.

Maria wore the beautiful white silk dress with the pink smocking that Mrs. Roosevelt had given her. The parents I invited to the party — one of whom had been a polio patient of David's — their children, and our friends and relations all good-humoredly came to the noisy, festive event. Mrs. Roosevelt was there, too. It was the only birthday celebration of Maria's she ever attended. When David arrived home for the cutting of the cake, I overheard one young mother ask his former polio patient, "Is *he* your *doctor*? He wouldn't be mine. He's much too good-looking." Maria loved the party, especially the unexpected (to her) arrival of her father in the afternoon. I remember the occasion with joy — and with a nod to Mrs. Roosevelt.

David's summer vacation, which began at the end of June, was spent on the hospital ship *Hope*, anchored at that time off the coast of Trujillo, Peru. He'd been invited by Neurological Institute colleagues. Much as I wanted him at home, I could understand his desire to be part of their team. There was an epidemic of infantile paralysis in and around Trujillo, and David's object was to introduce rehabilitation medicine to Peruvian physicians and teach some basic physical therapy techniques. He was nervous about leaving Mrs. Roosevelt in her precarious state of health, but the excellent hematologist Dr. George A. Hyman was on hand, along with the various specialists familiar with her case, who were following a "watch and wait" procedure.

Maria and I were to spend the few weeks of David's absence with Mrs. Roosevelt in Val-Kill. Before he left, she gave David a letter, on the envelope of which was written: "David To Be Read On the Plane *Not Before*."

Thursday night
David dearest,

I've just seen you for the last time I surmise till you come home so I write you these lines which I hope you will read when you are on the plane and all the hurry and worry is over. You will begin then to enjoy and savour the adventure of the trip and I hope it proves to be all you hope for and that you return refreshed in spirit and less fundamentally weary physically than you are and have been.

To me all goodbyes are more poignant now, I like less and less to be long separated from those few whom I deeply love. Above all others you are the one to whom my heart is tied and I shall miss you every moment till we meet again and I shall come down with Edna and Maria to greet you on your return. I will do all I can to help Edna, for I know this separation will be hard for her to bear.

On your side will you try to think out how to lighten your week a little? A woman needs companionship and a little more leisure than you have been able to find this past winter. We are all selfish when we love someone and want the one to give to us personally part of the time.

And now an end to preaching! I know what drives you have, and I am deeply appreciative and admiring of the standards and values you set for yourself. God bless you and keep you wherever you are, my prayers and thoughts will be with you constantly. Au revoir, and my love always.

E. R.

Enjoy life and take care of yourself.

Mrs. Roosevelt had never written "au revoir" to David before. It was not her last letter to him, but it was her farewell.

Maria and I settled into Val-Kill Cottage. I did not have David's and my usual room, but the small suite on the second floor. Maria slept under a faded print of the victorious U.S. armored warship, the *Monitor*.* Before Tubby brought a crib up from my parents' apartment, Maria slept in a very old one, which had been stored in the Big House in Hyde Park. It was in Val-Kill that Maria took her first independent steps, played games

---

*David and I purchased the print for sentimental reasons when John Roosevelt put it up for sale with many of his mother's Val-Kill possessions at the Hammer Galleries after her death.

with Maureen, tried hard to catch Duffy, the Scottie, picked flowers, petted the sheep, splashed in the pool, and, seated on the grass at the foot of Mrs. Roosevelt's chair on the back lawn, played with heaps of discarded envelopes Mrs. Roosevelt passed down to her as she opened the mail.

David wrote me every day from Peru, numbering his letters. He counted on my letters from home, happy when the mail caught up with him, and wrote charmingly to Maria. Mrs. Roosevelt wrote him often and one of her letters (July 3) ends:

Never did I feel stronger or better so you have no worries where I am concerned.

My love to you always and enjoy your work.

E. R.

FROM THE HOPE SHIP, TRUJILLO, PERU

Wednesday, 7/4/62

Dearest Mrs. R.—

Thank you for your good letter. Yesterday it came, the first mail since I left. There is more and more pressure of work, what for, I am not quite clear about. A daily clinic of proportion and kind you have seen in India or Karachi or Marrakech. Only they come from far away. . . . Each time one opens the door [of the onshore clinic] there is a fight to get in, and for us to keep the many mothers with polio babies out, except for one [at a time]. Much, much polio. I have 18 prospective therapists to teach 2 hours every day and medical students and where will it lead once I am gone? No successor in sight. Thank you for all the good news. It is a fantastic enterprise. It has caught the people here—Peruvians and U.S. staff—other specialities do much better than mine. Still this is only the end of the first week. I found nothing when I came, and now it hums in many directions.

Just my love.

I hear that by now you had your transfusion—I hope. I also

hope Anna is better. I was so dead tired when I saw her that I could barely speak.

Give my love to Edna and to Uncle David.*

Your
David

And my love to Maureen.

Mrs. Roosevelt had her usual Fourth of July picnic lunch around the swimming pool in Val-Kill. She'd invited two young men from the Soviet delegation to the United Nations to join us—she always liked having foreign guests on important American holidays. After the customary reading aloud of the Declaration of Independence, she escorted the Russians, along with Maureen, Maria, and me, to the Big House. I remember thinking that on the way there Mrs. Roosevelt was listless, but she later rallied. It was a wonderful experience to be shown through the family house by her.

On July 8, I received a letter from David. And on the same day, Mrs. Roosevelt wrote him:

> Edna is very happy with your letters and only afraid that now that you are on the Ship, they may take longer to reach her. She had dreaded this first week and thought it would seem very long but she tells me it has gone more quickly than she dared anticipate. The baby is sleeping well and eating well and seems her happy self.
>
> I'm so glad to hear from Edna that you find things better than you expected and that you like Dr. Walsh.** Tomorrow night you will have been gone a week and how much you have done and

---

*David Gray, Mrs. Roosevelt's uncle, was staying at Val-Kill for the summer. He was writing the biography of Eamon De Valera, former prime minister and then president of Ireland. Mrs. Roosevelt used to say that he'd been working on it for so many years, she doubted it would ever be finished. "Be glad he is taking his time" was David's answer. "When he finishes it, he will die."

**Dr. William Walsh was the head of the project: S.S. *Hope*.

seen since then! I hope you have had some rest and that the change is a relaxation. I was in N.Y. yesterday and all was well at the house.

I went in and had the type blood taken and on Monday the 9th at 10 a.m. they will do the transfusion at the office and let me go at 12 so I hope to leave the house on the return drive at 2:30.

The Wiltwyck picnic* has just come to an end and was a great success I think. Mr. Stix got a magician to come and perform for them but so many asked for the story, that I've promised to go over some afternoon later and read and provide ice cream and cake so it will be like another party!

. . . To-night the democratic state chairman Mr. MacKeon will be here. I meet after dinner with 30 of the County democrats. I think Edna is really getting rested. I couldn't feel better. Tell me how you are. Much love.

E. R.

Neither Maureen nor I knew anything about the transfusion. I had found it curious that for the first time a magician was hired to substitute for Mrs. Roosevelt to read to the Wiltwyck boys from Rudyard Kipling's *Just So Stories*, as she normally did at her picnics for them, but I didn't attach special importance to it. There were other indications, however, that something was wrong. Before lunch one Sunday, Mrs. Roosevelt closeted herself in a room with her sons Franklin and John, which was unusual. The three of them then entered the study to make a telephone call to Elliott. The rest of us went out to the porch, where the table was set for lunch, but we could not help hearing the gist of the message to Elliott, who evidently needed money. This time, his mother refused to deal with his problems, and her response on the telephone was emphatic. Her patience with him had expired, she said. She was preparing Elliott to face the reality that she could no longer sustain him in trouble and that he must look to his brothers if he needed help. I assumed that in

---

*The Wiltwyck School for Boys was an experimental type of reform school, to which young lawbreakers were sent by the courts for psychological rehabilitation.

preparing for the end of her life, she wanted to feel that Elliott would not be abandoned by his brothers. That was the promise she had elicited from Franklin and John behind closed doors. She wrote on July 10:

David dearest,

Edna reported that all goes well but you are not too luxurious. I only hope it is comfortable enough so you can sleep and that the food is fairly good.

Edna looks and feels better and the baby is adorable but I wish she'd learn to let Edna sleep til 7:30, just now she's taken to getting up at 5:30.

I had the transfusion last Monday, 2 full bags, so I should need nothing more for a long time. Anna reports a little improvement. Helen Robinson* died last Sunday but because her daughters were cruising in Greece the funeral will not be til Thursday. A long time to wait. I've left directions for burial the next day, Maureen suggested that it's awkward if there is a grave diggers strike, so we must hope to avoid that calamity!

David [Gray] seems to me much more frail and more in need of rest.

I went out over to New Paltz, Teachers College this A.M. and made 3 speeches to the retired teachers group, the Peace Corps group going to teach in Sierra Leone in secondary schools and then to early lunch with faculty and students. I ended at 2:15 and had had enough of my own voice!

We've been having a bad time over Elliott again, but I left it to the boys and they are coping quite successfully I think, tho' I don't believe Patty or Elliott enjoy it.

Thank you for your dear letter but I know you are busy and Edna gives us news. Take care of yourself, you have only been gone 10 days but it seems much longer!

*Mrs. Theodore Douglas Robinson, the daughter of Franklin Roosevelt's half brother, "Rosy" Roosevelt. She lived in Hyde Park, close to "Springwood," the FDR family house.

I send you much love and hope you find your 2 dear ones well cared for on your return. Devotedly,

E. R.

Tubby will get your car on Friday.

She wrote again on July 18:

David dearest,

It was wonderful to get your letter of the 4th and tonight the telephone message to Edna was reassuring for it sounded as though the unrest [in Trujillo] was growing ominous. Your letter to me seemed to indicate an impossible amount of work. I'm afraid that having left exhausted you will return even more exhausted. This can't be good for you. Your baby needs you and is so extraordinary but she has many years in which your guidance is essential. I realize more every day how much Edna needs and depends on you. I do not find her very strong, she hasn't half the endurance I had at her age. You are essential to this small family and I surmise no less important to Grania in the next few years, though she would probably not acknowledge it.

Edna's father and mother came for lunch today and the baby was delighted.

I work with Miss Denniston off and on and the book goes forward,* not as well as I would like but it moves. . . .

My loving thoughts fly to you many times a day and please be careful of yourself. Devotedly

E. R.

P.S. David [Gray] and Maureen would send love if here.

---

*Mrs. Roosevelt's last book, *Tomorrow Is Now*, was written in collaboration with Elinore Denniston and was published posthumously.

David's absence had not weighed as heavily as I thought it would, for I was happy in Val-Kill. I missed him very much but did not lack for friends or things to do. Being a full-time mother, the baby, not to mention David, had kept me busy all year and it had been months since I'd had the chance to sit down with a book. I delighted in looking after Maria, I loved Mrs. Roosevelt's company, and I enjoyed contact with Maureen, who had not spent nearly as much time in Hyde Park in summers past. My parents, warmly welcomed, came regularly for visits. Friends of ours drove up from the city, and I found Mrs. Roosevelt's guests interesting, as usual. Little Joan, John Roosevelt's youngest child, of whom I was very fond, often tagged along with Maria and me when she wasn't on horseback. And the baby was charming. Frequently after an early dinner, Mrs. Roosevelt drove to the city and back that same night to speak on behalf of Robert Morgenthau, who was running for governor of New York. Upset by how weary she looked at times, I asked Maureen why she didn't arrange to campaign for him during the day, rather than at night. Didn't I realize, Maureen confided, that Mrs. Roosevelt stayed close to Hyde Park during the day so that I would not be lonely? There were always new layers of subtlety to fathom in Mrs. Roosevelt's behavior.

Tivoli

One morning, Mrs. Roosevelt declared she would like to have a picnic that day in Tivoli, not far from Hyde Park. Her mother, aunts, and uncles had been raised in "Oak Terrace," as the house in Tivoli was called, and it was where she and her younger brother, Hall, had spent part of their childhood in the custody of their grandmother Hall. We set out around noon, when Maria napped. The occupants of our car grew silent as we pulled into the long driveway of Oak Terrace on that sun-drenched July afternoon. The house was now owned by an Estonian charitable organization. Mrs. Roosevelt was visibly pleased to see her childhood home once more. We parked by a picnic table under a tree. Mrs. Roosevelt cheerfully helped put out the sandwiches on the slatted wood table, which included unwrapping Tubby's sandwich for him. The entire time we were there, however, Uncle David Gray, too affected by memories of the olden days, when he had been married to Mrs. Roosevelt's aunt Maude, remained seated in the car, his back to the beautiful house he had known so long ago. His food had to be handed in to him through the car's open door. But Mrs. Roosevelt did not allow her uncle's sadness to affect her. She was remembering the good things that had taken place in Tivoli. She wanted to show the house to Maureen and me, and after lunch, failing to find someone who could allow us in, the three of us circled its exterior. Mrs. Roosevelt was animated. "There," she said, pointing to the windows of the basement laundry room on the side of the house, "was where the poor young laundresses worked long hours in the heat of the summer, pressing with steam irons the frilled petticoats of my aunts." She happily showed us a grassy mound. "And here, was where I slid down on the slippery grass on a wooden board to the bottom." Such a lonely story, I thought, yet I noticed how the recollection delighted her. It does not take much to amuse a child bent on being amused. She recalled that her aunts were good-natured and sweet to her. She showed us the windows on the top floor from which her two confined alcoholic uncles occasionally aimed their guns, taking potshots at her as she ran to and from the mailbox. "I had to run, dodging from tree to tree, to avoid being hit," she recounted. She told this hair-raising story with no hint of anger.

Mrs. Roosevelt did not want to leave before going into the house. We knocked at the front door, which was partly ajar, and when no one answered, we cautiously entered. The interior was dilapidated; the spacious entrance hall was empty of furniture except for two or three metal folding chairs and a long table. To one side of the superbly carved staircase, there was a Coca-Cola machine, where, Mrs. Roosevelt said, a beautiful piano had once stood. I could not help reacting sadly to the shabbiness of the formerly elegant surroundings, but it did not faze Mrs. Roosevelt. We took one last look and left.

I thought it was remarkable that she had not been sentimental about what my instinct told me was her farewell to Tivoli. I felt her spirit was still light on the return trip to Val-Kill, though no one spoke much. Uncle David finally broke the silence. "How could you stay there today, Eleanor?" She finally replied, "It was so long ago." I remembered she had the same realistic attitude when she had wanted to take me to see the Saint-Gaudens sculpture in Rock Creek Cemetery, which at a critical period had soothed so many of her solitary, unhappy hours and had helped give her the strength to carry on. You hold on to the good of a thing, the part that enriches you, and do not dwell on the sadness. It is unproductive.

Homeward-Bound

While there were days during my stay with Mrs. Roosevelt when she looked pallid, it was not obvious to me that she was critically ill. She carried that secret well—and I didn't want to know it. Family and friends continued to come to her cottage for lunches and dinners as well as for overnight stays; she drove down to the city on various political missions. She dealt with the mail and her household, kept up her personal correspondence, and occasionally stopped in local ceramic workshops for Christmas presents. She covered her feelings and fatigue well. But there was less bustle in Val-Kill during those summer days; it was relatively quiet for Mrs. Roosevelt, with just David Gray, Maureen, Maria, and me staying there, and Nina, Haven, and Joan about the place. Soon it would all change.

Mrs. Roosevelt had accepted dinner invitations for herself and for us one evening at the Italian villa–style house of Mrs. Lyman Delano in a neighboring Hudson River town. Usually, she was the first downstairs before dinner, utilizing spare moments at her desk or reading while she waited for the rest of us. This time she was so late, one of us was about to go upstairs, but then she appeared. She said she'd had a nap and had overslept. She looked ill. Was she sure she wanted to go? "Yes," she replied; she was already at the door. The dinner was pleasant and uneventful, but that night I wrote to David, saying, "Mrs. Roosevelt is not well." He said later that the letter had been forwarded to him in his hotel in Lima after he'd cut short his stay in Trujillo, and when it was slipped under his door and he read those words, he was already packed for his journey home. By the time Jimmy Roosevelt had contacted the State Department to locate him and advise him he was needed, David was airborne.

Forced to give in to her illness, Mrs. Roosevelt left Val-Kill for the city, sitting in the front seat of the station wagon, which was driven by Tubby. Her head rested on a large bed pillow. I thought I should stay in Hyde Park until we heard from David. Her Scottie had stood beside the car, looking up at his mistress as she was leaving. She was so weak, she could barely signal good-bye to him. Under the hematologist's care, Mrs. Roosevelt received a blood transfusion on July 31.

The baby record book I kept reads: "David came home in the early afternoon of August 1. I received his cable in the morning in Hyde Park. I quickly packed and Tubby took Maria and me home immediately. Mrs. Roosevelt was already in New York. We were in front of our house at 12 noon. Maria had been taken upstairs from the car, asleep. When David walked in to her at 1:30 she had just awakened and he found her sitting up in the darkened room, looking around. She was very glad to see him. So was I. Mrs. Roosevelt is very ill."

He'd come home not a moment too soon. Mrs. Roosevelt was in bed downstairs in her apartment. She'd had a bad reaction to the transfusion; after two days of a high, spiky fever, chills, and other disquieting symptons, David had her admitted to the hospital. On the sixth hospital day, after she'd had chest X rays and many laboratory tests, her temperature leveled off to normal and she was discharged, the diagnosis still unclear. She was advised to rest.

There was only one place Mrs. Roosevelt wanted to convalesce, one place she yearned to see again, and she seized the opportunity to return to Campobello. David said that for years she had wanted them to go there together; they had talked about it a number of times. He wrote, "In spite of her rapidly waning strength, she organized the trip most efficiently."

She was ready to set out two days after she left the hospital. Unknown to Mrs. Roosevelt, David had arranged with Franklin before we left New York to have a helicopter standing by should a quick return home become necessary.

Campobello

Mrs. Roosevelt longed to revisit the family summer house she loved on Campobello Island, despite the fact that the property had been sold.* Some years earlier, the wonderful, big Victorian house on Passamaquoddy Bay and everything in it, including part of FDR's collection of rare miniature books and the pony cart he had used as a boy, had been sold by Elliott to Armand and Victor Hammer. Though the Hammers were presently occupying the house, they made temporary arrangements to be guests of their neighbor, Harry Matlin, so that Mrs. Roosevelt could be there. She would not have gone otherwise.

Eleanor and Franklin had both been devoted to Campobello Island, located off the Maine seacoast village of Eastport and half in Canada, where they had spent splendid summers enjoying days of sailing, swimming, and picnicking with their lively group of handsome children. It was there that Franklin taught Anna and the boys to sail the *Half Moon*, and where Mrs. Roosevelt could relax in the company of the small group of other summer residents. She wrote:

Hyde Park and later Warm Springs had come to mean "roots" to Franklin. In some ways Campobello meant more to me. Franklin had been going to Campobello when he was two years old, and while our children were small we went there every summer. The house next to his mother's belonged to us, and some of the children

---

*In due course, the new owners presented the house and grounds to the United States and Canadian governments jointly. It is now the Roosevelt Campobello International Park and Natural Area, Campobello Island, New Brunswick, Canada.

have happy memories of it and of the life we lived there. Franklin was always on vacation when he came to Campobello, before he had infantile paralysis, and many of the children's happiest times were with him there.*

Mrs. Roosevelt preferred to treasure the comforting memories of Campobello rather than remember the anguished ones when her husband, involved in a romance, was reluctant to leave Washington to join her and the children, not to mention the harrowing period of his near-fatal illness there. Surrounded by nature, with brilliant sunrises and sunsets gloriously reflecting on the waters of the bay at its back door, the house was, in a way, Eleanor and Franklin Roosevelt's first home of their own. The young couple (especially Eleanor) had endeared themselves to their mother's next-door neighbor, Mrs. H. Kuhn, and when she died, she stipulated in her will that Sara Roosevelt could buy her cottage for the sum of five thousand dollars, provided that she purchase it for her son and daughter-in-law. In 1909, the capacious rustic house became theirs.**

Mrs. Roosevelt, Maureen, David, Maria, and I took an 11:30 A.M. plane to Boston for the first part of the trek to Campobello. In Boston, we had a two-hour wait in the airport for the flight to Bangor, Maine, where Tubby, who had driven on in advance, was to meet us. Normally, Mrs. Roosevelt would have refused special attention, but on this occasion she quietly accepted the private room the airline gave us in which to relax until boarding time. Nor did she object to the large airport car that transported us directly to the bottom step of the waiting plane. In Bangor, we transferred to Mrs. Roosevelt's station wagon for the three-hour drive to the ferry that was to take us to Campobello Island. Though Mrs. Roosevelt bore the entire trip uncomplainingly, her passivity made it very clear it was taking its toll. When we at last reached the ferry, we

---

*Eleanor Roosevelt, *This I Remember* (New York: Harper & Brothers, 1949), pp. 18–19.
**Joseph P. Lash, *Eleanor and Franklin* (New York: W. W. Norton, 1971), p. 163.

were confronted by a discouraging long line of waiting cars. And there, stretching temptingly before our eyes, was the newly completed but not yet opened Franklin D. Roosevelt Memorial Bridge linking Campobello Island and the coast of Maine with the Canadian mainland. Mrs. Roosevelt's visit coincided with the inauguration of the bridge and she had been scheduled to dedicate it. David left the car to speak with ferry authorities, and shortly after, we were waved onto the bridge and were the first to cross it.

At 7:00 P.M., we at last pulled up in front of the dark red-shingled house. Standing on the front steps to welcome her was Linnea Calder, Mrs. Roosevelt's former Campobello housekeeper and an island native, who had temporarily returned to help. Mrs. Roosevelt's first words to Linnea from her seat in the car were, "Has the crib been set up for the baby?" Such was our introduction to Campobello.

I am certain David told Mrs. Roosevelt the truth about her condition as far as it was known. While he did not mislead her, he did not emphasize the negative side. She was able to hope this stay would help her regain some of her strength, that the invigorating island air and sunlight, as well as peace and familiar surroundings, would revive her.

Maureen and I spent part of our first morning in the house tucking out of sight little white tags that the Hammers had dangling on chairs, tables, and the corners of carpets, reading: "Collection of President and Mrs. Franklin D. Roosevelt." The labels did not seem to bother Mrs. Roosevelt, but they bothered Maureen and me, and so we hid them. David said that the house had been "rather hard for Mrs. Roosevelt to take, that being a guest in a house Mrs. Roosevelt felt was hers was still hard to swallow." The affluent Hammers had had sets of porcelain creamers and sugar bowls with the Campobello house pictured on them made, which were then sold to tourists visiting the house. (David and I bought several sets of them at a cost of one or two dollars each.) Mrs. Roosevelt was too happy to be there to allow anything to annoy her. At last she had a chance to share with David—and with the rest of us as well, I believe— her favorite island sites.

David recorded in his notes:

She was eager to organize picnics but could not, and instead showed us the places she'd picnicked in the past and we drove to other points she liked best. She took us to see the places which were especially attractive to her, coves and inlets. . . . By then she could do hardly any walking. Before sitting down on the grass picnic area under a tree, one of her favorite sites in Campobello, we had to move through rather thick underbrush — one would sink into soft leaves and branches — she had to be lowered into a sitting position by me holding her and she had to be helped to stand up again in the same fashion. Not once, however, did she complain, and though her strength was rapidly dwindling, she was full of plans for the autumn and winter. At the same time, this must have been a visit of farewell. . . . The return to Campobello was a moving experience for her because every corner had its memories. Though she never put it into words, here she was going back in time.

When Maureen tripped on the underbrush on that picnic site on her way from the car, David was pleased to point out to Mrs. Roosevelt that even Maureen had difficulty in finding her footing on the uneven ground. He later thanked Maureen for her timely "demonstration." He seized every excuse to keep Mrs. Roosevelt's spirits up. Mornings, she read on the back porch, which overlooked the bay, or attended to some of her mail, as David, with Maria in her usual perch on his shoulders, and I went walking. We often stopped for berry picking. "Wild blueberries and raspberries grow in abundance behind this Campobello house," I noted in my baby record book, "and we return to the house with basketsful. Handing them over to Linnea, they reappear in delicious pies." While the Hyde Park butcher had packed supplies of meat and poultry to be taken for the Campobello stay, we concentrated on fish, Mrs. Roosevelt's favorite being fresh herring, which Linnea remembered had been her choice in the old days, as well.

One afternoon, Mrs. Roosevelt insisted upon taking us to the place where she'd loved to shop in the past — an English store on nearby St.

Andrews Island. I was happy when she said they carried a wonderful assortment of woolens. "We can use a lightweight summer blanket," I said. David did not think Mrs. Roosevelt would be strong enough to accompany us on foot on the island. Before boarding the motorboat tied up at the dock behind the house, David advised Maureen and me to make our entire land visit as short as possible, and to select our purchases in a matter of minutes. "If you return to the boat empty-handed, Mrs. Roosevelt will be disappointed that you found nothing you liked and will feel that by staying behind, she prevented us from doing any shopping. Never mind about looking for things you want. Buy the first things you see."

Leaving the shore, Mrs. Roosevelt savored the sight of Campobello Island from the water, enjoying the wind and spray as the boat sped across the bay to St. Andrews. She recounted past excursions, described the danger of falling into the water when it turned bitterly cold, and remembered some good fishermen's tales, as well. Upon landing, we left her seated alone, and in the English store, we hurriedly bought items available from the front counters. David rushed us relentlessly. We had a brief view of flower-covered St. Andrews — an island essentially a golf course — before returning to the boat. Mrs. Roosevelt was glad to see our packages. I said nothing about the blanket I had mentioned earlier. (Shortly after she was back in New York and before she was readmitted to the hospital for the last time, a large package was delivered to me from a department store. It had no card. In it was a lightweight summer blanket.)

She had wanted to take part in the inauguration of the Franklin D. Roosevelt Memorial Bridge but was unable to do so. In her place, James and Irene came to represent the family when the bridge was officially opened, and after spending the night, they left for New York. At breakfast one morning, Mrs. Roosevelt told us she felt obliged to invite her benefactors, the Hammers and their wives, to tea. "You will not want to be here when they come," she alerted us, and we were grateful to be elsewhere for that hour.

In their many intimate conversations on the sun-filled back porch of the Campobello house, David urged Mrs. Roosevelt not to lose hope; he had not. Nevertheless, she faced the gravity of her condition squarely, and when it was time to leave, she planned to motor back to Hyde Park so that she could stop along the way to say her good-byes to certain special friends. Trude Lash came up to go with her. On President Roosevelt's death years before, Mrs. Roosevelt had told the press, "The story is over." She felt the same now. The morning following her departure, Maureen, David, Maria, and I flew back to New York.

While Mrs. Roosevelt had reduced her schedule considerably, she had a semblance of normal activities as the end of August neared. She did some campaigning for reform Democrats in New York and entertained a number of guests in Val-Kill, as usual. How she garnered her strength for these undertakings was a marvel, but her good days alternated with those in which she had bouts of difficult breathing, extreme weakness, and the return of chills and high, spiky fever. Still, a note in my record book on August 30 has the optimistic comment: "Mrs. R. told me at lunch today that she bought a crib for Maria for Hyde Park."

On September 11, David took Mrs. Roosevelt to the hospital for further tests and consultations. Physical examinations again proved negative, but there was no doubt she was rapidly declining. We accompanied her to the AAUN's reception for the U.S. delegation to the Seventeenth General Assembly, but she was uncomfortable and couldn't wait to get home. She forced herself to do errands during the day—I think because she was afraid to stop—and when her fever went up and stayed elevated, she went to bed. On the evening of September 25, Mrs. Roosevelt was examined by the internist Dr. F. Randolph Bailey, with whom David had been having regular consultations, as well as with Drs. Hyman and Gellhorn.* Dr. Bailey agreed with the opinions of the team of physicians on the case as to procedures to be followed and medication to be given, and he made

---

*Dr. Alfred Gellhorn, an oncologist at Columbia, was Martha Gellhorn's brother.

added recommendations, which could be handled only in the hospital. On the afternoon of September 26, David had a meeting with Dr. David M. Karnofsky (of Memorial Sloan Kettering Cancer Center). That night, James was with his mother when David made urgent arrangements for Mrs. Roosevelt's admission to the hospital for the fourth time. Leaving Jimmy in her bedroom, with instructions to stay with his mother and prepare her for the fact that she would soon be leaving for the hospital, David went upstairs to telephone. Just as he was asking me to go to Mrs. Roosevelt in case help was needed to pack her things, Jimmy, plainly disturbed, came up with the news that his mother absolutely refused to go. David went back down to her, requesting that Jimmy and I stand by. We sat down together on the inner staircase of the house, just outside Mrs. Roosevelt's open door. David began to speak to her. Her response was bitter. She did not want to go. The room became silent. After a few moments, I heard David say to Mrs. Roosevelt, "If you don't go to the hospital, I will be down here nineteen times during the night." That was enough to change her mind. "Irene can pack my bag," she said, referring to her housekeeper. But her reply was wretchedly spoken—a general's surrender.

Mrs. Roosevelt entered Presbyterian Hospital for the last time on September 26, giving strict instructions to David that she was to have no visitors. She was too proud to be seen ailing. Adlai Stevenson was eager to call. She had wanted to meet him several times before, but his heavy schedule as UN ambassador had prevented it. Now that she'd been hospitalized, it was awkward for him to confess to the press that he had not yet seen her. One day, he announced himself in the hospital, only to be turned away. "Doctor's orders," he was told. He never quite forgave David for refusing him.

After further examinations and new laboratory reports, there was another medical group consultation on the evening of September 27.

Mrs. Roosevelt decided to celebrate her seventy-eighth birthday on October 11 by giving a children's party at Seventy-fourth Street by proxy, the event dulling news of her health, which would be reported in the following day's newspapers. Maria and several of Trude's grandchildren had been invited. There was the usual birthday cake and presents for each child, things that Mrs. Roosevelt had ordered. Curtis, his half brother Johnny Boettiger, and their wives joined the party to toast their grandmother. The natural gaity of the children did little to lift the gloom of her absence. On that same day, Drs. Bailey, Gellhorn, Gurewitsch, Hyman, and Kneeland* met again to review the situation, and a few days later, Anna arrived with her husband to stay in her mother's apartment. Dr. Halsted was included in the group of doctors that met on October 17. David's memorandum in Mrs. Roosevelt's medical file reads in part:

> Her present condition, the state of the diagnostic workup, her prognosis, and the next steps to be taken were discussed. Drs. Bailey and Gellhorn essentially agreed on the diagnosis as follows:
>
> An aplastic bone marrow which gives rise to leukemoid reactions in the blood, and which is responsible for the low platelet count, and could possibly be responsible for the temperature Mrs. Roosevelt has been running off and on since the beginning of July 1962. The lung infiltration could be explained on the basis of leukemia, but in the absence of a clearcut picture of leukemia in the bone marrow it is not possible to make that clinical diagnosis.
>
> Mrs. Roosevelt is suffering from a chronic blood loss. . . . Generalized tuberculosis could conceivably be responsible for the entire picture.
>
> The diagnosis and, therefore, therapeutic approaches were by no means clear.

Then David summarized Dr. Bailey's recommendations and stated further:

> He [Dr. Bailey] would at this stage be satisfied that further diagnostic procedures were not wanted, and that we should accede

---

*Dr. Yale Kneeland's speciality was infectious diseases.

to Mrs. Roosevelt's strong desire to be treated at home from now on. We would have to organize nursing around the clock, medical care on a daily basis by Dr. George Hyman . . . in addition to the daily supervision I will provide.

Dr. Halsted emphasized that Mrs. Roosevelt's children are fully aware of the grave condition of their mother. They also know of her strong desire to be discharged and treated at home and they are strongly in favor of it under these circumstances. Dr. Halsted himself was in favor of her discharge also.

I emphasized that the prognosis was grave, that three weeks of an intensive workup had not brought us therapeutically any closer to helping her present condition, and . . . felt that we should arrange for a transfer to her home. . . .

The likelihood that we were dealing with a leukemia-like condition for which we have no treatment, with the possible infections being purely secondary, was considerable. . . .

Today, October 18, she was returned to her home by ambulet[te] without undue difficulty.

Following my own brief evening visits to Mrs. Roosevelt's bedside after her homecoming (with David remaining after I left), I developed the habit of noting them on writing paper, folding and sealing each one afterward in an envelope. Writing out what happened in those last meetings was therapy for me, a way to relieve my sorrow, and sealing them into envelopes was meant to prevent the pain of rereading what I had written. The emotional distance of all these years makes it possible to quote some passages from them now:

October 18
David brought Mrs. Roosevelt home from the Medical Center today at 12:45 P.M. David had originally proposed to Mrs. Roosevelt that she come home tonight, when onlookers and press might not be around. But she was so eager to return here that she insisted on

[coming home] early in the day. Last night at 11, her nurse telephoned David on Mrs. Roosevelt's instructions, saying Mrs. R. did not want to make the trip via ambulance, but wanted to drive in her car (small), lifted by Tubby into the house. This was an impossible idea as Mrs. Roosevelt cannot sit up for any length of time, certainly not for the 30 minute drive. But David wanted to accede as much as possible to Mrs. Roosevelt's wishes so last night he arranged for an "ambulette."

David made endless preparations for her homecoming. It meant so much to her. And he had given his word to her weeks ago that she would not die in the hospital.

Among David's preparations this morning were his efforts to protect her from photographers.

The hospital staff had been extremely cooperative in whisking Mrs. Roosevelt out unseen through a back door to avoid the photographers standing in wait at the Harkness Pavilion entrance. It was a beautiful fall day, and enjoying the drive home through Central Park, she asked if she could be taken through it a second time. She told David that in the coming days, Tubby could take her out for drives. "This is not possible," I jotted down on one of my sheets, "but David said she 'must rest' for a few days."

Anna, Maureen, and I were expecting her momentarily. Anna and Maureen were waiting in her apartment. Suddenly, there was a noisy commotion in the street, which could be heard upstairs, and I went down. Anna and Maureen were already on the sidewalk. I don't know by what means members of the press had learned the time and date of her arrival in Seventy-fourth Street, but they appeared in full force in front of the building as the ambulette pulled up. David was very upset to find them there, thinking he'd managed to evade them. He knew Mrs. Roosevelt would hate to be photographed in her condition and could answer no questions. David got out of the ambulette to make his plea to the photographers. "Mrs. Roosevelt has always been so kind and available to you all these years," he began, "won't you please give her the courtesy to be

brought into her house without taking pictures?" Anna impatiently interrupted him. "They are newspapermen and must do their job," she said.
With that, Mrs. Roosevelt was carried out on a stretcher, and Maureen
had the foresight to attempt to throw part of the blanket covering Mrs.
Roosevelt over her face as flashbulbs popped until she was out of view. I
went quickly up to our apartment, but not before hearing Mrs. Roosevelt
say to David, "I *told* you to ask them to take only two pictures. Then they
would have gone away."* Maureen remembers that, in all the tumult of
her return, Mrs. Roosevelt commented that she was sorry she had forgotten to thank the stretcher-bearers.

Later that day and in a perfectly natural voice, Maureen telephoned
me to say, "Mrs. Roosevelt invites you and David to dine with her to-
night." (Anna and Jim were going out.) I could hardly believe my ears. I
later recorded my impressions:

> I was ill-prepared for the dying lady I saw tonight. A small table
> was set in her bedroom. I kissed her. She was too weak to respond
> but soon gathered her strength to ask, "What news do you have of
> Grania?" . . . David had arranged that all courses should be served
> at once as we should stay only 15 minutes. It was difficult for me
> to keep my control. Mrs. Roosevelt tried to manage her small meal
> on a bed tray by herself as best she could. She was so weak. Irene
> [housekeeper] fed her [her] dessert. [Mrs. R.] has always hated to
> eat alone, and now that she is at home, [she] invited David and
> me to dine with her.

David remained, but I left. While waiting at the elevator, I clearly
heard her say, apologetically, "Tell Edna this is my first night at home. I
shall behave better tomorrow." On the second evening she was at home,
I wrote:

---

*The front page of the following day's *New York Daily News* showed a ghastly close-up
of Mrs. Roosevelt, whom the blanket hid only minimally.

October 19

I spent the afternoon helping Maureen open and sort the countless birthday messages and get-well letters which arrived for Mrs. Roosevelt. . . . Maureen showed me a lovely letter President Kennedy had written Mrs. Roosevelt on her birthday, October 11. . . . The President's letter was written by hand and delivered by a representative of his to the hospital.

Mr. Colston Leigh, Mrs. Roosevelt's lecture agent, called for Elliott's number as he would like Elliott to take over some of Mrs. Roosevelt's speaking engagements. . . .

Trude was there in the day. Also Joe. Elliott will come for the weekend, and Franklin returns from a 5-day stay in London tomorrow. He just telephoned David. Maureen sent him daily night letters about his mother's condition.

Anna is cold and efficient. . . .

I heard Mrs. R. tell Curtis that she had to start doing things for herself again. She dozed most of the day.

Anna wasn't always cold. I believe her sometimes exaggerated efficiency was a defensive reaction to the mounting tension over the fact that her mother was dying. Assuming a role of command was probably helpful in dealing with her brothers. Sometime around ten o'clock in the morning, sad and lonely, she would drift upstairs and, reclining on our bed, would chat with me. They were aimless conversations, Anna just needing to have company. But I do remember the time she regarded a lovely ring on the little finger of her hand. "Father gave this to Princess Martha, and when he died, she thoughtfully sent it back to me. Wasn't it nice of her?"* Occasionally when her husband, Jim Halsted, went home to Birmingham, Michigan, for several days, Anna would have dinner with us. As we waited for David, she spoke of her early

---

*Princess Martha of Norway was one of President Roosevelt's favorite visitors to the White House, a sentiment perhaps borne out by his having given her a friendship ring.

childhood, the lack of intimacy with her mother; she said that her mother had not known how to supervise the care of her young children. She told of cruelties (unknown to her mother) suffered at the hands of a disciplinary nurse when she was very young, recounting an incident that had happened when she was three years old. Resentments lasted long with Roosevelts.

When Mrs. Roosevelt dozed in the afternoon, I helped Maureen and Anna read and sort the cards, messages, and letters of good wishes, expressed in all languages, that poured into our house by the thousands from every corner of the globe, including places one never heard of. Prayers of all religious faiths, even the most obscure, were being said for Mrs. Roosevelt, and printed copies of them were often enclosed in letters. Books arrived, containing hundreds of signatures from schools, communities, and congregations. The huge outpouring of love and admiration was based not on myth but on reality, Mrs. Roosevelt's goodness and accomplishments having touched and changed the lives of people everywhere. Some letters were poignantly funny.

Dear Mrs. Roosevelt:

My husband and I are conservative Republicans from Ohio. We have never really believed anything you have written or said. But I want you to know that I am praying for you. My husband is praying for you too, but he doesn't want anybody to know about it.

Dear Mrs. Roosevelt [written on an oversize get-well card covered with signatures]:

Here is a card signed by our whole family and a picture of us. After you have seen the picture, will you please send it back?

When David came home at night, I would accompany him downstairs for a few moments alone with Mrs. Roosevelt, and then he stayed on. This was the only way I saw her by then. On top of the daily activity of doctors and family conferences, a high degree of tension permeated the apartment. Eyeing the future, the Roosevelt offspring were vying among themselves. Who would be the family spokesman? Who would be in the best position to reap political gain or other rewards? Who was being unfair to whom? At a time like that, any person not directly involved is understandably in the way. It was soon apparent that Anna did not welcome my help. Her visits upstairs stopped. Indeed, she moved toward keeping the upstairs and the downstairs separate. Anna was testy about the visits of Joe and Trude, as well.

Resentment toward David, constrained in the past, could now be more openly expressed. The children had suffered him for so many years. Yet they could not dissociate him from their mother, helpless as she was, nor indeed from their own lives. Seeking David's consolation, Elliott came upstairs to sit with us—and Franklin's tenderness to both David and me was moving during such a sad time for him. But there was no denying that Anna's relationship with me cooled in direct proportion to her wrangling with David about his supervision of her mother's care. Though he didn't outrightly name himself, Jim Halsted wanted someone else to be in charge. The conflicts in this large querulous family produced a clash of opinions about how to handle their mother's illness. And David continued to plague them. As long as the medical diagnosis was not absolutely clear, he wanted to leave no stone unturned to continue optimum care for Mrs. Roosevelt, despite the family's wish to leave her in peace, as she herself desired, and have further medical procedures stopped.

Often in the past, I had heard David say, "A doctor's role is to preserve life and not to prolong dying." He strongly believed this. In Mrs. Roosevelt's case, however, with the diagnosis still not absolutely clear to him, he continued to pursue every possible avenue of inquiry.

My note of October 22:

Mrs. Roosevelt is still the same. The house grows more oppressive.... There are great comings and goings of family members and Trude and Joe. Elliott came to New York. Franklin Jr. arrived from London and returned to Washington after having visited his mother. He will be back in N.Y. today. Franklin came up to our bedroom around noon yesterday to talk to David. He cried. He spoke of how appreciative he and others are to David. He keeps the president informed about his mother.

About a month before this, near the end of September, I had gone alone to a dinner party. David joined me around ten o'clock, after seeing Mrs. Roosevelt. Among the guests was an internist from Johannesburg, Dr. Moses M. Suzman, who greatly interested him. They privately conferred.

David wrote in Mrs. Roosevelt's chart:

On the evening of November 4th I had a telephone call from Dr. Moses Suzman of Johannesburg. I had met Dr. Suzman some six weeks previously and had discussed with him the problem of Mrs. Roosevelt, without mentioning her name. Dr. Suzman told me [at that time] that he had seen similar pictures produced by tuberculosis of the bone marrow alone, without miliary spread in the lungs.* After reading up on the literature I thought that this possibility was indeed a likelihood. I persuaded the various physicians who were involved with Mrs. Roosevelt to start intensive antituberculosis therapy. . . . I then told Dr. Suzman over the telephone [November 4] the name of the patient I had been discussing with him.

Chest X rays were interpreted differently by the various radiologists and other specialists involved in the case. David reported on these findings:

---

*Miliary spread: tuberculosis in which the bacili are spread by blood from one point of infection.

But all of them agreed that it could possibly be an atypical spread of tuberculosis. For this reason the anti-tuberculosis therapy is reconfirmed.

For a long time we had not the slightest impression that anything we were doing had any effect on the infection. The x-rays of the chest seemed possibly to look a little better. This is quite questionable. Her temperature remained a septic one,* at least for several weeks.

When she was taken home at her urgent request on October 18th, it was felt that she was really discharged in order to spend her last days at home. . . .

On October 26th we had been told that two cultures taken on 9/27/62 had grown typical acid fast bacili. . . . In a consultation with Dr. Amberson,** he felt that the bone marrow tuberculosis was most likely secondary to the miliary spread, which now he was willing to accept from the atypical x-ray of her lungs. . . . Dr. Bailey and Dr. Hyman accepted Dr. Amberson's opinion that tuberculosis of the bone marrow was a possibility.

David had earlier thought tuberculosis might be a factor in Mrs. Roosevelt's illness. Perhaps he was more conscious of the possibility because he had long believed that she had been wrongly diagnosed as having pleurisy at the age of thirty-five, when she'd fallen ill during a trip abroad with FDR. When she explained the episode to him, David reasoned that Mrs. Roosevelt had had tuberculosis, not pleurisy, and that with her remarkably strong constitution, she'd been able to throw off the symptoms within a relatively short time. Thinking of tuberculosis as a possibility now, David became cautiously hopeful for the first time. He was determined to save her. Knowing Mrs. Roosevelt as he did, certain that if she knew she had a chance to live, she would grasp it, he was counting upon

---

*Indicating generalized bacterial invasion of the body.
**Dr. J. Burns Amberson was probably a TB specialist.

her phenomenal willpower to help fight the disease when he told her, "We have a cure for tuberculosis." It was wishful thinking. Sitting on the edge of her bed, bending low, he spoke into her ear: "We can cure you!" She replied, "David, I want to die."* If she could not live the useful life she wanted, she did not want to live at all.

David noted:

[On] November 6th, I saw Mrs. Roosevelt and noticed . . . that her general condition had deteriorated further. . . .

On November 7th in the morning her condition was about the same. . . .

At 6:15 as I was ready to leave [the office], I received a call from Dr. Hyman telling me that Mrs. Roosevelt had just ceased breathing. I rushed to her bedside and reached there at about 6:30. . . . Dr. Hyman [was] present, also John, his wife, and Anna. I was shown the statement which was to go to the press, describing Mrs. Roosevelt's end, which had been put together by Dr. Halsted. I made just a few small changes. Anna Halsted was preparing an announcement which at about 6:50 was telephoned to the wire services. Within a very few minutes it was announced to the world that Mrs. Roosevelt had died. I was working with Dr. Hyman on the death certificate, which he signed, and on which he put the diagnosis of aplastic anemia, disseminated tuberculosis and heart failure.

I wrote:

November 8
Our dear Mrs. Roosevelt died last evening. . . . Around a quarter of nine, I saw from my bedroom window the simple casket leaving the house, it being placed into the hearse, and Mrs. Roosevelt alone

---

*Author's interview (November 1997) with Maureen Corr, who was present during this exchange.

with David driving away from 74th Street for the last time. . . . The hearse stopped at the corner for a red light. I was surprised that traffic lights were still working. . . .
We leave for Hyde Park tomorrow.

This was the last letter I wrote to myself, which I then sealed. On December 15, David wrote to Joe Lash:

Dear Joe,

This is one o'clock in the morning. Fifteen hours ago we had a clinical pathological conference including the final results of the autopsy of Mrs. Roosevelt. I thought you would like to know.

I have been rushing the whole day. But now that I have some peace, an enormous sense of relaxation has come over me as a result of this conference. The pathological findings show without any question that Mrs. Roosevelt had a primary disease of the bone marrow, in which the bone marrow, to a very high extent, lost the capacity to form blood. Therefore the anemia. We know no treatment for this condition. It is really a miracle that she was able to carry on as actively as she did for as long as she did. The trip this spring to Israel was on borrowed time alright. No medical knowledge is available which could have saved her, even theoretically. The organism, however strong it had been, had been depleted of all reserves to such an extent that in the end, I mean about three months before the actual end, an old otherwise utterly innocuous tuberculosis gland, could spread tuberculosis infection into the bone marrow and in virtually all other organs of the human body other than the central nervous system. The resistance of the body had been weakened to such an extent that not the slightest resistance could be seen of the body to the infection. This is very rare. Even in the most advanced case of tuberculosis we see body resistance, attempts at encapsulating, localizing the infection. Here was none. Nothing could have been done to save her.

Incidentally, the man who examined her brain made this statement: that she had the brain of a young person. I thought you would like to know that too.

Just my love.
David

David wrote similarly to Franklin and Elliott:

... an old encapsulated, and otherwise perfectly harmless, tuberculous gland—originating most likely from this old tuberculosis which occurred during the first World War—could spread to the bone marrow and subsequently most every part of the body. . . . It then seems that when we found tuberculosis in the bone marrow, it was already the expression of the final, most violent stage of your mother's illness for which no remedy could possibly have been of value. . . .

On February 4, 1963, Franklin wrote us from Washington:

Dear David and Edna,

First of all, may I thank you, David, for sending me your letter about the final results of the autopsy. Your conclusions are certainly most reassuring. In this connection, may I say that at no time was there any question in my mind, that you and the other doctors you brought into Mother's case, did everything which modern medicine could do to preserve her life.

I hope you will always remember that she lived a very full and unusually constructive life—often a very exciting, and perhaps, most important—an unusually unselfish and good life. Toward the end, she knew and wanted it to be over, for she knew that she had done and had inspired about all that she could expect to achieve; and that her remaining strength would not have provided her with the energy to do much more than to observe from the sidelines—a circumstance which would have been hard to enjoy because she felt so deeply about the things and people she really cared for.

I wanted you both also to know that you brought her much happiness and comfort during the years in which you knew her. I think that, particularly, she enjoyed living close to you both through sharing the house in New York during the last two or three years. I appreciate not only what you, David, did for her in your professional capacity, but particularly, I always appreciate what you and Edna did for her happiness and her peace of mind through your devotion and affection during her later years.

Gabrielle* has sent to me, the enclosed letters, written by each of you to Mother. They were on top of the desk in her bedroom.** We, the executors, have decided to give to the Library, all such personal correspondence, including that from the family. These enclosed letters are particularly sweet and thoughtful; and I thought that you might wish to keep them, rather than have them go to the Library. But, on the other hand, I rather hope that you will return them to me; as I think it will be good for future generations of Mother's family, as well as for historians, to know that people like you, who were close to her, had so much love and admiration for her.

With my warm regards.

Sincerely,
Franklin D. Roosevelt, Jr.

David replied:

February 24, 1963
Dear Franklin:

Here are the letters you so kindly sent us, for you to do with them whatever you see fit. Thank you for your good letter. Yes-

---

*Gabrielle Gutkind, Mrs. Roosevelt's part-time secretary.
**As I have said earlier, Anna Halsted burned the bulk of David's correspondence, which she found in the drawers of Mrs. Roosevelt's desk in the city apartment. The ones to which Franklin refers above must have come from the desk in her Val-Kill bedroom.

terday was our fifth wedding anniversary. We got married in your mother's house, every detail arranged for by her. . . . We miss her every day, but somehow yesterday was particularly sad. But what is our loss in comparison to yours! . . . I don't think that I ever extended to you my condolences formally . . . I have certainly felt [them] for you. . . .

In the end, there is no question that she did want to go, but her zest for life was very strong indeed. She had taken in awhile back that there seemed to be no hope of pulling her out of the clutches of this illness. But whenever in the vacillating course of this illness she felt only a little better, her hopes soared. . . .

Her last trip from the Hospital in the ambulette, sitting halfway up, in the beautiful clear autumn weather, driving through the park, gave her a great boost. She was making plans again, she was hopeful again. . . .

All the data, including the autopsy findings, are unanimous that she could not have been saved. This may well be so, and probably is so. In the seven days' hospitalization after my return from Peru, and before going to Campobello, she responded well to anti-tuberculosis treatment. This treatment was stopped on the day she was discharged from the Hospital on August 10, 1962. It was resumed at my insistence on September 27th. The gnawing doubt persists in my mind that if she had continued therapy after August 10th, she might have, at that earlier stage, been able to conquer her infection. The pathologists do not think so. However, they are unable to explain the rather dramatic improvement between August 3d and August 10th, and for the two, three, or even four weeks thereafter. . . .

There was no question that medically she received competent care from as good medical brains as are available. And at this stage the knowledge of this fact just has to be enough to drown out these little voices of doubt. . . .

Funeral

In separate cars, Joe and Trude and David and I drove to Hyde Park for Mrs. Roosevelt's funeral. It took such an occasion to unite us.* Perhaps the sensitivity David showed to Joe during the period of Mrs. Roosevelt's acute illness softened him to us. We stopped on the road for dinner. After we arrived in Val-Kill, Franklin came over from his house, where the family had dined and were talking over their plans. The cottage was ominously quiet. Franklin and David went into the sitting room to confer.** Mrs. Roosevelt's coffin stood behind its closed doors. When the two men emerged, David and I retired to our room.

The weather on the day of Mrs. Roosevelt's funeral was overcast and foreboding. Every so often, it rained a few early-morning tears. Breakfast had been strange, with Anna solidly seated in her mother's place at the head of the table. The morning dragged on, punctuated by the arrival of Roosevelt friends and relations and some of the world's foremost figures, invited by the family to lunch before the funeral service. John F. Kennedy, president of the United States, arrived punctually with his wife, Jacqueline. There were two former United States presidents, Dwight D. Eisenhower and Harry S. Truman, the latter accompanied by Mrs. Truman and their daughter, Margaret. Vice President Johnson was present, as was the secretary-general of the UN, U Thant. They, as well as other leaders representing foreign countries and branches of the American gov-

---

*Joe Lash and David Gurewitsch were the two people in Mrs. Roosevelt's "adopted family" who were closest to her. David was very fond of Joe, despite the fact that Joe was distant with him, jealous of David as he himself states in his book *A World of Love: Eleanor Roosevelt and Her Friends, 1943–1962* (New York: Doubleday, 1984), p. 303. Joe believed that David had replaced him in Mrs. Roosevelt's affections. David had not replaced him. Mrs. Roosevelt loved both men, although differently.
**Mrs. Roosevelt had had a fear of being buried alive. I believe it was years before her illness that she had elicited David's promise to be absolutely certain of her death before her burial took place. She had evidently asked the same of Franklin, Jr. The formality of confirmation was the subject of the meeting between the two men in the sitting room the night before the funeral.

ernment, past, present, and future, crowded into John and Anne's small cottage. All had come to pay their respects to a private citizen, a woman who had never held an elected public office. Their presence testified to the profound influence President Roosevelt's widow had had in the world and the universal respect she had won.

There was a great milling about when drinks were served. David could not resist asking General Eisenhower why he had accepted Mrs. Roosevelt's resignation from the United Nations delegation, since she had been such a superb ambassador for her country. The former president shrugged good-naturedly and said, "Politics, you know." Overhearing this exchange, President Truman boasted, "I appreciated her. I named her First Lady of the World!" I watched President Kennedy, who stood in a corner of the enclosed porch, completely surrounded by a gathering of men seeking to attract his interest. With each draw on his long, thin cigar, he exuded power, and the expression on his face took on a hardness I would not have suspected. When asked, I went over to say a few words to Mrs. Kennedy, who was seated alone on a couch. The encounter was brief. She was shy, and I didn't have the energy to be social.

It was hard to relate to the situation. In that company of family, friends, and eminent people gathered in those familiar surroundings, David and I—and, I'm certain, others among us—were unconsciously expecting Mrs. Roosevelt's arrival. We listened for her quick step, her hearty laugh; we waited for her imposing presence for the occasion to begin. We waited in vain.

It rained again when the casket was lifted into the hearse in front of her cottage. Anna had efficiently organized the order in which the cars were to move from the house to St. James Church. Protocol regarding the position of each vehicle in the funeral cortege was carefully observed. Our car followed those of the Roosevelt family. When David and I were driven into the church grounds, we saw the president's limousine pull up and wait to one side until the family and intimates of Mrs. Roosevelt, including household staff, entered the church and were seated in the front pews. It seemed fitting that at Mrs. Roosevelt's funeral her friends and staff were given precedence over the president of the United States. Only in this country, I thought, would a president be expected to patiently wait his turn.

Prayers and Scripture were read and favorite hymns sung at the service, which was simple and short. Then we were driven to the Rose Garden on the estate, where Mrs. Roosevelt was to be buried beside President Roosevelt. As soon as the graveside ceremony began, the sun suddenly burst through the dark clouds, its symbolism causing many of us to smile. The brightness soon vanished and the storm again threatened. But only at the conclusion of the burial service, when the gathering turned to leave, did it begin to rain in earnest.

We were invited to dinner with the family in Franklin and Sue's house before returning to the city. At a given point, Franklin asked me to go outside with him. Tearfully, he told me, "David was more of a son to my mother than any of her sons." I was very touched. It was generous of him to say that.

David recorded his thoughts in connection with a talk he was asked to give about Mrs. Roosevelt shortly after she died. In this passage, he described the richness of her personality:

Much of Mrs. Roosevelt's influence was based on very solid strength. Her character was truly formidable. If one begins to think in what areas she excelled, the list of her qualities is awesome. She possessed each of these qualities to an unusual extent and the combination of all of them in one person is probably unique: courage, honesty, wisdom and common sense, perseverance, self-discipline, industry, modesty, compassion, love, and warmth. To these should be added simplicity and directness, bravery, tact and good manners, restraint, loyalty, and, of course, patriotism. For each of these qualities Mrs. Roosevelt could have been a symbol. . . . She had all the best qualities of youth and age. She had the curiosity of youth, the energy, the desire to learn and *the ability to change with new learn-*

ing—characteristics of youth—combined with the wisdom, patience, perseverance and experience of age. . . .

How unique she was. And what a life, without show or blemish, doing the right thing to a point that she could say only recently if she had her life to live all over again she would do nothing differently. What a glory to be able to say that, and this coming from such a modest, self-effacing, and matter-of-fact human being.

Years passed. We were parked in front of our house one night, prepared to go upstairs. David made no move to leave the car. He was quietly chuckling. "Why are you laughing?" I asked. After a moment, he turned to me with a wonderful smile, his eyes glistening. "I was just remembering Mrs. Roosevelt," he said.

EPILOGUE

AS A DOCTOR'S WIFE, I knew that members of the medical profession rarely think they ever become ill. Doctors perceive themselves to be invulnerable, in a category different from that of patients. David had neither time nor inclination for physical checkups. So I was stunned one morning in the summer of 1972 when he told me he had cancer. My heart began to pound. "How do you know?" I asked. He had not complained about any physical problem. "I've gone to various laboratories for tests" was the answer. "We had better see a doctor," I replied.

David's diagnosis was correct. After major surgery, a hospital stay, and a brief period of recuperation, David returned to a full work schedule. However, after one good year, he was back in the hospital as a patient. His internist, Dr. Hamilton Southworth, called me to his office one day. Before telling David, he gave me the news that the cancer had metastasized. "What shall we tell this brilliant, wise doctor?" he asked, leaving me no choice as to my answer. "The truth," I replied. "Give me half an hour with him and then come to his room," he said. David was alone when I entered. He spoke gently: "Dr. Southworth should not have asked *you* what to tell *me*. He should have asked *me* what to tell *you*." David's next concern was his elder daughter, who was in the waiting room. "What shall we tell Grania?" he asked.

We were closer than ever when he returned home, savoring every minute together. Maria was wonderful — tactful, loving, somehow knowing everything, as children do. We had daily visits from colleagues and friends. Finally, David was advised that he would have to return to the hospital imminently for additional surgery. "You will not find me there," he answered firmly. His time was clearly limited and he wanted to remain at home.

One evening, Grania called, wanting to stop by. Filled with emotion, David could not bring himself to see her, an immense sacrifice for him. Speaking to her over the telephone, he sent her his love in such a way that she understood he was saying good-bye. Earlier, he had repeated many precise instructions for me to follow after he was gone, to be certain I understood them. He was worried that "the ceiling will fall in on you." And not wanting me to lose years in mourning him, he told me, "Don't take too long. Cross the threshold!" Endlessly, he repeated the word *darling* to me. He said it was a pity that life was still so sweet.

Maria was asleep in her room for the night and the day nurse was gone when David died in the early-morning hours of January 30, 1974. I put on a heavy wool sweater and winter coat, but nothing could have stopped my trembling. Soon after, I woke Maria, braided her hair as usual, gave her breakfast on a tray in her room, and sent her quickly off to school before calling the doctor. By the time she returned home that afternoon, the house was filled with people. I went upstairs alone and told her, "Daddy died." Her face turned crimson. "I knew it!" she replied heatedly. "I *hated* it last night when he said to me, 'Maria, you are twelve and a half years old and already you can stand on your own two feet!'"

Some months later, I met an old patient of David's on the street. "How are you?" I asked. "Not well," she replied. "I am not seeing any doctor now." We looked into each other's eyes. She then added, "I keep thinking about your husband's funeral. Usually at funerals, they say too much. In the case of Dr. Gurewitsch, nothing said could have been enough."